Java™ Thin-Client Programming for a Network Computing Environment

JÜRGEN FRIEDRICHS ▪ HENRI JUBIN ▪ AND THE JALAPEÑO TEAM

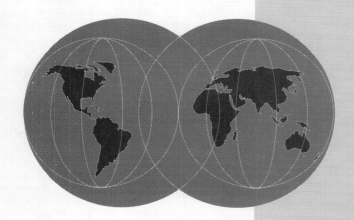

International Technical Support Organization
Austin, Texas 78758

ISBN 0-13-011117-1

90000

9 780130 111173

PRENTICE HALL PTR, UPPER SADDLE RIVER, NEW JERSEY 07458

Editorial/production supervision: *Maria Molinari*
Cover design director: *Jayne Conte*
Cover designer: *Bruce Kenselaar*
Manufacturing manager: *Pat Brown*
Marketing manager: *Kaylie Smith*
Acquisitions editor: *Mike Meehan*
Editorial assistant: *Bart Blanken*

 Published by Prentice Hall PTR
Prentice-Hall, Inc.
 A Simon & Schuster Company
Upper Saddle River, NJ 07458

Prentice Hall books are widely used by corporations and government agencies for training, marketing, and resale.
The publisher offers discounts on this book when ordered in bulk quantities.
For more information, contact Corporate Sales Dept.; Phone 800-382-3419; FAX: 201-236-7141
E-mail (Internet): corpsales@prenhall.com
Or write: Prentice Hall PTR, Corp. Sales Department, One Lake Street,Upper Saddle River, NJ 07458

Printed in the United States of America

10 9 8 7 6 5 4 3 2 1

ISBN   0-13-011117-1

Prentice-Hall International (UK) Limited, *London*

Prentice-Hall of Australia Pty. Limited, *Sydney*

Prentice-Hall Canada Inc., *Toronto*

Prentice-Hall Hispanoamericana, S.A., *Mexico*

Prentice-Hall of India Private Limited, *New Delhi*

Prentice-Hall of Japan, Inc., *Tokyo*

Simon & Schuster Asia Pte. Ltd., *Singapore*

Editora Prentice-Hall do Brasil, Ltda., *Rio de Janeiro*

Contents

Chapter 14
Java in the IBM Network Station, 227

Appendix A
Brief HTML Reference, 247

List of Figures

List of Tables

Preface

In an astonishingly short period of time, Java has emerged as a major force in the computing landscape, both as a programming language for the '90s and as a new platform for the development of heterogeneous network-centric systems. Along with the rise of Java has come the idea of network computing.

This redbook looks at these two major forces by positioning network computing within the enterprise and showing how Java can be used to build sophisticated applications in the network computing arena. Using a scenario centered around the Lunar Medical Center, this redbook shows how to design and develop Java-based applications, applets and complete systems and highlights many of the related issues and alternatives that must be examined before an organization can feel "safe" with the new technologies.

Developing applications with Version 1.0 of IBM's versatile VisualAge for Java Integrated Development Environment is the focus of this redbook. It will help you install, tailor and configure the new IBM Network Station 1000 to run Java-based applications and applets and show you how to work with the new Lotus eSuite Java-based application on the Network Station.

The Team That Wrote This Book

This redbook was produced by a team of specialists from around the world working at the International Technical Support Organization, Austin Center.

Figure 0–1 The Jalapeño Team

Shown above: the team that worked on this book. Clockwise from top-left: Gerardo Bazalar (Peru), Bob Brown (Australia), Jürgen Friedrichs (Germany), Burkhard Volkemer (Germany), Jose Swanepoel (France), Henri Jubin (France) and Dennis Remmer (Australia).

Jürgen Friedrichs is a project leader in the OO/AD group at the International Technical Support Organization (ITSO), Austin Center. Before joining the ITSO in 1997, Juergen worked in Technical Marketing Support for OS/2, Warp Server and TCP/IP in Germany.

Henri Jubin is currently working for the International Technical Support Organization (ITSO) in Austin, where he covers the area of Object Oriented Technology. Henri has previously worked in various support and consulting positions within IBM France. He has dealt with topics such as Object Oriented Technology and OS/2.

The Jalapeno Team:

Bob Brown is a Principal Consultant with the Distributed Systems Technology Centre (DSTC), based in Brisbane, Australia. He has been associated with computers in various ways for 14 years. He has worked as a computing researcher in the United Kingdom and as a lecturer in computing throughout Asia. At the DSTC, Bob works on controlling technology transfer from the centre to industry and is the manager controlling DSTC's relationship with IBM. Bob's varied activities also include managing nodes on the Australia-wide Asynchronous Transfer Mode-based Experimental Broadband Network and presenting workshops on Java.

Dennis Remmer is a Principal Consultant with the Distributed Systems Technology Centre (DSTC), based in Brisbane, Australia. He has over seven years of experience in systems design, implementation and integration in the areas of databases, geospatial information systems (GIS) and network computing. He holds degrees in Computer Science and GIS from the University of Queensland. Dennis has previously worked at Unisys Corporation and ARC Systems, an Australian GIS company. His role with the DSTC encompasses consultancy, software development, course development, and instruction in network computing and distributed system technologies.

Gerardo Bazalar is an IT Specialist in IBM of Peru. He has one year of experience in electronic and network computing business. He holds a degree in Information Engineering from the Catholic University of Peru. He is also a professor in that university in the Compilers and Interpreters area. His areas of expertise include software development, consultancy and emergent technologies.

Burkhard Volkemer is a consultant for the IBM Global Services at the department for telecommunication and media in Frankfurt/Germany. Before joining IBM in 1996, he was working at the European center for particle physics (CERN) in Geneva/Switzerland, where he earned his Ph.D. in physics. In IBM Global Services, Dr. Volkemer has been working on the analysis and design of telecommunication applications and their implementation.

Jose Swaenepoel is a AS/400 System Engineer in France. He has worked with customers and Business Partners since 1988. His skill areas include Application Development, Performance tuning and communications. In January 1998 he joined the IBM EMEA West Region AS/400 Java team. He has previously written a book intended to Business Partners on Communication APIs.

Thanks to the following people for their invaluable contributions to this project:

Bob Maatta is a Senior Software Engineer from the United States at the International Technical Support Organization, Rochester Center. He writes extensively and teaches IBM classes worldwide on all areas of AS/400 client/server. Before joining the ITSO three years ago, he worked in the U.S. AS/400 National Technical Support Center as a Consulting Market Support Specialist. He has over 20 years of experience in the computer field and has worked with all aspects of personal computers for the last 10 years.

Brian White Eagle is a software engineer in the Network Computer Division's Advanced Solutions Center from Austin, TX. His current responsibilities include hardware and software enablement on the Network Station, which includes smart cards on the Network Station 1000 using the OpenCard Framework. He is a recent graduate from the Massachusetts Institute of Technology with a Bachelor of Science in Computer Science and Electrical Engineering.

Sandeep Singhal is a Research Staff Member with IBM's T.J. Watson Research Center. Dr. Singhal's research focuses on network protocol design and implementation for enabling high-performance applications such as distributed multimedia, simulation, and virtual environments in heterogeneous network and computing environments. His other interests include large-scale software engineering and object-oriented design. His current work addresses issues facing the implementation of client/server applications for "pervasive computing" devices. His previous networking research has been adopted in the "Tom Clancey's Politika" video game shipped by Red Storm Entertainment and in the DoD military simulation High-Level Architecture. Dr. Singhal has served on DARPA Technical Advisory Boards and National Research Council efforts to define the modeling and simulation research agenda for the 21st century, Singhal earned his Ph.D in Computer Science from Stanford University in 1996 and an M.S. in 1994. He earned a B.S. in Computer Science, B.S. in Mathematical Sciences, and a B.A. in Mathematics from Johns Hopkins University in 1992.

Chris Ritchie is a technical consultant for the Network Computer Division Advanced Solution Center (ASC) in Austin, Texas. He has worked for IBM for 14 years and has experience in high performance graphics device driver development, X Windows Server development, Xlib protocol transport mechanisms, Microsoft Windows NT graphics device drivers, MPEG hardware and software technology, Java integration support, and thin client architecture. He is currently a member of the ASC SWAT team responsible for pre-sales customer support and solution development.

Donna Van Fleet, Rebecca Austen, Lauren Kingman, Paul Buck, RG Keen

Comments Welcome

Your comments are important to us!

We want our redbooks to be as helpful as possible. Please send us your comments about this or other redbooks in one of the following ways:

- Fax the evaluation form found in "ITSO Redbook Evaluation" on page 333 to the fax number shown on the form.

- Use the electronic evaluation form found on the Redbooks Web sites:

  For Internet users   `http://www.redbooks.ibm.com`
  For IBM Intranet users   `http://w3.itso.ibm.com`

- Send us a note at the following address:

  `redbook@us.ibm.com`

Chapter 1

Introduction

- ▼ A THIN CLIENT APPLICATION—THE LUNAR MEDICAL CENTER STORY
- ▼ ABOUT THE BOOK
- ▼ WHO SHOULD READ THIS BOOK
- ▼ ASSUMPTIONS
- ▼ HOW TO USE THIS BOOK

Novus ordo seclorum, cum grano salis

— A new order of ages, with a grain of salt

Network computing, Java, the Internet, client/server, distributed systems, *ad infinitum*—technologies and techniques that promise a new, cheaper, more efficient and easier way of computing, that we must approach with caution and understanding.

Java is a modern programming language that supports development and deployment of network computing applications. There are literally hundreds of books on Java, some specialized, many generic. Almost all neglect to provide a sound basis for understanding the fundamentals of network computing and the basic reasoning behind why you should use Java for developing and deploying your applications. The focus *ad nauseum* has been on language syntax, which is fine in

1

isolation. Often missing are the nontechnical issues, the helicopter view of the network computing domain that makes it clear where to position Java, how to integrate it with existing technologies, and what you need to consider to allow for a rapidly changing future.

When a "normal" monolithic application runs on a computer, all the components of the application work within the same memory space, and the computer manages the interplay of program modules in a well-understood and time-honored fashion.

Writing an application for a network computing environment involves the factoring of the application's functionality into components and with the deployment of these components on devices that are most appropriate for their requirements. An application deployed across multiple, (perhaps geographically) separated systems is referred to as a *distributed* application.

Distribution brings with it a number of questions that must be answered before the system can be fully implemented: how can the components of the application communicate, interact with other programs, and make use of external facilities? What are the new "rules" for developing applications for a potentially unlimited number and class of users? How can the new failure modes introduced by the distribution process be handled?

Java is still very young, but under the impetus of the Internet and the World Wide Web, it is maturing rapidly. No programming language is perfect, and in this regard, Java is certainly not unique! Java has a number of very good points, and some that are currently the subject of some debate. As a modern language designed from the ground-up to be an object-oriented language for network computing, it does represent a powerful weapon in the armory of the distributed systems warrior.

The Network Computer (NC) is another arrow in the quiver for all those who are charged with building complex, enterprise-wide systems. It offers a powerful, lower-cost alternative to today's networked desktop hardware. Even more importantly, the network computer in its various guises represents choice and freedom: system designers are now free to choose their hardware and software systems according to the idea of *fitness for use*, rather than attempting to mould and shoehorn inappropriate devices into their designs.

Predicting the future is always a risky proposition, but one thing seems clear: both Java and the idea of network computing are now here to stay. We hope this book will help you find your way through the battlefield.

A Thin Client Application—The Lunar Medical Center Story

To illustrate the techniques and technologies discussed in this book, gaze into the proverbial crystal ball, and imagine a future moonbase medical center—The Lunar Medical Center (LMC)—which needs to provide services to the lunar community.

Figure 1–1 The Lunar Medical Center

The LMC system designers have chosen to adopt a network computing strategy and need to implement numerous applications—administrative, device-monitoring, public access, and so forth—using a network computing-centric programming language. Having conducted a comprehensive study of the technology options, Java has emerged as the only serious contender for the job.

In the LMC's medical departments, access terminals are expected to support work 656.7 hours a day, 365 days a year and allow for easy replacement in case of failure. The Network Computer is the solution chosen by the *Lunar Medical Center*.

Because many people have to share information, the data must be stored on a system that can be accessed by multiple departments. Java provides several communication and access solutions, such as Java Data Base Connectivity (JDBC), Sockets, and Remote Method Invocation (RMI). It is up to the LMC designers to investigate the pros and cons of each method and to determine the most appropriate solution for their needs. To achieve this goal, they have chosen to prototype two aspects of the LMC system—the patient check-in facility and the patient record view/edit facility—using the various options available to them.

About the Book

This book is about developing thin-client Java applications for a network computing environment, such as your local network, whole enterprise, or even the Internet. Thin-client is a technique that, among other things, attempts to minimize the resource requirements of the application at the desktop. Thin-client computing aims to help you to build a system that doesn't require a system configuration that NASA would be proud of!

This book's intention is to furnish Java knowledge with a foundation in network computing. In the chapters that follow, you will gain a clear understanding of network computing, the features and issues related to distributed systems, the role of Java as one of the key technologies in this domain, and developing distributed client/server applications with Java. The focus is on architecting thin-client 100 percent pure Java applications by example, both generically and through a packaged Java development environment: IBM's VisualAge for Java.

Several different communication mechanisms for implementing a distributed Java application are considered: Hypertext Transfer Protocol (HTTP), Remote Method Invocation (RMI), Sockets, and Java Data Base Connectivity (JDBC). The new class of Java-centric network computing desktop devices—the Network Computer (NC), in particular—is discussed, along with the nature of these devices, and the issues associated with deployment of Java applications for such technology. IBM's Network Station is presented as an NC case study.

This book, in combination with some Java language reference documentation such as that provided in the Java Development Toolkit (JDK) electronic document set, will give you the knowledge required to implement thin-client, distributed Java applications and to be able to put what you've created in context.

Structure of the Book

Chapter 1, Introduction

This chapter is the introduction and highlights the remaining chapters in this book.

Chapter 2, Network Computing and Network Computers

This chapter positions Java and Network Computers (NCs) within the broader framework of network computing, by discussing what network computing is, its implications, benefits and problems, along with an overview of the Network Computer Technical Standard, NC products, variations, and usage.

Chapter 3, Distributed Applications

This chapter looks at some of the various issues associated with the development of systems based on the network computing paradigm. It also examines the features and facilities of Java that make it such an excellent platform for the development of distributed systems.

Chapter 4, HTML-Based Clients

This chapter investigates the implementation of simple client applications using HTML and JavaScript. This facilitates using browsers as the data entry interface, as they are readily and inexpensively available and deployable.

Chapter 5, Java-Based Clients

This chapter has three aims. The first is to introduce Java and take a brief look at its features and facilities.

A second aim is to introduce the Java-based LMC patient record retrieval and update application that is used as the vehicle for discussion in the remainder of the book.

The final aim of the chapter is to provide a short overview of some Java facilities supporting enterprise-wide network computing—the "ecology" of Java: its features, properties and related technologies.

Chapter 6, Design Decisions

This chapter looks at the design of the object model underlying many of the applications and also examines how the LMC's network designers investigated the various network architectures and technologies to see which were most appropriate for their environment.

Chapter 7, Java Servlets and HTTP Communication

Chapter 4 examined the implementation of very thin clients using HTML and JavaScript. Chapter 5 examined a Java Applet implementation of the same client application. This chapter examines the corresponding server application for the clients, which takes the syntactically valid data from the client, stores it to our chosen storage mechanism (either the filing system or a database), and provides some feedback to the browser.

Chapter 8, Java Servers Using JDBC

This chapter introduces Java Database Connectivity (JDBC), the Java API for standardized SQL-based database access. JDBC provides a uniform interface to a wide range of database systems and a common foundation on which higher-level tools and interfaces can be built. Java-based middleware services that utilize the powerful data storage and retrieval facilities of database systems can be developed for our distributed applications.

Chapter 9, Java Servers and Socket Communication

This chapter deals with methods available in Java to slice monolithic applications into functional units which communicate through a network, thus making it a distributed application. The chapter introduces the Internet Protocol (IP) and its API using sockets. Sockets provide the functionality to transport data blocks or data streams over the network and thus represent a very elementary service for distributed computing.

Chapter 10, Java Servers and RMI Communication

This chapter introduces Remote Method Invocation (RMI). As its name suggests, this technique offers a way to invoke Java methods remotely. Using RMI allows development of *easily* distributed applications that can execute and communicate on multiple systems on the network.

Chapter 11, Client Diets

This chapter examines techniques and issues that need to be considered in order to produce optimized code—in terms of both speed and size—to maximize the "thinness" of Java solutions and to ensure that they make best use of the available resources.

Chapter 12, Tasty Additions

This chapter introduces Java programming for accessing smart cards and the serial port on the Network Computer.

Chapter 13, NC Deployment: Using IBM Network Stations

This chapter analyzes the IBM Network Station as an NC solution in the Network Computing world and investigates how it should be configured for commercial use. Performance tips and techniques are also provided.

Chapter 14, Java in the IBM Network Station

This chapter discusses how to successfully run Java in an NC, using the IBM Network Station as an example, along with some tips and techniques for avoiding problems.

Appendix A, Brief HTML Reference

This appendix provides an overview of some of the more important HTML tags used in the book.

Appendix B, Java Development: Using VisualAge for Java

Appendix B is a useful introduction to VisualAge for Java. It covers the VisualAge family, an overview of VisualAge Java, the Integrated Development Environment (IDE) and the Enterprise Access Builders (EAB). The chapter discusses various processes and windows that are used in the development of windows and applications using VisualAge for Java. A self study example is furnished as an exercise.

Who Should Read This Book

This book should prove an excellent resource for many information technology professionals, including programmers, architects, consultants, system administrators, and others. It is meant for those wanting a solid grounding in Java for network computing applications.

Anyone developing software for the Internet and the World Wide Web, for their enterprise networks (or intranets), or for any networking situation will find the material timely and relevant.

Although the discussion is centered on Java and the network computer, the fundamental concepts are applicable to any modern distributed system programming language and associated technology. The book collects a wide body of knowledge and presents it in a cohesive and realistic manner.

Assumptions

This book assumes a basic knowledge of the Java language, HTML, object orientation, and window-based GUI concepts.

Although the book provides a case study in Java development using an integrated development package, any other package, or indeed Version 1.1 of the "vanilla" Java Development Toolkit, may be utilized. The book does not provide a detailed syntax of commands, JDK classes and methods; so the reader will find a Java reference very useful. Many reference books exist, but the online documentation is perfectly adequate.

How to Use This Book

This book is not intended to be read in a linear fashion. It is anticipated that the reader will find certain chapters more relevant to their work than others and thus may want to "dip into" the book in their own order.

Readers are recommended to read this chapter, and especially "A Thin Client Application—The Lunar Medical Center Story" on page 3. This will provide the background that ties many of the chapters together.

Certain groupings of chapters may suggest themselves, however.

Readers new to network computing should first read Chapter 2, to establish a "feel" for the area. "Client-Server Computing with Java" on page 61 also provides a useful starting point.

Readers charged with implementing Java-based, network-aware systems should read Chapter 3 through Chapter 10. Chapter 6 also covers the design of applications for a network-computing-based enterprise.

The details of programming for the IBM Network Station are examined in Chapter 2, and Chapter 12 to Chapter 14. Chapter 9 also contains a relevant discussion. Chapter 14 looks at the new Lotus eSuite Java-based software suite for the Network Station. Programmers of the Network Station should also examine Chapter 11, which looks at how to optimize code to achieve peak performance.

Network Computing and Network Computers

▼ WHAT IS NETWORK COMPUTING?

▼ PROBLEMS WITH NETWORK COMPUTING

▼ A NETWORK COMPUTING STRATEGY

It is very important to differentiate *network computing* from *Network Computers*. The latter is a class of computing devices specified by The Open Group that have emerged on the market in recent years, attracting much of the media attention and therefore a place in the hearts and minds of the IT community. Network computing has a more fundamental reason for existing than to simply replace the "standard" desktop PC or workstation. It is a much broader space, encompassing techniques and technologies for development and deployment of information, systems and applications for a network of users.

This chapter positions Network Computers (NCs) within the broader framework of network computing by discussing what network computing is, its implications, benefits and problems, and provides an overview of the Network Computer Technical Standard, NC products, variations, and usage.

What Is Network Computing?

For a start, network computing is nothing fundamentally new. By definition, a network of computers is two or more computers connected in such a way as to be able to share information and resources; hence network computing is computing that uses the resources and facilities of the network. We have been able to construct networks of computers to facilitate such sharing for many years; however, in architecting such networks we've had to cater to the specific flavors of technology provided by the vendors, and in doing so limit our scope, ease of integration, and capacity for change and choice.

> ### The Earliest Thin Client?
>
> Jan 1940: At Bell Labs, Samuel Williams and George Stibitz complete the "Model I Relay Calculator." Rather than requiring users to come to the machine to use it, the calculator (acting as a server) is provided with three remote keyboards, at various places in the building, in the form of teletypes (acting as thin clients). Only one can be used at a time, and the output is automatically displayed on the same one. In September 1940, a teletype is set up at a mathematical conference in Hanover, New Hampshire, with a connection to New York, and those attending the conference can use the machine remotely. Extract from "A Chronology of Digital Computing Machines (to 1952)," maintained by Mark Brader at:
> `http://www.best.com/~wilson/faq/chrono.html`

Network computing effectively started with mainframes, which utilized non-programmable display-only terminals, a server-centric processing environment, centralized systems management, and proprietary applications highly dependent on the operating and physical system specifics.

With the advent of more powerful devices such as PCs, Macintoshes, and workstations, users became empowered with powerful computational devices and display technology. Systems management was decentralized, and specific servers were deployed in proprietary networks.

There are pros and cons associated with each of these. Although decentralizing systems management allows for contained local networks with devices more self-manageable by their users, administration costs increase dramatically, and security and control decreases over installed software and configuration. Use of proprietary networks and applications increases the risk and cost when the need to change arises.

Modern network computing has the potential to deliver a great deal, employing increasingly universal interfaces such as browsers, simplified and standardized access, system-independent development languages, middleware to manage distribution, and centralized systems management.

Directly or indirectly, computing is now a fundamental part of daily life. The technology has become exponentially more capable, and the social and commercial benefits of accessing and sharing information are being realized. The IT market is maturing from the specialized industry it once was in order to provide services and systems as general commodities. The focus is on the information; therefore, the technologies required to facilitate our access and sharing must work well and, in most cases, be hidden from the user. The key is hiding complexity while providing performance, functionality and integration, all at low cost.

Network Computing Ideals

In network computing Shangri-La (*a remote, beautiful, imaginary place where life approaches perfection*):

- We connect using widely accepted and standardized network protocols and services.

- We use well-defined and trusted industry standards.

- We can easily and effectively distribute our resources, data, functions, and processing.

- We partition and deploy our application functionality where appropriate (thin clients, servers, application services, and so forth.).

- Our applications are distributed, object-oriented, component-based, designed with user profiles in mind, and architecturally neutral.

- We have cost-effective graphical devices for our users and performance-rich server devices to do the hard work.

- Users can access and share data and applications transparently and irrespective of geographical location.

- We deploy our information using widely accepted and standardized data formats.

- Our environment is secure and well-managed.

- The combined environment is at the user's or system's disposal as if it were a single computer ("the network is the computer").

- We can interchange devices and software services seamlessly.

- We support growth and a changing future.

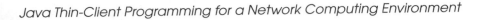

For most users, network computing must be at least as robust as traditional computing. Unfortunately, we're not there yet, and it's not that easy.

Network Computing Reality

In the last fifteen years or so, several key developments have supported the growing reality of network computing through:

- Adoption of key communication protocols and standards (such as TCP/IP and HTTP), and data format standards (such as HTML).

- Methodologies and technologies to support distribution of applications (such as remote procedure calls—RPCs, and distributed objects).

- Programming languages supporting development of applications for a heterogeneous hardware and network environment (such as Java).

- Vendor collaboration, cooperation-operation and consolidation, often under the aegis of industry standards bodies and consortia (such as the International Standards Organization—ISO, The Open Group, and the Object Management Group—OMG).

- The massive uptake of computing by the general population due to simplification of interface and access, increasing power and range of available hardware and software, and reduction in cost.

- A corresponding need to better manage this newly empowered user base, to reduce total cost of ownership and improve resource utilization.

Underlying the adoption of network computing are the recent developments in high-speed networking technologies such as Asynchronous Transfer Mode (ATM) and GigaBit Ethernet. It is now possible to effectively centralize resources that previously needed to be distributed simply for performance reasons. The increased reliability of today's networks also makes possible the centralized management of geographically distributed systems.

Centralization of resources and their management is one reason why the network computing model is claimed to have a lower total cost of ownership than previous networking schemes that have been used. Other benefits also accrue: centralized applications can be rolled out throughout an organization much faster by fewer staff than would otherwise be the case, and reliability is also much greater. In addition, it becomes easy to implement an enterprise-wide security scheme (perhaps based on the use of SmartCards), a very difficult task in the best of circumstances.

A further major factor is leading us to consider network computing and its associated ideas: dissatisfaction with the resource requirements and stability of today's software and operating systems. There is growing evidence that today's enterprise systems (populated as they are by powerful, general-purpose computers) may not be able to successfully scale to meet the demands being placed upon them. Because of this, architects are beginning to look long and hard at the idea of fitness for purpose. Instead of employing general-purpose devices that are underused, costly and potentially unstable, network computing promises to allow an architect to choose a more specialized device appropriate for the task at hand.

Although we are still quite a long way from Shangri-La, the phenomenal growth of the Internet is spurring the adoption of network-ready and mobile systems, and is also acting as a breeding ground for the required developer skills. The network is now firmly embedded in the popular psyche.

Problems with Network Computing

The complexities involved with any environment incorporating multiple flavors of hardware, operating system, and network infrastructure are a significant concern and not easily dealt with:

- How to transact, schedule, audit, and synchronize tasks in an environment with any number of different states?

- How does an application or system tell the difference between a resource that is not responding because it is being heavily used and a resource that doesn't respond because it has failed or is unavailable?

- How to manage byte-ordering and data format differences between systems?

- How can the user maintain productivity when the server or network goes down?

- How to control and manage distributed resources effectively?

- How to technically implement the organizational security requirements in the system, such as authentication, authorization, encryption, and so on?

- In addressing these and other problems, how can complexities be kept transparent to the user or system?

> **Note**
>
> The ideal distributed or networked system hides complexity by keeping data-handling, location, failure management, and so on transparent to the user or system. There is a set of transparencies specified by ISO, known as the Reference Model for Open Distributed Processing (RM-ODP), which define the ideal distributed system characteristics. RM-ODP is a useful metric for evaluating middleware and network computing technologies.

Middleware is the layer of technology that sits above the physical. It manages many of the aforementioned issues by providing standardized services and interfaces to the applications, and is a crucial component in the architecture of a network computing environment. Chapter 3, "Distributed Applications" on page 23, covers middleware and distributing applications in much more detail.

New strategies and skills are required. The developer experience necessary to engineer "thin" or network-based client/server applications has been lacking. Developing applications for a network computing environment requires a fundamental understanding of the benefits, problems, options, and techniques associated with this new paradigm. Network computing is massively challenging for IT businesses and their models of commerce and operation.

The Network Computer (NC)

The Network Computer is an end-user display device with computational ability, specifically designed for a network computing environment, supporting (at least) a standard profile of features. The NC is more than a terminal due to its processing ability, but is currently less capable than a PC or workstation. It is a low-cost hybrid, built from the ground up with the network and a class of applications in mind. One of the key characteristics of network computing is that most application and system resources are located on servers in the network; so NCs are often called "thin clients." The resources needed to support client-side application components are significantly less than if the application was "monolithic" and required a self-contained, full system.

NCs are currently finding a place as a niche device class in the corporate market and they show potential in the entry-level Internet market. They potentially span a range of devices from simple palmtop organizers through specialized "executive" terminals for call-center applications incorporating telephones and simple processing capabilities, to powerful general-purpose desktop devices. NCs provide a clear upgrade path for current users of non-programmable terminals, a capable option where PCs and workstations are overkill, and can coexist-exist with devices currently in use, such as PCs. Determining correct role requires defining user types and function, careful design and consideration of the applications, data-handling, security, and management.

It is important to remember that NCs are not necessarily applicable (at least currently) to all situations, such as:

- Tasks where data processing is highly disk or CPU-intensive, such as image processing

- Situations where data sets may be very large and thus the requisite network support may be prohibitively expensive or difficult to provide, such as multimedia development

- A security environment where stations require isolation

- Situations requiring specific applications not available for Network Computer hardware

- Situations requiring specific hardware not available for the NC

- Situations where stations are mobile and likely to be frequently disconnected from a supporting network for substantial periods of time

The Open Group Network Computer Technical Standard (see `http://www.open-group.org/onlinepubs/9627999/toc.htm`) defines the minimum set of requirements that must be met by a product in order for that product to conform to an Open Network Computer Product Standard.

The Open Group is a leading vendor-neutral, international consortium for buyers and suppliers of technology. Formed in 1996 by the merger of the X/Open Company Ltd. (founded in 1984) and the Open Software Foundation (OSF, founded in 1988), The Open Group is supported by most of the world's largest user organizations, information systems vendors, and software suppliers. Its activities and output include open systems specifications, a branding scheme, collaborative technology development and advanced research, and assisting user organizations, vendors, and suppliers in the development and implementation of products supporting the adoption and proliferation of systems that conform to standard specifications.

NC Objectives

The NC provides an architecturally neutral application framework with the ability to launch applications from any server. NCs are appropriate devices for deployment of "thin" client applications.

The direct objectives of the NC standard are:

- Facilitate a broad application base

- Encourage interoperability

- Provide for simple and unified systems administration

- End-user ease of use

- Lower the total cost of ownership for desktop computing devices

Indirectly, the Standard:

- Provides a common foundation of popular and widely used features and functions

- Provides guidelines to content and service providers

- Does not specify implementation of compliant devices

- Does not preclude additional features outside the scope of the standard

NC Capabilities and Architecture

The Technical Standard specifies the basic capabilities of a Network Computer, shown in Figure 2–1 below. The four main functional requirements are:

- Provide a user interface with a minimum set of characteristics:

  - Support a text input mechanism (note that the standard does not specify a keyboard)

  - Support a pointing capacity (note that the standard does not specify a mouse)

  - Display with a resolution of at least 640x480 pixels, or equivalent (including NTSC, PAL and SECAM television display resolutions)

  - Audio output

- Process incoming and outgoing resources using the Uniform Resource Locator (URL) scheme:

  - Support the HyperText Transfer Protocol (HTTP) and Secure HTTP (HTTPS) schemes transmitted using the Transmission Control Protocol (TCP) over Internet Protocol (IP) -based networks

  - Be able to send e-mail using the Simple Mail Transfer Protocol (SMTP), supporting Multipurpose Internet Mail Extensions (MIME), and conforming to Internet Engineering Task Force (IETF) mail format standards

  - Optionally support file transfer using the File Transfer Protocol (FTP)

- Optionally support terminal sessions using Telnet
- Process and present resources:
  - Support character set encoding
  - Support text and HyperText Markup Language (HTML)
  - Support Graphics Interchange Format (GIF) and JPEG images
  - Support Sun Audio and Microsoft Waveform audio formats
- Execute Java:
  - Java Virtual Machine (JVM)
  - Java class libraries
  - JDK 1.1 base conformance

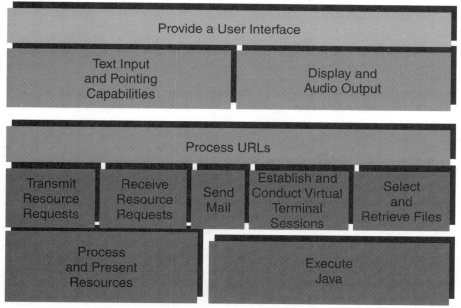

Figure 2-1 Network Computer Abstract Architecture

The physical architecture of NCs vary from vendor to vendor. Supporting the specification is possible in many ways. Some technologies and initiatives that are emerging in the marketplace include:

- Many different CPU architectures
- Java chips

- Lightweight NC operating systems (NCOS), downloaded from the server at start-up or booted from ROM

- Various lightweight desktop environments

- Various authentication and user preference mechanisms, such as SmartCards and server profiling. An extension to the NC standard, the OpenCard smart card initiative, is discussed in Chapter 12's subsection "Sample SmartCard Application" on page 189.

- Caching mechanisms using extra memory, disk, flashROM or some other technology

- Tuned software kits that allow legacy machines (such as 386 PCs) to be resurrected as NCs

Different types of NCs exist in the marketplace, and are planned for release, including:

- Pure NCs—devices created from the ground up to support the NC Technical Standard. Currently, the devices typically boot a modified lightweight operating system from an appropriate server and download their JVM and class libraries. Second-generation devices may implement their Java requirements in hardware or ROM.

- Enhanced (or Hybrid) Terminals—typically (based on) X-terminals whose local operating systems have been improved to include a Java Virtual Machine. The IBM Network Station falls into this category.

- Net-PCs and Windows Based Terminals (WBTs)—effectively PCs running Windows and leveraging Java, supporting centralized "Zero" administration

- Internet Access Devices (IADs) and Set-Top Boxes (STBs)—devices that connect to television systems and provide access to the Internet through built-in Web browsers

- Personal Digital Assistants—hand-held devices that rely on a wireless or wired network environment

- Intelligent Telephones—devices that combine executive telephones with network access

NC Product Example: The IBM Network Station 1000

The IBM Network Station series traces its evolutionary line back to X-terminal technology and is designed to provide an upgrade path for existing terminal users to support modern network computing capabilities.

Figure 2–2 The IBM Network Station

The Network Station is an example of a hybrid NC, which combines traditional support for terminal and display protocols, such as X (using either a built-in Window Manager or one deployed on the host system), VT320, 3270 and 5250, with the ability to execute native Java. Windows applications are supported through Windows-terminal-type functionality, using WinCenter or something like it.

Table 2-1 The IBM Network Station Series 1000 at a Glance

Connection support	Ethernet, Token-Ring
Terminal support	3270 5250 VT320 X-Windows server
Java Virtual Machine	Version 1.1.4
Web browser	Multiple supported
Windows applications	Through multiuser implementations of Windows NT on a PC Server
Memory	32 MB EDO (base) expandable to 64 MB 2 SIMM Sockets Optional 512 KB SRAM cache memory
Connectivity	Ethernet 10/100 Mb or Token-Ring 4/16 Mb
I/O Ports	One serial, one parallel
Video support	Minimum: 640x480 VGA Maximum: 1600x1280 SXGA 2 MB (base) VRAM

Table 2-1 The IBM Network Station Series 1000 at a Glance *(continued)*

Monitor support	Video graphics array (VGA) Super video graphics array (SVGA) Super extended graphics array (SXGA)
Smart card support	T=1 hardware support
Input devices	102-key PC keyboard, two-button mouse
Audio support	16-bit audio
Physical specifications	System unit, excluding base: Height: 243.0mm (9.56 inches) Depth: 292.0mm (11.5 inches) Width: 50.8mm (2.0 inches) Weight: 1.45kg (3.2 lbs.) Power consumption: 40 watts max.

The IBM Network Station kernel is a cut-down version of the Berkeley UNIX operating system that fits into less than 2 MB. This kernel provides an operating system and hardware access for the application software. Figure 2–3 illustrates the general architecture of the Network Station.

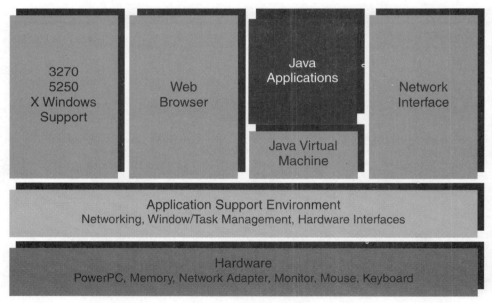

Figure 2–3 IBM Network Station Architecture

A Network Computing Strategy

Given that the world is moving increasingly towards network computing as a way of working, and given that the underlying technology changes on a regular basis, what is the best way to move forward?

- Fitness for purpose is the key philosophy, and network computing suggests that supporting mixed technologies for different users and tasks is possible, based on careful planning and cost analysis.

- Centralized systems management is a good idea for the enterprise.

- For solutions to become decreasingly dependent on physical system specifics and increasingly dependent on a robust network computing environment, we need to be cognizant of standards. Vendors should support standards.

- Supporting the ideals of the NC Technical Standard has merit because the technologies required for conformance are in wide use and are increasing exponentially as the Internet grows.

- Any NC device must meet the needs of the business and enterprise and must be deployed based on a clear understanding of user function.

- Java directly supports the development of network computing applications. NCs are a device class that inherently support Java.

Chapter 3

Distributed Applications

▼ THE MONOLITHIC, NONDISTRIBUTED ALTERNATIVE

▼ A LOOK AT SOME ISSUES

▼ CONSIDERING DISTRIBUTED SYSTEMS DESIGN & DEVELOPMENT STRATEGIES

▼ IN SUMMARY

In common with their competitors, the Lunar Medical Center is facing increasing interplanetary competition, market dynamics, shortening product life-cycles, and the ever-increasing pace of technological change. These forces are putting increasing pressure on their need to manage and manipulate information. In response, their business applications are becoming far more complex than they have ever been.

The Center's system developers are beginning to find it very difficult to create a single, do-it-all, monolithic application. They are turning to the techniques promoted under the banner of distributed systems to help them maintain their competitive position in their industry.

23

The Monolithic, Nondistributed Alternative

Before looking at network computing systems, perhaps now is a good time to examine the current state of affairs.

The monolithic, nondistributed system represents the most "traditional" of all possibilities. It corresponds to a single application, executing completely on a single system, closely coupled to the data upon which it operates. Structurally, the client may possess lax internal structuring with no clear division between the various functions.

Although this is often regarded as a "quick and dirty" solution, there are a few advantages to this style of development:

- This approach may allow for rapid development. This can be especially important for tailor-made solutions or those which have to be developed or prototyped rapidly.

- This approach corresponds to the normal mode of development that has been undertaken for many years. It is relatively simple, or is at least well-known by developers.

- A great variety of toolsets provide direct support for straightforward monolithic development. Support for the development of distributed systems, which are still felt to be more "esoteric," is still distinctly lacking.

- A single monolithic application especially developed for a given platform may give performance that is hard to achieve by any other strategy.

There are also many drawbacks to this style of development:

- The complexity of a monolithic application makes development difficult, and while a good tool such as VisualAge for Java can provide a degree of assistance to the programmer, development can easily get "out of hand."

- The amalgamation of various functions into a single application makes for a very complex system; this may make comprehension difficult, and thus maintenance is often problematic. In addition, monolithic applications are typically not built with reference to a standard "framework," and so each is effectively unique, compounding the problem.

- A monolithic application is required to handle all aspects of processing; so it will typically have large resource requirements, both in terms of memory and CPU processing power.

- Initial deployment and the mechanisms whereby upgrades are introduced can often be problematic.

- It is often very difficult to make use of preexisting functionality within a monolithic application. In large organizations, it is common to find that problems are often "solved" several times—each time in a unique way. This wastes time and money and may directly impact reliability.

- Developing a single monolithic application for a heterogeneous mix of client platforms requires significant effort, both to ensure that a proposed design is appropriate and also during any subsequent porting activity.

- Reliability may be a problem in some circumstances. Trivially, if a monolithic application crashes, all processing stops. Gracefully handling the issues of reliability and scalability, if at all possible, is very hard.

Any good points associated with this methodology are completely swamped by the numerous drawbacks described.

A Look at Some Issues

While distributed systems are usually applied to solve complex situations, they also tend to be inherently more sophisticated than a more traditional monolithic system would be. Some of the issues include:

Extensibility

"Change is the normal state of the universe." Any new system must be engineered to cope with this fundamental fact. Over time, new features will be required, some of which will be substantial and may require a number of subsystems to cooperate. The various software and hardware ecologies are also forever changing and this fact needs to be considered. A common example of the need for extensibility occurs when a system is required to work with suppliers' or other third-party systems.

Scalability and Performance

An expanding user base needs to be accommodated. System changes require ever greater processing power and network bandwidth to service. Performance issues can be addressed by installing server clusters.

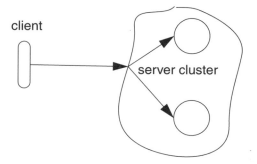

Figure 3–1 Server Clusters Can Cater for Performance Issues in a Transparent Way

It is also necessary to consider the required partitioning of the total system according to criteria such as the size, location, and complexity of the data being manipulated. Applications can also be pooled to achieve greater performance.

Reliability

Crafting a mission-critical application requires careful consideration. Server replication is often used, together with a failover mechanism to ensure that if one copy of the server is unavailable, another is able to take up the load. It is also often necessary to define classes of service to allow a system to degrade gracefully in the face of errors (it is still possible for a distributed order entry application to continue, albeit in a degraded state, for example, if an image of a part cannot be retrieved from an image server).

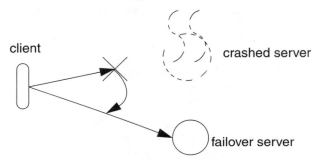

Figure 3–2 A Failover Server Can Transparently Take Over from a Crashed Server

Network partitioning is another potential problem that must be considered. Although network equipment is generally reliable, if a network divides itself into sections as a result of a component failure, each section having a member of a server pool, the two servers can continue to accept work. This may lead to inconsistencies in the total data set that will only be discovered when the two parts of the network are rejoined. Reconciliation strategies to recover from partitioning can be difficult to define.

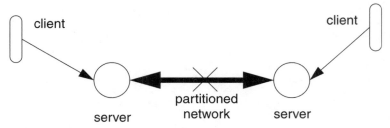

Figure 3–3 Recovering from a Network Partition is a Difficult Task

Security

Security can be an extremely complex matter and is one with a number of faces: privacy, authentication (is an object really what it claims to be?), authorization (what are the operations permitted for this resource?), auditing, proof, and so on. Security is a pervasive aspect of all systems, distributed or not, but those who are unfamiliar with distributed systems are often taken aback that "a surprisingly large portion of the entire infrastructure must be trustworthy, including pieces that you might not have realized were critical" (see Peter G. Neumann (moderator), *The Risks Digest*, Volume 19: Issue 11, http://catless.ncl.ac.uk/ Risks/19.11.html).

Support for existing systems

Nearly all systems have older components or are required to interact with existing systems. The need to cater for legacy systems can introduce considerable complexity or overhead into a system design. It is often the case that complete integration cannot be achieved (reading data may be possible but not update, for example).

Administration

In a busy network, servers need to be monitored, started, stopped, backed up, and restored. Bandwidth bottlenecks occur and need to be diagnosed and corrected (a process which may involve comprehensive reorganization). System administration must be supported by a powerful and diverse toolset.

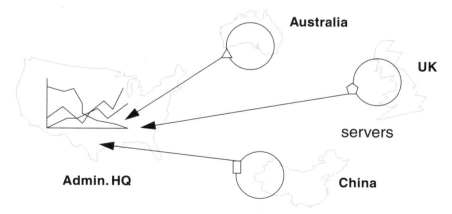

Figure 3–4 Distributed Administration is Vital for Large Distributed Systems

Transparency

Each of the preceding issues are complex when considered separately, but when considered *en-masse*, they can be overwhelming. An effective system architecture will allow the designers to focus on the requisite business tasks and not be overly concerned with the mechanics of dealing with the various issues outlined earlier in this section.

The "holy grail" of distributed systems is often described as "single computer image," meaning that the overall system should appear to the developer no different from a single, powerful and highly reliable computer. It is common to hear distributed systems designers refer to: access, location, failure, migration, replication, persistence, and transaction transparencies.

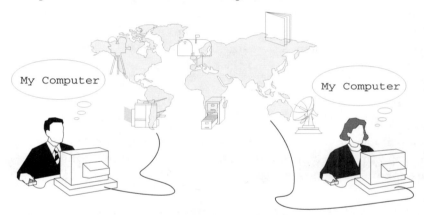

Figure 3–5 The Single Computer Image Concept

The current state of the art cannot deliver this, but the gap between this ideal and reality is steadily closing.

Maintenance

Complex systems are often very dynamic things. Bugfixes, updates, and so forth frequently need to be distributed. This in turn introduces the problem of component version control. For example, the code comprising a server application may be updated to reflect a new business policy, and this change may require the associated client applications to be updated. It can take a fair amount of time to complete the update. Mechanisms are needed to prevent different component versions from working with each other as the update progresses.

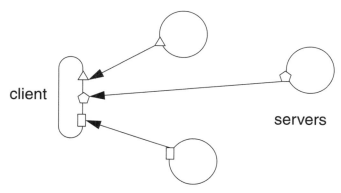

Figure 3–6 A Client Able to Deal with Multiple Versions

It can be very difficult to maintain full backwards compatibility between components while at the same time introducing required changes.

Chapter 5's subsection "Some Java Facilities Supporting Enterprise-Wide Network Computing," on page 98, takes a brief look at some of the tools and environments that exist to assist in the development of distributed systems.

Considering Distributed Systems Design & Development Strategies

Traditional design and development strategies create monolithic, do-it-all applications. This becomes increasingly inappropriate as an enterprise grows in complexity. Modern object-oriented development preaches that applications should be developed as logical groups of cooperating components. Distributed systems design also takes this approach but extends it slightly: Distributed systems should be constructed with functionality provided to clients by logical groupings of cooperating services.

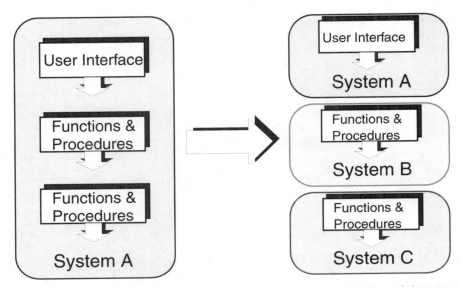

Figure 3–7 The Decomposition of a System into Distributed Cooperating Services

Services are active components that can be accessed to obtain well-defined functionality. Services are usually structured so that each can be accessed in a standard manner, thus reducing complexity.

Figure 3–8 on page 30 shows how this decomposition can be achieved. In this figure, a widget is composed from two parts: a square and a triangle. Each part is furnished by a specialized server. The client requests parts from the servers and assembles them according to its built-in rules.

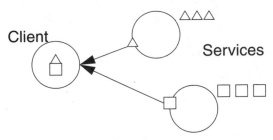

Figure 3–8 Clients and Services

Once an application is decomposed into clients and services, it becomes appropriate to consider where each service should be located.

A simple approach would be to place all data in one place and provide an appropriate service to mediate requests for that data. With this organization, all processing appropriate to that data would be performed in the client.

Although appropriate for some situations, this organization has a number of problems. It is common for business rules to change rapidly. (Discount rates, tariffs, the effects of inflation, and so on can change daily in some industries. Tax rates also change frequently.) Embedding these business rules within a client application creates serious inflexibility at worst or a maintenance nightmare at best.

The problem is that the client is relatively "fat." Data retrieval and processing functions are collocated, and the latter cannot be modified without also affecting the former.

Current thinking teaches that the reverse of this is preferable. In much the same way that a database is "normalized" to remove undesirable duplication of data and thus increase flexibility, so a distributed system is factored to separate its component parts into individual services. An application then becomes an amalgamation of a client and various services.

The factoring procedure also frequently introduces an intermediate "middleware" service layer, resulting in "three-tier client/server distributed computing."

The middleware layer in this discussion performs an additional (and common) function on behalf of the client: to encapsulate and apply the current set of business rules to the data obtained from the various servers in the system.

Middleware has an additional function in many circumstances; According to *Byte* magazine (see "The Muddle in the Middle," *Byte* magazine, April 1996), "Middleware is software that allows elements of applications to interoperate across network links, despite differences in underlying communications protocols, system architectures, OSes, databases, and other application services."

By imposing a well-defined middleware system on all the services in a system, it is possible to ensure that they are all manipulated and structured almost identically. The use of middleware can thus help to maintain order in a large enterprise and can prevent things from getting "out of hand."

Standardization is obviously important when middleware is considered. There are now many commercial middleware toolsets on the market helping to facilitate the development of appropriately structured distributed systems. De facto industry standard systems such as the Distributed Computing Environment (DCE) and, more recently, CORBA, the Common Object Request Broker Architecture, are helping practitioners of distributed computing create structured, effective systems. In addition, there are international standards such as the International Standards Organization's "Reference Model of Open Distributed Processing" (see http://www.iso.ch:8000/RM-ODP).

Middleware is also a favorite tool of Business Process Engineering (BPE) consultants.

With the introduction of middleware, and the relocation of the appropriate processing activities, the client portion in our example becomes a much "thinner" application that is reduced to simple retrieval and display functions.

Figure 3–9 on page 32 shows how the introduction of a middleware layer encapsulating the business logic works. The client no longer interacts directly with the various servers in the system but instead asks the middleware component to operate on its behalf.

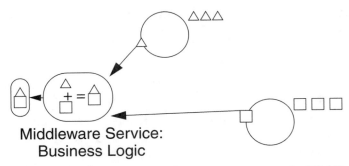

Middleware Service:
Business Logic

Figure 3–9 Isolating the Business Logic into Middleware

This "three-tier" architecture has a number of additional advantages:

- Multiple applications can reuse services, and this can help new applications be developed much more rapidly.

- It becomes possible to modify and maintain services with little impact on the rest of the system.

- Business rules can operate using data from multiple data sources.

- Changes to the underlying infrastructure (such as a database) can be made without rewriting client applications or intermediate services.

- Services can be distributed across a mix of different processing sites, giving flexibility and facilitating effective performance tuning.

The tiered architecture also makes it relatively easy to incorporate existing legacy systems. The legacy system can be presented as a service by a wrapper. As a veneer around the legacy system, the wrapper specifies what services are offered to the clients. As shown in Figure 3–10 on page 33, the wrapper also helps to present a uniform "face": It appears as simply another service in the system and can be accessed in a standard fashion.

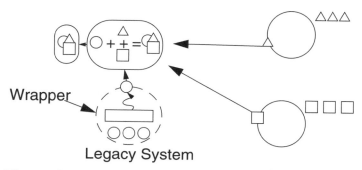

Wrapper

Legacy System

Figure 3–10 Using Wrappering to Incorporate Legacy Systems

It is also possible to generalize from three to an arbitrary number of tiers, and this is sometimes useful, particularly when organizational boundaries are being crossed and it is necessary to incorporate an existing system already structured into tiers as a service in a larger system.

An alternative—and common—view of this situation is the "peer-to-peer" organization. In this case, the distinction between client and server is less sharp: A component may offer services to a client, and to fulfil that offer, may be a client of another server.

A further major design issue related to the design of distributed systems concerns the asynchronous delivery of events. Events allow systems to respond to relatively infrequent occurrences of a situation with efficiency. In an enterprise network, events may include:

- A notification that a printer has jammed, which requires clearing and restarting

- The output from a database trigger highlighting that the level of a given product in the warehouse has reached a predefined reorder point

- An important announcement has been posted to the staff notes database

It is important, both from the point of view of ease of development and from that of efficiency, that the repeated checking for the occurrence of a situation of interest be avoided. The delivery of event notifications is a difficult topic and can complicate a design quite substantially.

In Summary

While the monolithic way of structuring enterprise-wide applications has some commendable points, it also has many problems and can effectively be ruled out for most network computing environments.

The technique of building distributed systems divided into clients and tiers of services is substantially more complicated, but is clearly more powerful and fits into the network computing world cleanly.

Industry-standard middleware software and internationally accepted techniques are increasingly being used to structure and define multi-tiered environments.

## Chapter 4

HTML-Based Clients

▼ Browsers and Web Servers

▼ HTML Overview

▼ Client Intelligence—JavaScript

This chapter investigates the implementation of simple client applications using HTML and JavaScript. This facilitates using browsers as the data entry interface because they are readily and inexpensively available and deployable.

The Lunar Medical Center check-in application as a whole consists of the data entry form, feeding its data to a server implemented as a Java servlet, which stores its data on the host system (using one of a number of storage mechanisms) and responds to the client. The total functionality of the application is partitioned to several layers, deployed where appropriate. Figure 4–1 illustrates this distribution of components.

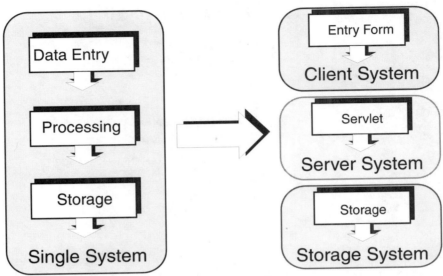

Figure 4–1 Check-In Application Distribution

Hypertext Markup Language (HTML) is the current language of choice for publishing resources on the network. It is a nonproprietary format based on the Standardized Generalized Markup Language (SGML) and is promulgated by an international industry consortium—the World Wide Web Consortium (W3C). Using HTML to design the client component of your application is a very simple and portable solution.

> *Note*
>
> SGML is an ISO standard (ISO 8879:1986). SGML allows you to define the logical structure of a document type in a very rigorous way using a Document Type Definition (DTD). Once a DTD such as HTML has been defined, it becomes possible to structure a document according to the specified rules.

Browsers, the applications most used today to access and display resources on the network, provide an excellent platform for the client components of simple client/server applications.

Simplifying network access and standardizing a "universal" data format has proven to be a very popular idea, gaining momentum exponentially and giving us the Internet we know today.

Browsers and Web Servers

Browsers were born out of a desire to integrate formerly separate network access functions within one simplified interface. They first appeared early in 1992. Most modern browsers, such as those produced by Netscape, Microsoft, Sun and others, provide several key functionalities.

- Display of resources coded using HTML.

- Support for some form of scripting mechanism (such as JavaScript) which allows additional code to be included in an HTML document. Scripting languages typically provide enhanced access to objects within the browser interface and HTML document, as well as many generic language features. Scripts are very useful for validation of data on an HTML-based client prior to interaction with a server.

- A Java Virtual Machine (JVM) for execution of Java applets. Applets are not stand-alone Java applications; they rely on a context to support their execution. The browser supplies the context, which provides strong security to restrain the applets from certain sensitive operations, such as access to the file system on the client, and a restricted set of network operations.

- Browsers that support a JVM often provide additional proprietary Java class libraries to extend Java's features and functionality. Netscape's Internet Foundation Classes (IFC) and Microsoft's Advanced Foundation Classes (AFC) are examples.

- Support for browser plug-ins. Plug-ins are proprietary software programs that extend the capabilities of browsers in a certain way—giving them the ability to play audio or view movies, for example.

Browsers request resources from servers using one of a number of supported network protocols, the predominant being the Hypertext Transfer Protocol (HTTP). Important aspects of HTTP are discussed in Chapter 7.

Requests are made using a structured naming convention, known as Universal Resource Identifiers (URIs). Every resource available on the network—HTML document, image, video clip, program, and so on—has a unique address that may be encoded by a URI. A Uniform Resource Locator (URL), the most common form of network URI, typically consists of three pieces of information:

- The naming scheme of the protocol or mechanism used to access the resource

- The name of the system hosting the resource

- The name of the resource itself, with its absolute location on the host system

> ── *Note* ───
>
> Uniform Resource Locators (URLs) are one subtype (and the subtype most commonly used in this book) of the more general URI naming scheme. Book ISBN numbers are also a type of URI.

Some example URL-type URIs are:

```
http://www.dstc.edu.au/index.html
http://www.pc.ibm.com/networkstation/news/station/index.html
http://jf0150b.itsc.austin.ibm.com/servlet/ProcessSQL
ftp://ftp.dstc.edu.au/incoming/readme.txt
jdbc:db2://juergen.itsc.austin.ibm.com:8888/sample
```

The basic operation of the Web server is to supply the requested HTML resource/s to the client. Figure 4–2 shows the general relationship between browsers and Web servers.

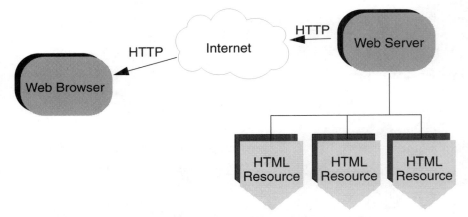

Figure 4–2 General Architecture of Browsers and Web Servers

Many Web servers also provide a number of mechanisms for interfacing with server-side applications. This is usually done for processing input from the client and dynamically constructing responses (typically in HTML) interpretable by the client browser. Such mechanisms include:

- The Common Gateway Interface (CGI) for interfacing regular programs with the Web server.
- Server plug-ins, similar in concept to browser plug-ins. An example is a plug-in allowing the Web server to interface directly with a Rational Database Management System (RDBMS).
- Java servlets—Java components written to accept and respond to HTTP requests.

Figure 4–3 shows that the general architecture of browsers and Web servers has evolved, and continues to do so.

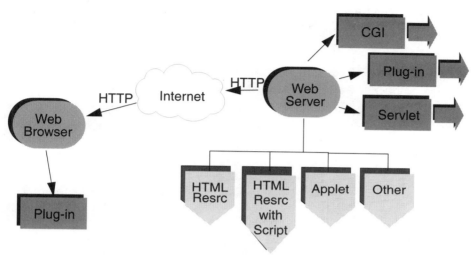

Figure 4–3 Growing Architecture of Browsers and Web Servers

HTML Overview

HTML is a widely accepted way of formatting documents that can be created and processed using a range of tools, from simple text editors to sophisticated graphical authoring tools. Web pages are the most common use of HTML.

HTML consists of a series of *tags* taking the general form of:

```
<TAG tag-attributes> my text </TAG>
```

The above example shows an *opening tag*, the tag's attributes, some content, and a *closing tag*. When coding HTML, blocks of text are *tagged*. Appendix A, "Brief HTML Reference" on page 247, provides an overview of the most commonly used tags, grouped in a number of general functional categories.

HTML Conformance

The HTML Standard, like most things in this industry, gets revised from time to time in order to adopt new features, and to deprecate or remove dated ones. Most of the currently deployed HTML resources have been coded using version 3.2 or below of the HTML Standard. The most recent W3C work has resulted in a much expanded Standard—HTML 4.0. In addition to the text, multimedia, and hyperlink features of the previous versions of HTML, HTML 4.0 supports more multimedia options, scripting languages, style sheets, better printing facilities, documents that are more accessible to users with disabilities, and internationalization.

HTML 4.0 is not yet widely adopted; so code conformance to HTML 3.2 will ensure the widest support. Third parties have also extended the Standard with their own tags, which may or may not be supported by all browsers. If you intend developing 100 percent pure HTML, these browser-specific extensions should be avoided.

Developing in HTML

There are a number of ways to create a Web page (generate HTML code), such as:

- Manually, using a text editor. This method requires a browser to view the HTML code and relies on the developer's ability to design from scratch. Clear knowledge of HTML tags and techniques will result in clean minimal code with a low download time. To improve readability while developing, there a number of text editors which support automatic code indentation and construct color-coding, and several are available as *shareware* from the Internet.

- Visually, using a Web page design package. This method generally requires desktop publishing skills, as such packages bear close resemblance to this class of software. The benefit here is that a Web page can be created without a fundamental knowledge of HTML. Work is simply saved as it would be with any other document-creation package; the difference is that the saved file is in HTML format. Such packages support rapid development and provide user-friendly facilities to implement otherwise complex components of a Web page. The main problem is that the HTML code generated by these packages is typically less than optimal.

- By converting other document formats. Many modern word processor, desktop publishing, spreadsheet, and database packages provide a means to export their native formats to HTML. For example, a table of information for a Web page could be generated by exporting a spreadsheet or database query results as an HTML file. As with the visual method, the generated code is often "heavier" than necessary.

- Dynamically, as output from an application. The results of an application can be easily output in HTML format and streamed by the Web server back to the client browser. This is the art of developing Web server applications, and it requires clear knowledge of HTML and the utilized Web server/application integration mechanism (CGI, servlets, and so forth.)

- Automatically, as the output from an HTML-format documentation mechanism. An example is the Java utility, `javadoc`, which creates documentation from Java source code.

As you begin to develop more complex Web-based applications, you will find yourself adopting a hybrid approach, using a mix of tools and techniques that best suits the particular job.

Simple Example

Here is a very simple HTML file (which is saved as `index.html`). Note the basic structure.

```
<HTML>
<HEAD>
    <TITLE>Lunar Facilities</TITLE>
</HEAD>
<BODY>
    <H1>Welcome to the Moon</H1>
    <P>Available facilities are:</P>
    <UL>
      <LI><A HREF="medical.html">Lunar Medical
            Center</A></LI>
      <LI><A HREF="gym.html">Lunar Gymnasium</A></LI>
      <LI><A HREF="bar.html">Lunar Bar and Grill</A></LI>
    </UL>
</BODY>
</HTML>
```

Observe that there are two main sections within enclosing <HTML> and </HTML> tags—a header section and a body section. Most activity will occur in the body section of the HTML code. Within the body section, observe the use of level 1 heading, paragraph, unordered list, list item, and anchor (hyperlink) tags.

Note the hyperlink tags in this example. Simple references are used to linked files (for example `medical.html`) because the linked file is placed in the same host system directory as `index.html`, and the browser knows to fully qualify the shorthand URI at request-time. The browser knows that the shorthand location is *relative* to the location of the linking document. In other words:

```
<A HREF="medical.html">Lunar Medical Center</A>
```

...is effectively the same as:

```
<A HREF="http://www.moon.xyz/medical.html">Lunar Medical Center</A>
```

> **Note**
>
> The URI `http://www.moon.xyz` is a fictitious location; so your code and display should reflect the URI of the actual system you use for deployment.

Figure 4–4 shows how the file will appear in a browser, along with arrows which indicate the relationship between the HTML code elements and the display.

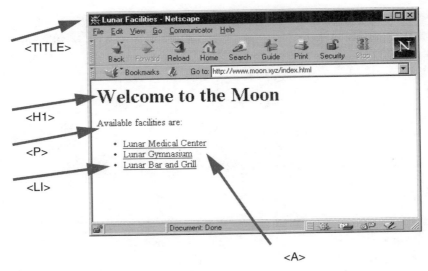

Figure 4–4 Simple HTML Example

Forms and Tables

Let's extend the Moonbase system by implementing the Medical Center check-in facility (`medical.html`). HTML form tags will be used to provide a means for entering the data to register a patient into the Medical Center. The code also uses the table tags to produce an attractive layout of the window.

```
<HTML>
<HEAD>
    <TITLE>Hospital Check-In Form</TITLE>
</HEAD>
<BODY>
    <CENTER>
    <H1>Lunar Medical Centre Check-In</H1>
    <FORM NAME=checkin METHOD=post ACTION=http://server.moon.xyz/servlet/Process>
    <TABLE WIDTH="90%" BORDER=1 CELLPADDING=10>
        <TR>
          <TD ALIGN=CENTER COLSPAN=2>
             <P>Enter your details and press the <I>Submit Details</I> button</P>
          </TD>
        </TR>
        <TR>
          <TD ALIGN=RIGHT WIDTH="50%">
            <P>Last Name: <INPUT TYPE=TEXT NAME=lastname SIZE=20 MAXLENGTH=40></P>
            <P>First Name: <INPUT TYPE=TEXT NAME=firstname SIZE=20 MAXLENGTH=40></P>
            <P>Date of Birth (DD/MM/YYYY):
               <INPUT TYPE=TEXT NAME=dobday SIZE=2 MAXLENGTH=2>/
```

```
             <INPUT TYPE=TEXT NAME=dobmonth SIZE=2 MAXLENGTH=2>/
             <INPUT TYPE=TEXT NAME=dobyear SIZE=3 MAXLENGTH=4></P>
          <P>Social Security (###-##-###):
             <INPUT TYPE=TEXT NAME=ssec1 SIZE=3 MAXLENGTH=3>-
             <INPUT TYPE=TEXT NAME=ssec2 SIZE=2 MAXLENGTH=2>-
             <INPUT TYPE=TEXT NAME=ssec3 SIZE=3 MAXLENGTH=3></P>
        </TD>
        <TD ALIGN=LEFT WIDTH="50%">
          <P>Sex: Male <INPUT TYPE=RADIO NAME=gender VALUE=M>
                Female <INPUT TYPE=RADIO NAME=gender VALUE=F></P>
        </TD>
      </TR>
      <TR>
        <TD ALIGN=CENTER COLSPAN=2>
           <P><INPUT TYPE=submit VALUE="Submit Details">
              <INPUT TYPE=reset VALUE="Reset Details"></P>
        </TD>
      </TR>
    </TABLE>
    </FORM>
    </CENTER>
</BODY>
</HTML>
```

Figure 4–5 shows how the file will appear in a browser. Note the relationship between the form and table code elements and the subsequent display.

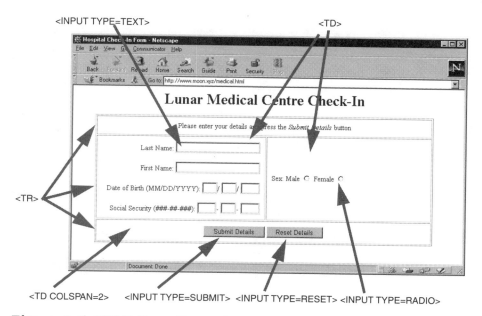

Figure 4–5 HTML Form Example

Let's examine some interesting aspects of this example.

The Table

```
<TABLE WIDTH="90%" BORDER=1 CELLPADDING=10>
   :
</TABLE>
```

This definition results in a table that must: span 90 percent of the browser window width (maintained regardless of the current window size), have a border one pixel wide, and surround (pad) each cell's contents with 10 pixels of space.

When the browser constructs a table, it examines each row definition before determining the number of columns to display in the table. The check-in table has three rows. The middle row has the most with two table data cells; so the table's display column count is two. In order to implement the first and third rows of the table, which appear to only have one column, a table data cell that *spans* two columns is created with the following code:

```
<TD ALIGN=CENTER COLSPAN=2>
```

The Form

```
<FORM NAME=checkin METHOD=post ACTION=http://server.moon.xyz
/servlet/Process>
   :
</FORM>
```

This FORM definition has several important aspects other than the form's name:

- When the form is submitted (by pressing the input button tagged as SUBMIT-type on the form), the data will be sent to the application Process through the *http* protocol, to the server location *servlet*, on the server machine, *server.moon.xyz*.

- The data will be submitted using the *post* method.

Servlets and form submission methods are discussed in Chapter 7.

To Validate or Not to Validate...

An important aspect of the code implemented so far is that there is no *validation* of the data that is entered and submitted. The assumption is that the server application (http://server.moon.xyz/servlet/Process) will verify that the required fields have been entered, the dates are correct, and so on.

Assuming that this is true, regardless of whether the server reports back an error or success, a *new page* must be instantiated in the browser for the HTML response from the server. This means that if there is an error, the user must go back a screen, reenter, revalidate, and so on. Not only may this become awkward for the user, but each submission will result in additional network traffic. This might become an issue for applications that submit large datasets.

There are two aspects to validation—*syntax* and *semantics*. In terms of general distributed system design, having this validation on the server/s is a reasonable separation of functionality, and results in a very *thin client*. With the Lunar Medical Center browser/HTML-based check-in application, the preference is to check the data *syntax* prior to submission so that problems can be reported to the user while on the same screen. Once users are ready to submit syntactically valid data, they only have to do it once, and the server can determine the *semantic* correctness (whether meaningful or not) of the data (usually a database function).

HTML itself does not provide any mechanisms for such functionality. The combination of HTML in association with a supported *scripting language* such as JavaScript provides a powerful way to locate some intelligence in the client application.

Client Intelligence—JavaScript

JavaScript (formerly Netscape's *LiveScript* and the basis for the forthcoming standards-based *ECMAScript*) is the most popular scripting language for the World Wide Web. JavaScript is embedded within hundreds of thousands of Web pages.

JavaScript looks a little like Java. Their expressions and flow of control are almost the same, and the general language syntax is similar; but other than these incomplete syntactic resemblances, JavaScript and Java are entirely unrelated. The naming of both is also purely (and unfortunately) coincidental.

In contrast to Java's compile-time system of classes built by declarations, JavaScript supports a run-time system based on a small set of data types representing numeric, Boolean and string values. JavaScript has a simple instance-based object model, but it still provides significant capabilities. Table 4-1 compares and contrasts JavaScript and Java.

Table 4-1 JavaScript and Java

JavaScript	Java
Textual source interpreted by browser	Intermediate binary bytecode (compiled from textual source) interpreted by Java VM
Object-based (code uses built-in extensible objects, but no classes or inheritance)	Object-oriented (object classes with inheritance)

Table 4-1 JavaScript and Java *(continued)*

Code integrated with, and embedded in, HTML	Code is distinct (but can be accessed from HTML using <APPLET> tag)
Variables not declared	Variables must be declared
Dynamic binding (object references checked at run-time)	Static binding (object references must exist at compile-time)

JavaScript can handle interactive events such as mouse-clicks, form input and page navigation. Event-handlers are embedded in HTML code as additional attributes of tags to which JavaScript code is assigned for execution. The general syntax is:

```
<TAG tag-attributes eventHandler="JavaScript Code"></TAG>
```

It is good design practice to assign the event-handler code to a JavaScript function so the same code can be used for other items and events. This assists with code readability. Events apply to HTML tags as follows:

Table 4-2 Browser/HTML Events and Associated JavaScript Event-Handlers

Event	JavaScript event-handler
Blur - occurs when the user removes input focus from a form element	onBlur()
Click - occurs when the user clicks on a form element or link	onClick()
Change - occurs when the user changes the value of a text, text area or select element	onChange()
Focus - occurs when the user gives the form element input focus	onFocus()
Load - occurs when the user loads the page in the browser	onLoad()
Mouse Over - occurs when the user moves the mouse pointer over a link or anchor	onMouseOver()
Select - occurs when the user selects a form element's input field	onSelect()
Submit - occurs when the user submits a form (typically by pressing the Submit form button)	onSubmit()
Unload - occurs when the user exits the current page in the browser	onUnload()

JavaScript can be associated with an HTML form to verify that a user enters valid information into a field. Since JavaScript runs locally within the browser, the Java-Script can check the entered data and alert the user if the input is invalid.

While the simplicity of JavaScript is appealing, there are some caveats:

- Be aware that not every browser supports the language, and if it does, use of the language is optional. Users may have their JavaScript disabled.

- There is an additional resource load on the system (through the browser) if JavaScript is enabled. This load varies depending on the system and the application.

- Although scripts can provide an impressive amount of local processing power and can allow for a high degree of user interactivity, an HTML and JavaScript-based application may still provide an interface that is somewhat less rich than for a traditional application.

- It can be difficult to map an application's required functionality onto the facilities provided by a World Wide Web browser.

Use JavaScript appropriately, and ensure it meets the needs of the application and is supported by the intended user base.

Simple JavaScript Examples

JavaScript is embedded directly into the HTML page. To see how it works, let's revisit the Lunar home page and insert some simple JavaScript (shown in bold type). Don't worry about the language syntax at this stage, just observe the way JavaScript is introduced into the HTML.

```
<HTML>
<HEAD>
    <TITLE>Lunar Facilities</TITLE>
</HEAD>
<BODY>
    <H1>Welcome to the Moon</H1>
    <SCRIPT LANGUAGE="JavaScript">
      <!-- Hide
      document.write("We hope you enjoy your stay.")
      //-->
    </SCRIPT>
    <P>Available facilities are:</P>
    <UL>
      <LI><A HREF="medical.html">Lunar Medical Center</A></LI>
      <LI><A HREF="gym.html">Lunar Gymnasium</A></LI>
      <LI><A HREF="bar.html">Lunar Bar and Grill</A></LI>
    </UL>
</BODY>
</HTML>
```

Figure 4–6 shows how the new file will appear in a browser. Note the additional output produced by the JavaScript.

Figure 4–6 Simple JavaScript Example

Obviously, this is a trivial example. Let's investigate something that regular HTML could not achieve. A useful extension to the previous example would be to associate some opening and closing times for each Lunar facility and create a variable to hold the current time. When the user selects one of the facilities that is "closed," a pop-up window appears with an appropriate message.

In the following code, notice the use of a *function* defined in JavaScript. It looks much the same as a function, procedure or method defined in any other language. Functions should be defined in the header section of the HTML because there is a guarantee that they are loaded and checked by the browser before any user interaction can occur. Notice also how the function is called from an event-handler associated (in this case) with the hyperlink tag objects.

```
<HTML>
<HEAD>
   <TITLE>Lunar Facilities</TITLE>
   <SCRIPT LANGUAGE="JavaScript">
     <!-- Hide
     function checkOpen(venue) {
         openTimes = new Array(8,12,16);
         closeTimes = new Array(15,19,23);
         if (now < openTimes[venue])
           alert("Be aware that this facility opens at " + openTimes[venue]);
         else
           if (now > closeTimes[venue])
```

```
            alert("Be aware that this facility closed at " + closeTimes[venue]);
        }
        //-->
    </SCRIPT>
</HEAD>
<BODY>
    <H1>Welcome to the Moon</H1>
    <SCRIPT LANGUAGE="JavaScript">
        <!-- Hide
        today = new Date();
        now = today.getHours();
        document.write("The current time is: " + now)
        //-->
    </SCRIPT>
    <P>Available facilities are:</P>
    <UL>
        <LI><A HREF="medical.html" onClick="checkOpen(0)">
            Lunar Medical Center</A></LI>
        <LI><A HREF="gym.html" onClick="checkOpen(1)">Lunar Gymnasium</A></LI>
        <LI><A HREF="bar.html" onClick="checkOpen(2)">
            Lunar Bar and Grill</A></LI>
    </UL>
</BODY>
</HTML>
```

Figure 4–7 shows how the application will appear in a browser for a customer who has attempted to visit the Lunar Bar and Grill before hours! Note the additional output produced by the JavaScript.

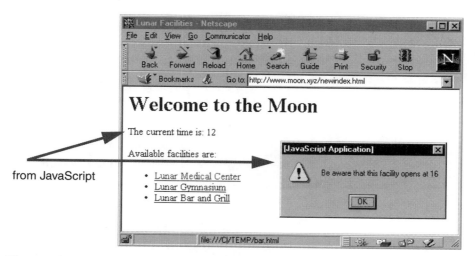

Figure 4–7 Intermediate JavaScript Example

Using JavaScript

When a page is loaded in a browser, a number of objects are created corresponding to the page, its contents, and other pertinent information. JavaScript organizes all browser and Web-page objects in a hierarchy, each having certain properties and methods. Every page (in a browser) has the following objects:

window The top-level object which contains properties and methods that apply to the entire window (`self` is a synonym for the current window; `top` refers to the topmost browser window; `parent` refers to a window containing a frameset)

location Contains properties for the current URI

history Contains properties representing URIs the user has previously visited

document Contains properties for the content in the current HTML document

The objects in the browser exist in a hierarchy that reflects the hierarchical structure of the HTML page itself. In the strict object-oriented sense, this type of hierarchy is an *instance* hierarchy, since it concerns specific instances of objects rather than the object classes. Figure 4–8 illustrates the instance hierarchy for a sample HTML document.

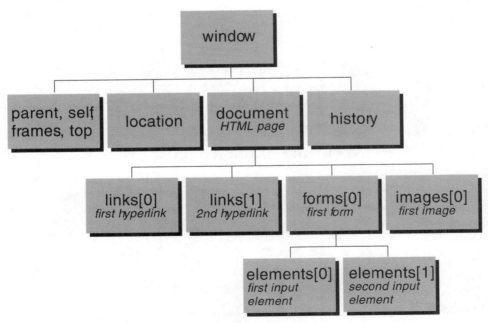

Figure 4–8 JavaScript Instance Hierarchy

A browser constructs the display of an HTML file in a *top-down* fashion, sequentially moving through the code and building the layout as it goes. JavaScript similarly constructs its instance model by examining the HTML top-down. In a Web page, the top-level object is known as the document object. The first image is known as images[0], the first link as links[0], the second as links[1], and so on. Note that reference numbering starts at zero, not 1.

To reference an object in JavaScript code, its *fully qualified* reference is used. The window object is not required if the current window is being referred to. For example, the first hyperlink would be:

```
document.links[0]
```

Forms have their own subhierarchy, with the first form known as forms[0]. The first input element in that form is elements[0]. The fully qualified reference to this element would be:

```
document.forms[0].elements[0]
```

To access what has been entered into the form element, the object's value is referenced:

```
document.forms[0].elements[0].value.
```

To avoid having to use fully qualified references, which can quickly become tedious, the object's *name* (as defined in HTML) may be used. For example, consider an HTML fragment used in the Medical Center patient check-in facility:

```
      :
<FORM NAME=checkin METHOD=post ACTION=http://server.moon.xyz/servlet/Process>
      :
  <P>First Name: <INPUT TYPE=TEXT NAME=firstname SIZE=20 MAXLENGTH=40></P>
      :
```

Instead of referring to the *First Name* form field's data value in JavaScript as:

```
document.forms[0].elements[1].value
```

the following could be used:

```
document.checkin.firstname.value
```

A very useful object available is the predefined window object. JavaScript allows creation, population, and closure of additional browser windows (including pop-ups) using several methods available on this object. The alert() method in the previous JavaScript example is a window object method that provides a pop-up facility.

To illustrate, the previous example may be altered slightly to allow loading of the linked facilities into a new browser window. The code below highlights (in bold type) five simple modifications, and Figure 4–9 on page 53 shows the result of clicking the Medical Center hyperlink. Notice that a reference to the current object (this), in this case the hyperlink object, is now passed to the event-handler function. The object's href data value may now be accessed for the window object open() method in the function.

```html
<HTML>
<HEAD>
    <TITLE>Lunar Facilities</TITLE>
    <SCRIPT LANGUAGE="JavaScript">
      <!-- Hide
      function checkOpen(field,venue) {
          openTimes = new Array(8,12,16);
          closeTimes = new Array(15,19,23);
          if (now < openTimes[venue])
            alert("Be aware that this facility opens at " + openTimes[venue]);
          else
            if (now > closeTimes[venue])
               alert("Be aware that this facility closed at " + closeTimes[venue]);
          newWindow = open(field.href);
       }
      //-->
    </SCRIPT>
</HEAD>
<BODY>
    <H1>Welcome to the Moon</H1>
    <SCRIPT LANGUAGE="JavaScript">
      <!-- Hide
      today = new Date();
      now = today.getHours();
      document.write("The current time is: " + now)
      //-->
    </SCRIPT>
    <P>Available facilities are:</P>
    <UL>
      <LI><A HREF="medical.html" onClick="checkOpen(this,0)"
         >Lunar Medical Center</A></LI>
      <LI><A HREF="gym.html" onClick="checkOpen(this,1)">Lunar Gymnasium</A></LI>
      <LI><A HREF="bar.html" onClick="checkOpen(this,2)">Lunar Bar and
         Grill</A></LI>
    </UL>
</BODY>
</HTML>
```

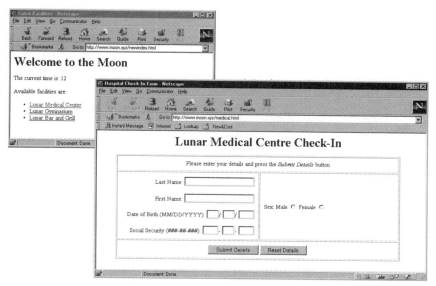

Figure 4–9 Intermediate JavaScript Example Using New Window

Another useful object available to JavaScript code is the `location` object, which holds the address of the loaded HTML document in its `href` data value. For example, the Medical Center check-in page's `location.href` value would be `http://www.moon.xyz/medical.html`. New values can be assigned to `location.href` to immediately load a new page into the browser window.

Other features and facilities available with JavaScript include access to frames, the browser status bar, layers, time-out mechanisms, built-in string, date and math objects, and many more. As with HTML, it is not the purpose of this book to give a full reference to all features. The best place to find the most current JavaScript reference is on Netscape's Website at:

`http://developer.netscape.com/docs/manuals/communicator/jsref/`

## Chapter 5

Java-Based Clients

▼ A Brief Overview of Java

▼ Client-Server Computing with Java

▼ The Lunar Medical Center's Java Application

▼ The Lunar Medical Center's Java Applet

▼ Some Java Facilities Supporting Enterprise-Wide Network Computing

▼ In Summary

This chapter has three aims. The first is to introduce Java and take a brief look at its features and facilities.

A second aim is to introduce you to the Java-based Lunar Medical Center patient record retrieval and update application that is used as the vehicle for discussion in the remainder of the book.

The final aim of the chapter is to provide a short overview of some Java facilities supporting enterprise-wide network computing—the "ecology" of Java: its features, properties and related technologies.

A Brief Overview of Java

The "traditional" description of Java is:

"Java: A simple, object-oriented, network-savvy, interpreted, robust, secure, architecture neutral, portable, high-performance, multithreaded, dynamic language." (from: The Java Language: An Overview,
`http://java.sun.com/docs/overviews/java/java-overview-1.html`).

This audacious statement covers practically the whole arena of development! Each claim will be briefly examined in turn.

Simple

The Java language is certainly simpler than its C or C++ forbears, but it is important to keep in mind that development is a hard activity, regardless of the language used. Programming for network computing remains an even harder activity than developing for "simple," non-distributed environments.

Object-Oriented

In common with most modern programming languages, Java is object-oriented from the ground up: Almost everything in Java is an object, and what isn't can be wrapped and hidden behind an object interface. In contrast to the earlier language C++, there are no nonobject-oriented features in the language. This accounts to a large degree for the enhanced robustness of systems developed in Java.

Network-Savvy

Straight "out of the box," Java provides facilities for building sophisticated, object-oriented distributed systems using Remote Method Invocation (RMI). Java also supplies the facilities for working with World Wide Web browsers and with legacy systems such as FTP and Telnet.

Starting with Version 1.2, Java will also offer an implementation of the Common Object Request Broker Architecture (CORBA) standard.

Interpreted, Portable and Architecture-Neutral

Rather than being compiled into the native code for a given architecture, in a break from tradition, Java is compiled into a compact intermediate code that has no direct correspondence to any given item of hardware. This intermediate code is instead executed under the auspices of an interpreter known as the Java Virtual Machine (JVM). The JVM is a relatively straightforward program that can be easily ported from one machine architecture to another with only minimal change. It is this fact that accounts for the portability of Java code and for a large part of its appeal.

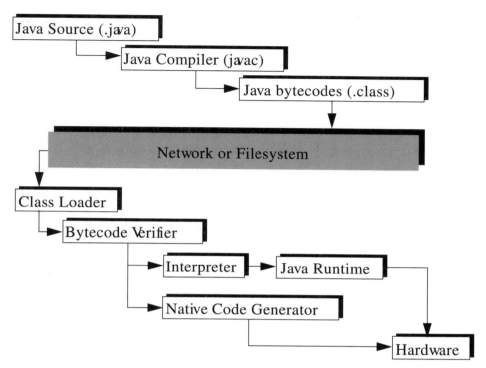

Figure 5-1 Java's Architecture-Neutrality Arises from the Use of Byte-codes

Java's portability also stems from the inclusion of a number of standard library facilities that all Java environments are required to provide. Given this, developers do not have to worry about the existence or quality of a given entity: If the desired functionality is defined as part of the standard facilities, it can be relied upon; otherwise it will have to be supplied by the developer according to need.

Robust and Secure

Java was originally intended for the creation of embedded code (code that would be incorporated into devices such as dishwashers and toasters). Given this, it is no surprise that the design of the Java language makes it easy to create code that is relatively error-free: Consumers would not be happy if their toaster continually produced burnt toast because of a developer error!

Java has no pointers (sometimes called "the goto of the data structure") and handles memory allocation and deallocation "behind the scenes." These two features remove many possibilities for error. Other language features, such as exception handling, bounded arrays and a built-in string type, also make it easy to create well-behaved code.

Security is an area where the Java engineers have devoted a lot of time and effort.

As shown in Figure 5–1 on page 57, downloaded code is verified prior to execution to ensure a base level of trustworthiness.

- The bytecode verifier ensures that bytecode is structured correctly and is not likely to induce problems at run time. These tests are required because it is assumed that bytecode may be designed to be malicious or that an uncaught compiler error may manifest itself and thus cause problems.

- A large number of tests are carried out, including: ensuring that no instructions are likely to index beyond the limits of an array, that the run-time stack is always correctly formatted (the number of stack pops are equal to the number of pushes) and that types are always used in appropriate ways (no attempt is being made to use an integer as a reference to an object, for example).

- A number of security policies embedded within the virtual machine are enforced as well. Rather than being given unrestricted access to the full resources of the machine on which it is executing, downloaded Java code is fairly constrained in what it may do. Among other things, a downloaded applet cannot access the host machine's filesystem; it cannot connect to an arbitrary server on the internet, and it cannot execute a native command in the host system.

- The combination of JVM and security policies is commonly called the "sandbox." Java code is constrained to execute like a baby playing in a sandbox: The baby cannot destroy delicate objects outside the sandbox, just as the Java code cannot adversely affect the host system, either maliciously or unintentionally.

With the sandbox ensuring that Java code cannot act as a virus, or behave badly in some other fashion, users are free to use downloaded code without worry.

Additional security mechanisms are also being introduced into Java. A key mechanism is the "digital signature" for applets. This is intended to provide a means whereby the author and the integrity of the applet may be established. A digital signature is essentially a mathematical code applied to the applet, which results in a value that is carried around with it. *Any* change made to the applet (including attempts to change the signature itself) will result in a different value for the signature. When a browser downloads an applet, it attempts to recalculate the signature. If the value it generates is different from the one that is carried around with the applet, then the applet is assumed to have been tampered with, and the browser will not execute it.

If a valid digital signature indicates that the applet's author is trusted, and the code is unaltered from the time of signing, it is reasoned that the code may safely be given additional abilities (access to limited portions of the native file system, for example).

Security is the leading differentiator between Java and Microsoft's competing technology, ActiveX (which allows for the execution of downloaded native code without the security constraints imposed by the Java sandbox).

High-Performance

Java is an interpreted language and as such faces a performance penalty when compared with languages like C or C++ that are traditionally compiled prior to execution. For the small, highly interactive uses for which Java has so far been employed, this is not a great problem, but as the use of Java becomes more widespread, performance becomes a potential problem.

Java supplies two mechanisms to obviate this problem: the Just-In-Time compiler (JIT) and the new "HotSpot" technology.

A JIT boosts execution speed by converting Java bytecode to native code "on the fly," which can then be directly executed instead of being interpreted as bytecode by the Java Virtual Machine.

Sun's new HotSpot Virtual Machine technology uses a process called "Adaptive Optimization":

- As an application runs, the JVM detects the frequently used "hot spots." It then immediately uses this information to optimize those critical portions of the code.

- Because run-time information is available, the hotspot compiler can do a better job than a static compiler.

- Because optimization saves a considerable amount of time in the overall lifetime of the application, very aggressive and time-consuming optimizations can be performed and still result in a net reduction of the execution time.

It is claimed that Java performance will soon be on a par with that of compiled C++.

Multithreaded

Instead of only allowing a single operation to be performed at a time, Java provides threads to allow the application designer to specify that operations may be performed "in tandem."

On a single CPU system, of course, tandem execution is implemented by fast switching between threads and is an illusion, but when multiple real CPUs are present, threads can actually be executed in parallel, and a substantial speedup can result (if the JVM is written to take advantage of multiple CPUs).

In addition, the presence of threads as a part of the language definition allows the application designer to more closely model a real-world problem.

Dynamic

Recognizing that downloading code across the Internet can be a very slow proposition, the designers of Java have incorporated a dynamic loading feature into the JVM. A class is only loaded—for an applet, fetched from the server—when it is actually needed at execution time. Since 80 percent of the program is typically catered for by only about 20 percent of the application code, this can result in a substantial time saving.

After looking at these features, it should now be clear to you that Java represents a powerful tool for application development. Several features make it close to ideal for developing in a network computing arena.

It must be said that Java is currently not problem-free, however. It is still a young language, and this is reflected in the rate of change of development tools, libraries, and so forth. As with any complex piece of software, different ports and versions of the JVM and the core class libraries also exhibit different bugs. Crafting a fully portable Java application still remains an art form, although this is improving rapidly and may in any case be very much simpler than for some languages.

Most people's initial contact with Java is through the Sun Java Development Kit (JDK). While perfectly adequate for experimentation and the development of simple applications, it is not an industrial-strength tool. Many developers fairly rapidly adopt more sophisticated tools such as IBM's VisualAge for Java, which is what we used in this book. VisualAge for Java is discussed in Appendix B, "Java Development: Using VisualAge for Java" on page 255.

The "100 percent pure Java" initiative is currently of some importance in getting developers to focus on the portability of Java. Simply developing in Java does not guarantee that a program will be correctly portable: A developer that assumes his or her code will always run inside a 1024 by 1024 pixel display will give a "poor" user with a somewhat smaller 640 by 480 pixel monitor quite a surprise! As part of the 100 percent pure Java initiative, Sun has developed a testing and certification mechanism that is intended to ensure that a certified Java application will run on the widest range of systems possible and avoid such nasty surprises.

It must be said that while the 100 percent pure Java initiative is a useful way of focussing developers on the issues of portability, it is not 100 percent of the solution for many enterprises. The need to interface with existing legacy systems, the need for more performance than can currently be delivered by Java, the need to retrain staff, and so on, means that most systems will remain impure for a fair time to come.

Since its introduction in May 1995, Java has become the most rapidly adopted programming language in computing history. All major computing platform vendors have signed up to integrate Java into their products, paving the way for widespread deployment of Java-based applications.

We look at more of the 100 percent pure Java ecology in Chapter 5's subsection "Some Java Facilities Supporting Enterprise-Wide Network Computing" on page 76.

Client-Server Computing with Java

Java is often proclaimed as the premier tool for developing distributed applications. Java's binary-level portability gives Java a unique position in the world of distributed computing—for the first time, programmers have been freed from having to worry about differences between architectures and operating systems and can now concentrate on writing great applications (or applets!).

This section provides brief overviews of some of the facilities provided by Java for client/server programmers. You will see in-depth use of some of these tools and technologies in later chapters.

Applets

Applets are essentially executable content: applications that are embedded within, and rely on, the support of a context to provide services such as printing and display management. The context is usually a World Wide Web browser such as Netscape Navigator, HotJava or Internet Explorer.

Applets were the first manifestation of the value of Java for creating portable, distributed applications.

Applets are typically used to "spice up" a page written in HTML with animations or "ticker tape" text displays, but they can do much more, as you will see in this book.

One of the simplest Java applets is:

```java
import java.awt.*;

public class Simple extends java.applet.Applet
  {
  private String message;
  public void init ()
    {
    message = getParameter ("MESSAGE");
    }
  public void paint (Graphics g)
    {
    g.drawString (message, 50, 50);
    }
  }
```

There are two fundamental things to note about this example:

- The class `extends java.applet.Applet`. This is required to allow the context to work with the applet.

- The class has no `main()` method. Instead the functionality is spread across the two methods `init()` and `paint()`.

This applet is referenced by the following HTML file, `Simple.html` (for more details on this, see Chapter 4, "HTML-Based Clients" on page 161):

```html
<APPLET CODE="Simple" WIDTH=200 HEIGHT=100>
<PARAM NAME="MESSAGE" VALUE="Hello, World">
</APPLET>
```

When the HTML page is loaded by a browser and the applet is first started, the browser calls the applet's `init()` method. In this simple applet, this method looks into its associated APPLET tag for a PARAM section with the name MESSAGE and retrieves the associated value. When the browser later instructs the applet to show itself within the 200 by 100 pixel area reserved for it, the `paint()` method is called, producing the following:

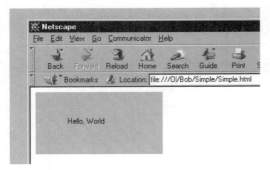

Figure 5-2 The Simple Applet Running Inside a World Wide Web Browser

An applet may implement other methods: start() and stop() are used by the context to tell the applet when the user's focus includes it (and thus whether the applet should continue its activities or suspend them and wait for the user's focus to return). Other miscellaneous methods allow an applet to identify itself and to provide usage information.

Sockets in Java

If you need electrical power, you plug your appliance into a standardized electrical socket and access the electricity supply service. In the future, it is reasoned, a computing application that needs to access computing power will simply be plugged into a standardized computing socket. A socket has two components: an address (typically the location of the computer on which the code is running) and a port (which allows a given address to provide multiple services, if necessary).

This concept has proven remarkably enduring, and sockets are a facility provided by almost all operating systems, from mainframes to Personal Digital Assistants (PDAs).

Java provides a simple-to-use socket facility in its java.net package. This is most useful for connecting to legacy systems such as those based on the Telnet remote access protocol.

The following code fragments (from an example so traditional that it is almost *de-rigueur*) are taken from a simple sockets-based server. The server simply accepts a string from a client, assumes that it represents a person's name, and responds with "hello, *name*." Note that in this, as in all the following fragments, much associated error-handling code is excluded.

```
import java.io.*;
import java.net.*;

public class Server
  {
  public static void main (String [] args)
    {
    ServerSocket listen_socket = null;
    try
      {
      listen_socket = new ServerSocket (8888);
      for ( ; ; )
        new Thread (new Connection (listen_socket.accept ())).start ();
      ...  // code elided
```

The ServerSocket that is created in this fragment is using port 8888 to listen for connecting clients.

As the server accepts a connection, Java's socket system creates and returns a new socket specifically for the connection between the server and the particular client.

The server also creates a new thread specifically to service the client. The new socket is passed to the constructor of the associated Connection class from which the thread is created.

Once the thread is started, the server returns to listening for more clients.

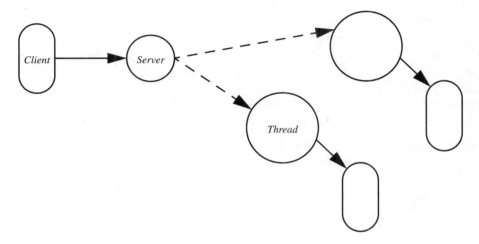

Figure 5–3 Servers Create Multiple Threads to Handle Multiple Clients

Allowing the server to off-load processing to multiple threads enables it to respond as rapidly as possible to new connection requests, something it could not do if it were also directly concerned with the processing associated with each client's connection.

The socket passed to the thread has an input and an output stream associated with it. The Connection class' constructor obtains these streams, and the Connection.run method uses them to take data from, and to pass results back to, the client. The low-level details of performing network I/O are hidden from the method.

```
class Connection implements Runnable
  {
  private DataInputStream in;
  private DataOutputStream out;
  private Socket client;
  public Connection (Socket client)
    {
    try
      {
      this.client = client;
      in = new DataInputStream (client.getInputStream ());
      out = new DataOutputStream (client.getOutputStream ());
      }
    catch (Exception e)
```

```
          { /* code elided */ }
        }
    // called by Thread.start () to start execution
    public void run ()
      {
      try
        {
        String name = in.readUTF ();
        out.writeUTF ("Hello, " + name + ".");
        }
      catch (Exception e)
        { /* code elided */ }
      }
    } // end of Connection class
```

The corresponding client application is much simpler (largely because it does not have any need to deal with multiple threads), as is shown in the following code fragment:

```
import java.io.*;
import java.net.*;

class Client
  {
  public static void main (String [] args)
    {
    Socket server = null;
    try
      {
      server = new Socket (args [0], Integer.parseInt (args [1]));
      DoHello (args [2], new DataInputStream (server.getInputStream ()),
                      new DataOutputStream (server.getOutputStream ()));
      }
    catch (Exception e)
      { /* code elided */ }
    finally
      {
      try { server.close (); } catch (Exception e) { /* ignore */ }
      }
    System.exit (0);
    }

  private static void DoHello (String name,
                              DataInputStream in, DataOutputStream out)
    {
    try
      {
      out.writeUTF (name);
      System.out.println (in.readUTF ());
      }
    ...  // code elided
    }
  } // end of Client class
```

Java also provides for creating client/server systems utilizing *datagrams*—a very low-level communication facility. This is not examined in this book.

Chapter 9, "Java Servers and Socket Communication" on page 141, discusses how sockets can be used to implement one of the possible solutions for the needs of the Lunar Medical Center.

Accessing an HTTP Server with Java

Java provides a specialized mechanism for connecting to World Wide Web servers. Although it is based on the sockets facility examined earlier, it is even more straightforward to use, as the following example shows:

```java
import java.net.*;
import java.io.*;

public class URLReader
  {
  public static void main (String [] args)
    {
    BufferedReader in = null;
    try
      {
      URL IBMJava = new URL ("http://www.ibm.com/java");
      in = new BufferedReader (new InputStreamReader(IBMJava.openStream ()));
      String line;
      while ((line = in.readLine ()) != null)
        System.out.println (line);
      }
    catch (Exception e)
      { /* code elided */ }
    finally
      {
      try { in.close (); } catch (Exception e) { /* code elided */ }
      }
    }
}
```

This straightforward code fragment will open a connection to a Web server and retrieve the file referenced by the URL http://www.ibm.com/java one line at a time through a Java stream. This code provides the basic communication framework for an application similar to a World Wide Web browser.

Java provides additional facilities to enable finer interaction with a World Wide Web server. These are not examined here.

Object-Object Communication: Remote Method Invocation (RMI)

Sockets are a straightforward and efficient scheme for getting components to "talk" to each other. They can also be difficult to use in complex situations, such as when it becomes necessary to invent a special-purpose "application-layer protocol" for the client and server to use to coordinate their activities. The design and implementation of this protocol can be a challenging and time-consuming task that, when it comes down to it, has little to do with the real task of the distributed application.

RMI is a 100 percent pure Java mechanism that obviates the need for application developers to also become protocol developers by arranging for the "nuts and bolts" of communication to be completely hidden. RMI makes it possible for a developer to call a method of an object that may be located in another Java Virtual Machine (perhaps running on a different computer) in precisely the same way that he or she would call a method of a local object. This removes the burden of handling communication and lets the developer concentrate solely on application development.

Chapter 10's subsection, "RMI: An Easy Way to Implement Java Client/Server Applications" on page 151, discusses RMI in detail and shows how the Lunar Medical Center can use RMI in their system as an alternative to sockets.

Connecting to the Database: JDBC

Through the JDBC facility (found in the `java.sql` package), Java provides a straightforward and uniform interface to a very wide range of SQL databases.

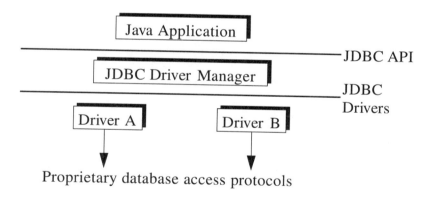

Figure 5–4 JDBC Provides a Uniform Interface to Proprietary Databases

It has been said that much of the popularity of Java is due to the early availability of this facility, allowing developers to access enterprise databases right from the beginning.

Any application using JDBC goes through a number of major stages:

1. Cause a database-specific JDBC driver object to load. By convention, this is typically done in a static block so that the driver is loaded immediately

when the application is loaded. All JDBC drivers are constructed so that they initialize themselves when first loaded.

2. Ask the `DriverManager` to use the loaded driver to create a connection to the database.

3. Prepare a SELECT (or UPDATE or DELETE) statement, and then issue it to the database.

4. Process the results of the statement. This is achieved through a `ResultSet` object, which provides a facility to allow for the sequential processing of the result (or more usually, the table of results).

This sequence is exhibited in the simple example (which queries a remote IBM DB2 database) below:

```java
import java.sql.*;
import java.util.*;

public class SQLQuery
  {
  private static final String DRIVER = "COM.ibm.db2.jdbc.net.DB2Driver",
    URL = "jdbc:db2://juergen.itsc.austin.ibm.com:8888/sample",
    USER = "db2admin",
    PASSWORD = "password";

  // convention: load & initialize JDBC driver at class load time
  static
    {
    try
      {
      Class.forName (DRIVER);
      }
    catch (ClassNotFoundException x)
      {/* code elided */ }
    }

  public static void main (String [] args)
    {
    Connection connection = null;
    Statement statement = null;
    ResultSet result = null;
    try
      {
      Properties info = new Properties ();
      info.put ("user", USER);
      info.put ("password", PASSWORD);
      connection = DriverManager.getConnection (URL, info);
      statement = connection.createStatement ();
      String SQLSelectStmt = "SELECT COUNT (*) FROM patient";
      result = statement.executeQuery (SQLSelectStmt);
      int number = result.next() ? result.getInt (1) : 0;
      System.out.println (number + " records found.");
```

```
    }
  catch (Exception e)
    { /* code elided */ }
  finally
    { /* code elided */ }
  }
}
```

Although the structure of JDBC, with its proliferation of objects—DriverManager, Driver, Connection, Statement, ResultSet, and so forth—may seem cumbersome at first glance, it actually allows for maximum flexibility. This flexible structure is a major reason why JDBC can provide a powerful interface to the many disparate SQL-based systems that exist today.

JDBC's capabilities are discussed in Chapter 8, "Java Servers Using JDBC" on page 123, alongside the Lunar Medical Center's use of JDBC.

The Lunar Medical Center's Java Application

Chapter 1's subsection, "A Thin Client Application—The Lunar Medical Center Story" on page 3, introduced the various applications developed at the Lunar Medical Center. This section takes a brief look at the construction of the "main" Java module, the Patient Record display/edit application.

The application was constructed using IBM's VisualAge for Java and appears on the CD-ROM accompanying this book.

Since the application is predominantly GUI-based, VisualAge's visual composition editor was used to create a large proportion of the application. VisualAge for Java is covered in depth in Appendix B, "Java Development: Using VisualAge for Java" on page 255.

The figures from Figure 5–5 on page 69 to Figure 5–9 on page 73 show how the various Java screens appear in the visual composition editor and also show how the components were linked together to provide the appropriate functionality.

Figure 5–5 on page 69 shows the construction of the initial screen. This is the screen that greets a user when the Java application starts execution. The screen asks for a user identification and a password and will not allow the user to progress until a known user ID and the appropriate password are entered.

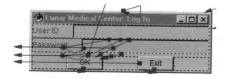

Figure 5–5 Construction of the Initial Log-In Screen

> **Note**
>
> In the version on the CD-ROM, this screen does no actual checking other than to ensure that an ID and a password have been entered.

The cluster of connections linking the OK button to the two text boxes ensure that the button is not enabled until *both* fields contain characters. The connections are arranged such that whenever the content of either text field changes, a method will be called to examine both fields and then decide whether or not the button should be enabled. The simple method that makes this decision—enableLoginOK— is shown below:

```
private boolean enableLoginOK (TextField userID, TextField passwd)
  {
  boolean userIDOK = userID.getText ().length () > 0,
          passwdOK = passwd.getText ().length () > 0;
  return (userIDOK && passwdOK);
  }
```

The simplicity of this code shows how the visual composition editor can reduce the amount of Java programming needed to create an application.

Note that instead of creating a new instance each time the screen is needed, the screen is merely set to visible, having been pre-allocated in a non-visible state. When closed, the screen is not destroyed but merely rendered invisible until the next time it is needed. This mechanism is used throughout the application and potentially reduces the amount of memory allocation/collection that needs to be performed, resulting in a smaller memory footprint and possibly more efficient execution.

Although the number of connections appearing at the top center of Figure 5–6 on page 70 may appear daunting at first glance, they are fundamentally quite simple and serve a similar purpose to the cluster of connections described earlier: to ensure that the "Find Patient Record" button is only enabled when a valid Social Security Number is entered.

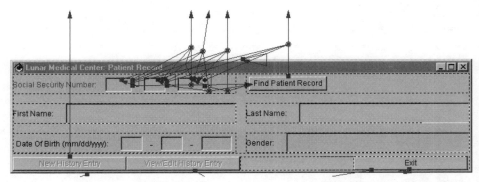

Figure 5–6 Constructing the Main Patient Record View/Edit Screen

When the **Find Patient Record** button is pressed, the following method is called:

```
public void findPatientRecordFromSSN (String first, String middle, String last)
  {
  Frame f = getFrame2 ();
  Cursor oldCursor = f.getCursor ();
  try
    {
    f.setCursor (Cursor.getPredefinedCursor (Cursor.WAIT_CURSOR));
    SocialSecurityNumber SSN =
      new SocialSecurityNumber (new Integer (first), middle, new Integer (last));
    setPatientRecord ((PatientRecord) Communicator.readPatientRecord (SSN));
    getTextField2 ().setText (getPatientRecord ().getFirstName ());
    getTextField21 ().setText (getPatientRecord ().getLastName ());
    Date date = getPatientRecord ().getDateOfBirth ();
    getTextField53 ().setText (date.getMonth () + 1 + "");
    getTextField521 ().setText (date.getDate () + "");
    getTextField511 ().setText (1900 + date.getYear () + "");
    getTextField4 ().setText
      ((getPatientRecord ().getGender ().equals (new Character ('M')) ?
                                         "M" : "Fem") + "ale");
    getButton10 ().setEnabled (true);
    getButton11 ().setEnabled (true);
    }
  catch (BadSSNFormatException b)
    {
    doUserMistake ("Invalid Social Security Number.", first + middle + last);
    }
  catch (PatientRecordException pre)
    {
    doUserMistake ("Invalid Social Security Number.", first + middle + last);
    }
  catch (Exception e)
    {
    doExceptionHandling (e);
    }
  finally
    {
    /* DO NOT MODIFY THIS */
    f.setCursor (oldCursor);
    }
}
```

This code is relatively straightforward. You should note the use of the Communicator object (described in Chapter 6, "Design Decisions" on page 81) to perform the actual retrieval of the data corresponding to the given Social Security Number. Once a PatientRecord object has been found, it is used to populate the appropriate fields of the GUI.

This method also illustrates how the two dialogs shown in Figure 5–9 on page 73 are used.

The screen shown in Figure 5–7 on page 72 is shown in response to the "View/Edit History Entry" button being pressed. It shows a summary list of history entries and allows one to be selected for viewing or further editing.

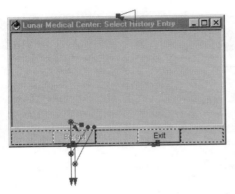

Figure 5–7 Construction of the "Select History Entry" Screen

Figure 5–8 on page 72 is the History Entry Screen shown either in response to the **Select** button in the above dialog being pressed—in which case the screen is first populated with the data from the selected history entry record— or as a result of the **New History Entry** button shown in Figure 5–6 on page 70 being pressed— when a "fresh" screen is shown populated only by the current date.

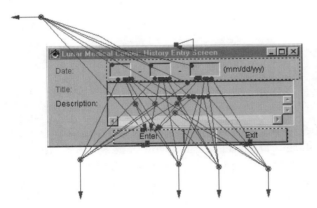

Figure 5–8 Construction of the "History Entry" Screen

The two dialog screens in the following figure are used whenever the application needs to issue a one-line warning to the user (the top screen) or announce that an error or run-time exception has occurred (the bottom screen). The bottom screen (referred to as Frame4 in the visual composition editor) has a scrollable text area (TextArea2) that allows for a large amount of textual information to be displayed.

This proved useful during development: the output from the printStackTrace method associated with the parameter is printed in the TextArea. This is potentially such a valuable technique that the code for the method Doctors.doExceptionHandling is excerpted here:

```
private void doExceptionHandling (Exception e)
  {
  StringWriter sw = new StringWriter ();
  PrintWriter pw = newPrintWriter (sw);
  e.printStackTrace (pw);
  getTextArea2 ().setText (sw.toString ());
  getFrame4 ().setVisible (true);
  }
```

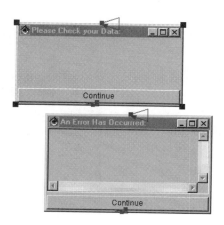

Figure 5–9 Constructing Two Error/Warning Screens

The Lunar Medical Center's Java Applet

Chapter 4, "HTML-Based Clients" on page 161, introduced the simple patient HTML and JavaScript-based check-in facility developed at the Lunar Medical Center. This section takes a brief look at the construction of an equivalent application written as a Java applet.

The applet was constructed using IBM's VisualAge for Java and appears on the CD-ROM accompanying this book.

The applet makes use of the Java-based servlet discussed in Chapter 7, "Java Servlets and HTTP Communication" on page 99.

Many of the fundamentals regarding the construction of Java components have already been examined in Chapter 5's subsection, "The Lunar Medical Center's Java Application" on page 69.

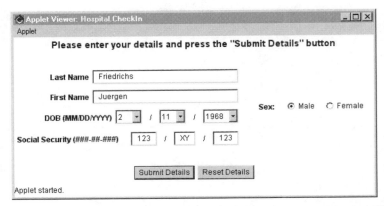

Figure 5–10 The Hospital Check-In Applet Running in the Applet Viewer

Figure 5–10 shows the Check-In applet running in the applet viewer. The function and layout of this applet are very similar to the HTML version developed in Chapter 4, "HTML-Based Clients" on page 161. The Java version is rather "fatter" than the simple version introduced in that chapter. There are, however, several reasons to consider building a more resource-hungry component:

More Flexible

While using JavaScript in an HTML document allows for some basic checking regarding the data entered in a form, a Java applet offers a potentially much more powerful validation mechanism.

Larger Choice of Communication Types

An HTML document has to communicate either with an CGI script or with a Java servlet running on a Web server. Java applets can do the same, but can also communicate either through sockets, RMI, JDBC, or perhaps even CORBA.

Smoother Application Flow

With Java, it is possible to construct a user interface much more like what a user would usually expect.

Easier Access to Local Hardware

It is much easier to provide access to hardware-specific functions (such as the SmartCard Slot on the IBM Network Station) through a (signed) Java applet instead of writing a browser and platform-specific plug-in.

The Check-In applet consists of one class called CheckIn. Depending on what Communicator class is chosen for use, the applet will make use of either the Java servlet, the socket based server, the RMI server, or will go directly to the database through JDBC.

```
/*
 * The following import statement decided the Communicator type used.
 * Just import ONE of the possible Communicators!
 */
// import com.ibm.austin.itsc.javanc.Servlet.Communicator;
import com.ibm.austin.itsc.javanc.Jdbc.Communicator;
// import com.ibm.austin.itsc.javanc.Sockets.Communicator;
// import com.ibm.austin.itsc.javanc.RMI.Communicator;
```

Comparing Figure 5–11, showing the Check-In applet in the VisualAge for Java's visual constructor, to Figure 5–6 on page 70 shows that the complexity of visual development has been drastically reduced.

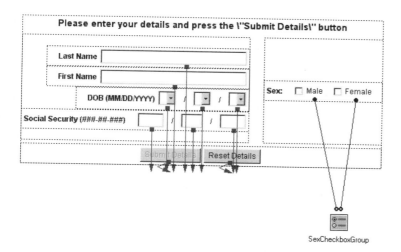

Figure 5–11 Check-In Applet Displayed in VisualAge's Visual Composer

The reason for the difference is mostly because the main Java application GUI *and* behavior has been developed graphically with the visual constructor. The Check-In applet is determining and keeping the state of most entry fields such as names, date of birth and Social Security Number in hand-written code.

In the applet, all that is required is to connect events to existing methods to check their states (such as isSSNOK(), which is used to check the Social Security Number input fields for validity). These methods then explicitly check the state of any associated field as required. This makes the visual representation clearer at the cost of more hand-written code.

The submitDetails() method is invoked by the actionPerformed() method nominally associated with the "Submit Details" button. It collects the values of all entry field and stores them in a PatientRecord instance which is then passed to the appropriate Communicator class to be sent to the server.

```java
private void submitDetails ()
  {
  try
    {
    //copy all data in a PatientRecord
    PatientRecord aPatientRecord=new PatientRecord
      (
      getFirstNameTextField ().getText (),
      getLastNameTextField ().getText (),
      getDOBDChoice ().getSelectedItem (),
      getDOBMChoice ().getSelectedItem (),
      getDOBYChoice ().getSelectedItem (),
      (getMaleCheckbox ().getState ()) ? 'M' : 'F',
      getSSN1TextField ().getText (),
      getSSN2TextField ().getText (),
      getSSN3TextField ().getText ()
      );
    //Send the PatientRecord using the Communicator
    Communicator.writePatientRecord (aPatientRecord);
    //Clear form after posting
    resetDetails ();
    }
  catch (Exception e)
    {
    e.printStackTrace ();
    }
  }
```

Some Java Facilities Supporting Enterprise-Wide Network Computing

This section provides a brief introduction to some of the tools and facilities that comprise the ecology of Java that are not examined further in this book.

These facilities allow a designer to create powerful 100 percent pure Java solutions.

Enterprise JavaBeans

An ambitious API describing the facilities needed to create, deploy and manage cross-platform, enterprise applications. This API extends that provided by Sun Microsystem's standard JavaBeans component APIs.

Lotus eSuite

Lotus eSuite is a set of business productivity software designed exclusively for the network computing environment.

There are two parts to the eSuite: the eSuite WorkPlace and the eSuite DevPack.

The WorkPlace is a Java-based, desktop environment with a set of pre-configured Java business applets, including: calendar, mail, word processor, spreadsheet, presentation graphics, Web browser, file manager, file viewer, and terminal emulation.

The DevPack portion is a set of Java-based applets that can be used as modular building blocks by application developers who needs to create more interactive and dynamic Web applications.

Java Naming and Directory Interface (JNDI)

Provides unified access to multiple naming and directory services across the enterprise.

Java IDL

Provides interoperability with CORBA, an upcoming industry standard for object-based heterogeneous computing.

InfoBus

Enables dynamic exchange of data between JavaBeans within a virtual machine. The InfoBus provides the idea of a bus into which components can be plugged and which provides a simple standardized data exchange protocol.

Java Transaction Service (JTS)

Defines a standard transaction management API for Java applications.

The San Francisco Project

A framework for the development of high-level business processes such as warehouse management, general ledger and order management. At over 500,000 lines of Java, the San Francisco project is claimed to be the largest Java-based development to date.

JavaBeans Activation Framework (JAF)

The JavaBeans Activation Framework (JAF) provides standard services to allow the determination of the type of an arbitrary piece of data. It also encapsulates access to the data, allows a component to discover the operations available on the data and makes it possible to instantiate the appropriate JavaBeans component to perform these operations.

JavaOS

As the name suggests, this is a new operating system optimized to run Java on a variety of computing and consumer platforms. Two flavors are planned: JavaOS for Consumers & JavaOS for Network Computers. They will be codeveloped and comarketed by IBM and Sun Microsystems.

Aglets

Java applets primarily address the need for extensibility at the client side. Java servlets have an analogous role for servers. IBM's aglets take Java onto the next stage and make maximum use of Java's architecture neutrality and portability. An aglet is a Java object that can move from one host to another. An aglet that executes on one host can suddenly halt execution, transfer itself, or be transferred, to a remote host, and resume execution there. When the aglet moves, it takes along its program code as well as its data.

The Java aglet API (J-AAPI) has been submitted as a proposed standard to the Object Management Group (OMG).

JavaPC

JavaPC converts PCs into network computers. Since it has a relatively light system requirement, JavaPC allows an enterprise to further recoup its investment in older equipment. JavaPC offers a migration path towards a complete network computer environment.

Project Java Activator

This software gives the ability to specify the use of Sun's implementation of the JVM in Internet Explorer 3.02 or later, and Netscape Navigator 3.0 or later, in preference to the browser's default JVM. This allows an enterprise to standardize on a single virtual machine and thus avoid compatibility problems.

As can be seen from the above list, the 100 percent pure Java ecology is constantly changing and being augmented with more standard APIs, tools and complete systems.

In Summary

As the Lunar Medical Center's systems get increasingly more complex, the facilities introduced in this chapter will prove invaluable in allowing their designers to create structured, powerful systems based upon standard interfaces and technologies.

By utilizing these standards, the designers will be able to concentrate on their core work: producing effective applications for their business without being distracted by low-level details and unnecessary minutiae.

Chapter 6

Design Decisions

As described in "A Thin Client Application—The Lunar Medical Center Story" on page 3 of this book, the Lunar Medical Center's design staff decided to build a number of applications, including a patient check-in module and a Patient Record view/edit module. There was some discussion among the LMC's designers regarding the best technologies to use and the best network architecture to use.

This chapter looks at the design of the object model underlying many of the applications and also examines how the LMC's network designers investigated the various network architectures and technologies to see which were most appropriate for their environment.

Designing the Object Model for the Lunar Medical Center's Systems

Health care on the moon base is free! The underlying object model that describes the data for the Lunar Medical Center is therefore quite simple since the designers don't have to think about billing and other unpleasant issues. What remains is a system for documenting a patients' medical history.

The basic patient data that must be kept is: Social Security Number, name (actually two items: first name and last name), date of birth, and gender. This data is encapsulated into a class called PatientRecord:

```
public class PatientRecord implements Serializable
    {
    private String firstName,
                   lastName;
    private Date dateOfBirth;
    private Character gender;
    private SocialSecurityNumber SSN;
    private Vector history;

    // code elided...

    public void setSSN (Integer SSNFirst, String SSNMiddle, Integer SSNLast)
      throws BadSSNFormatException
      {
      setSSN (new SocialSecurityNumber (SSNFirst, SSNMiddle, SSNLast));
      }
    public void setSSN (String SSNFirst, String SSNMiddle, String SSNLast)
      throws BadSSNFormatException
      {
      setSSN (new SocialSecurityNumber (new Integer (SSNFirst),
                                        SNMiddle, new Integer (SSNLast)));

      }
    }
```

The above code fragment shows an important technique used by the LMC's designers for all their classes. All data fields are private and can only be accessed in a limited number of ways through the constructor and so-called getter and setter methods. Rather than allowing unrestrained access to the data fields, which can lead to data corruption, parameters can be "groomed"—examined for correctness—before any permanent changes are made to the internal data fields. By following this technique, the LMC's designers can be assured that illegal values will not be stored and that corruption will not occur. It can be argued that access to the fields is rather slower than for direct access. The LMC's designers felt that this potential drawback was more than outweighed by the overall gain in security, readability and maintainability.

Associated with each patient is a medical history. A medical history consists of a variable number of history entries. The attributes of a history entry are a date, a title and other data (perhaps a detailed description of the diagnosis, prescription or treatment) giving the reason why the history entry is being made.

The LMC's designers decided to model a history entry as a separate `HistoryEntry` class:

```
public class HistoryEntry implements Serializable
  {
  private Date date;
  private String title,
               description;

  public HistoryEntry (Date date, String title, String description)
    {
    setDate (date);
    setTitle (title);
    setDescription (description);
    }

  // code elided...
  }
```

This code fragment shows another important programming method ascribed to by the LMC's designer: Note how the constructor simply refers to the setter methods elsewhere in the class. This is a useful technique that helps reduce duplicated code and thus increase reliability and maintainability.

The lunar Social Security Number is a complex entity. It is formed from the concatenation of three fields:

1. A three-decimal-digit integer

2. A two-character alphabetic field

3. Another three-digit integer

To model this complexity, a separate class was created for the Social Security Number.

The class was named `SocialSecurityNumber`, naturally!

```
public class SocialSecurityNumber implements Serializable
  {
  private Integer firstField,
                 lastField;
  private String middleField;

  // code elided...
```

The patient's Social Security Number is an important entity used as a unique key throughout the systems to identify particular patients.

All classes are annotated as being `Serializable`. This allows the LMC's designers to use a simple file-based serialization data storage mechanism, should they so desire.

Figure 6–1 on page 84 depicts the resulting object model graphically and shows the relationships between the components.

Note that while the `PatientRecord` contains a single instance of a `SocialSecurityNumber`, it may contain an unbounded number of `HistoryEntry` records, and that this relationship is modeled by a Java Vector object.

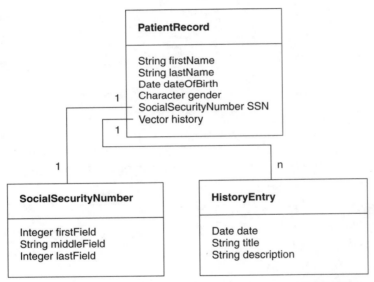

Figure 6–1 Simple Object Model for the LMC's Systems

A further point to note about the data classes of the fields contained in the LMC's classes—all are objects: Character not char, Integer not int, and so forth. The basic Java types have been avoided. The designers considered that it would preserve the maximum amount of flexibility if objects were used throughout their definitions. There is a minimal potential loss of speed associated with this decision, but as with the discussion surrounding the use of getters and setters, the loss of efficiency is felt to be acceptable if compensated for with flexibility.

There exist a number of other support-oriented classes, such as the `PatientRecordException` and `BadSSNFormatException` classes. These have been omitted from the above diagram to preserve its clarity.

As the LMC's designers undertook their work, they made the decision to standardize on the use of JDBC for their data access mechanism and on DB2 for a bulk data-storage facility. This necessitated translating the above data model into an appropriate relational form. You can read more about how this was achieved in Chapter 8, "Java Servers Using JDBC" on page 123.

Designing the Applications: Considering Alternatives

Various options regarding the structures and communication mechanisms present themselves to the designers of the Lunar Medical Center's network computing systems. After a lot of deliberation and a number of meetings, the design team drew up a number of profiles, shown in Figure 6–2 on page 85 through Figure 6–4 on page 86.

These profiles highlight various alternative technologies for client-side presentation systems, for intermediate services, and for back-end data storage systems. The profiles also specify the various alternative communication mechanisms that may be interposed between the layers.

The LMC's designers considered various two-tier and three-tier solutions (see Chapter 3, "Distributed Applications" on page 23, for a discussion of these terms). The various profiles show how complete systems could be composed using the various options available.

The code for many of the alternative implementations can be found on the CD-ROM associated with this book.

Profiles Describing the Check-In Applet

Consider the possibilities for implementing the initial check-in system. Figure 6–2 on page 85 describes an applet that makes use of JDBC directly in a two-tier architecture.

Presentation	Mechanism	Data Storage
Applet	**JDBC**	**DB2 Database**

Figure 6–2 Profile for a Two-Tier Browser-Based Solution

The profile in Figure 6–3 on page 86 shows that it is also possible to write an applet within a three-tier architecture. In this case, the Java applet would work with a Java-based servlet, which in turn would use JDBC to communicate with the actual data storage mechanism.

Presentation	Mechanism	Service	Mechanism	Data Storage
Applet				
HTML Form	**HTTP**	**Servlet**	**JDBC**	**DB2 Database**
HTML & JavaScript				

Figure 6–3 Profiles for the Three-Tier Browser-Based Solutions

The same figure highlights other alternatives for implementing the presentation (client) system: the use of a pure HTML form or the combination of HTML and JavaScript. In either case, HTTP is the communication mechanism.

Various factors influence the choice of one possible architecture over another and these options—and the implications of choosing one way over another—are presented later within this chapter.

Profiles Describing the Main Patient View/Edit Application

The situation regarding the application is analogous to the applet.

The same three-tier versus two-tier decision is possible, and the same advantages and disadvantages regarding the individual technologies apply. Figure 6–4 on page 86 shows the appropriate profiles for the "main" Patient Record view/edit application.

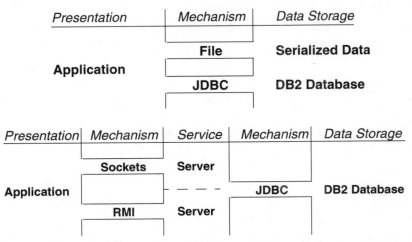

Presentation	Mechanism	Data Storage
	File	**Serialized Data**
Application		
	JDBC	**DB2 Database**

Presentation	Mechanism	Service	Mechanism	Data Storage
	Sockets	**Server**		
Application			**JDBC**	**DB2 Database**
	RMI	**Server**		

Figure 6–4 Profiles Describing the Application-Based Alternatives

Profiles Considered but Not Implemented

The LMC's designers also considered a number of potential designs, but did not take these past the design stage. Figure 6–5 on page 87 shows these discarded possibilities.

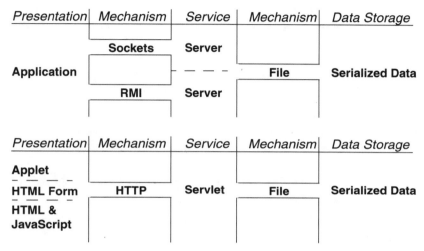

Presentation	Mechanism	Service	Mechanism	Data Storage
	Sockets	Server		
Application		– – – –	File	Serialized Data
	RMI	Server		

Presentation	Mechanism	Service	Mechanism	Data Storage
Applet				
HTML Form	HTTP	Servlet	File	Serialized Data
HTML & JavaScript				

Figure 6–5 Alternate Profiles Considered by the LMC's designers

The trial architecture is flexible enough to allow these possibilities to be evaluated, should the need arise.

Additional Factors to be Considered

The LMC's designers not only need to examine the direct technical issues associated with their systems. There are many associated issues, including:

- Benchmarking, profiling and optimization: establishing the "cost" of the various Java operations and components and determining bottlenecks in executing systems.

- Compilers and other development tools: their maturity, support, abilities, market penetration, support, and so forth.

- Maintainability: how to make code easier to document, understand and modify

- Support and staffing: where to go to get help when support is needed

Optimization is a potentially important issue. Much has been written regarding the "evils" of unwarranted optimization:

Rules of Optimization:

  Rule 1: Don't do it.

  Rule 2 (for experts only): Don't do it yet.

   - M.A. Jackson

"More computing sins are committed in the name of efficiency (without necessarily achieving it) than for any other single reason - including blind stupidity."

   - W.A. Wulf

"We should forget about small efficiencies, say about 97% of the time: premature optimization is the root of all evil."

   - Donald Knuth

In the network computing arena, many optimization issues will become important: Many devices will be relatively small systems with slow CPUs and/or small amounts of memory and storage capabilities. It may be that the LMC's developers will be forced to consider optimization issues sooner than they would if they were building for a network of high-powered PCs or workstations.

Some of the optimizations and issues looked at by the LMC's design team are examined in Chapter 11, "Client Diets" on page 167.

The Lunar Medical Center Implementations

To account for the various possibilities described in the various profiles, the LMC's designers have factored out all the I/O mechanisms into a separate class called Communicator, outlined here:

```
class Communicator
  {
  public static PatientRecord readPatientRecord (SocialSecurityNumber SSN)
    throws PatientRecordException;
  public static void writePatientRecord (PatientRecord patientRecord)
    throws PatientRecordException;
  }
```

In the diagrams throughout this section, you will see a Communicator class represented as:

Figure 6–6 Representation for a Communicator Class and Mechanism

Implementing a new Communicator simply requires creating a new class with different implementations for the requisite methods. This architecture allows for the input/output mechanism used by a component to be easily changed as required without affecting the bulk of the application, as illustrated by the following figure:

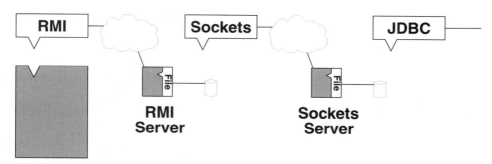

Figure 6–7 Alternative Plug-Ins

To determine which one of several alternative Communicator classes—and thus, which mechanism—is actually used by a component, the designers have utilized Java's package and import mechanisms.

A version of the Communicator class that performs I/O of patient records to files would be created in a package called File. A component that needs to perform file-based I/O would import com.ibm.austin.itsc.javanc.File.* and thus obtain the correct implementation, even though several alternatives may be present along the application's CLASSPATH.

```
//  import com.ibm.austin.itsc.javanc.Servlet.Communicator;
//  import com.ibm.austin.itsc.javanc.Jdbc.Communicator;
//  import com.ibm.austin.itsc.javanc.Sockets.Communicator;
//  import com.ibm.austin.itsc.javanc.RMI.Communicator;
import com.ibm.austin.itsc.javanc.File.*;
public class Hospital
   {
```

In the event (judged unlikely by the designers) of a single component needing to do I/O using more than one mechanism, Java's normal fully-qualified name-resolution scheme can be used (com.ibm.austin.itsc.javanc.File.readPatientRecord has a different fully-qualified name from the com.ibm.austin.itsc.javanc.Jdbc.readPatientRecord analogue; so this naming scheme allows Java to clarify the two methods).

An alternative structuring mechanism would have involved defining a Communicator *interface*. Whenever an I/O mechanism was needed, an object implementing the Communicator interface would be provided as a parameter to the constructor of the class needing to perform the I/O. The advantage of this is that the decision regarding which mechanism to use is delayed until the class is executing, rather than being made at load-time. The LMC's designers did not feel that this ability was needed for their systems and so chose the more static method detailed above.

A Communicator class can be used to provide an I/O mechanism at the client side and also to perform the same function for a middle-layer server that needs to work with a data storage facility, such as a file store or a JDBC database.

While various possibilities exist for implementing the middle layer to data storage layer communication, the LMC's designers standardized on JDBC for all their servers.

In general, JDBC is a very appropriate "thin" technology:

- JDBC is a standard part of the Java environment and can thus be expected to be available on all client platforms.

- Much of the work of communication is in the JDBC library, not in the actual applet. Since library code tends to be more optimized, this solution may need fewer resources overall.

- Since JDBC encapsulates the required communication, the developers will have to write less code, and this may lead to a a more reliable solution.

- Since JDBC provides standard ways to assist in manipulating data, the LMC's developers will not have to "reinvent the wheel" and will be able to efficiently manipulate the data returned by the server.

- JDBC support is available for many databases. The LMC's designers can use their existing DB2 database system for their trials while at the same time remaining flexible with respect to the actual database used in the final version of their system. JDBC also lets the LMC keep an upgrade path open, should one be needed in the future.

Each middle-layer server introduced into the LMC's systems utilizes the same JDBC Communicator to work with the same DB2 data store. This gives the LMC's designers maximum flexibility.

Nondistributed Full Application Based on Files

The first implementation decision facing the LMC's designers is whether or not to eschew distribution completely and instead create a simple, file-based version of the application, perhaps running "on top of" a shared filesystem.

To implement this alternative, the LMC's designers produced a Java serialization-based Communicator class. Serialization provides a simple method for saving and retrieving objects based on a standard file format. The use of serialization freed the LMC's developers from the need to develop an application-specific datafile format.

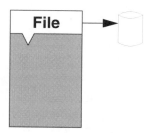

Figure 6–8 Factored, Nondistributed Application

Advantages of this alternative include:

*   Development may be quicker

*   Developers tend to be more familiar with nondistributed systems and so are more plentiful in the job market

*   There are many toolsets on the market that can be used to support development

*   The system may reach performance limits that may be hard to attain by any other strategy

The various drawbacks include:

*   Complexity

*   Administration is often problematic

*   Comparatively large resource requirements (both in terms of memory and CPU processing power), difficulty of dealing with heterogeneity and reliability

Perhaps the most serious drawback of this alternative is that of maintenance. It will be extremely difficult to modify the LMC's systems to cope with changes in regulations, increasing competition, and so on.

HTML Only at the Browser with a Servlet at the Server

This is one alternative implementation that the LMC's designers have experimented with.

This is perhaps the "thinnest" of all possible alternatives. Although lacking in some user-interface details, the client-side system requirements are little more than what is needed for the browser containing the HTML source.

Two major drawbacks are apparent:

- The lack of client-side validation of any entered data causes a "chunky" user interface experience.

- The servlet will have to perform validity checks on the data sent to it from the client-side form. This increases the servlet's complexity and may increase its resource requirements.

The advantage of this mechanism is that, since it requires the least from the host client system, it is the most "portable" of all solutions.

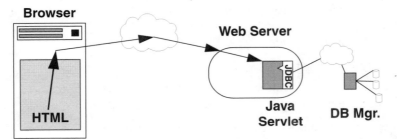

Figure 6–9 HTML, JavaScript POST Data to the Servlet through the Browser

This alternative is examined in Chapter 4, "HTML-Based Clients" on page 35.

The HTML code for this implementation appears on the CD-ROM accompanying this book.

HTML and JavaScript with HTTP to a Servlet

This alternative moves (some portion of) the validation processing from the servlet back to the client.

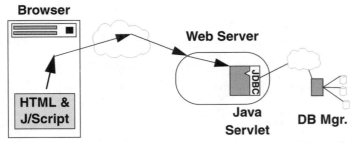

Figure 6–10 HTML, JavaScript POST Data to the Servlet through the Browser

This is the "thinnest" of all the alternatives that provide a fully-featured user experience. JavaScript imposes an additional resource load on the system that may vary depending on the browser, the system, and the JavaScript application. This alternative thus might not be appropriate for highly resource-constrained situations. In addition, Java is now widely supported, whereas the availability of JavaScript may prove problematic for some client configurations

This alternative is also examined in Chapter 4, "HTML-Based Clients" on page 35.

The code for this alternative implementation appears on the CD-ROM accompanying this book.

Applet at the Browser with HTTP Connection to Java Servlet

This is a more heavyweight alternative implementation that essentially provides the same functionality as the previous version.

One potential advantage of a purely Java-based solution is the ability to remove the browser "from the equation" and simply run the applet within the applet viewer environment. This may work out cheaper and could perhaps require fewer system resources, but at the cost of some flexibility.

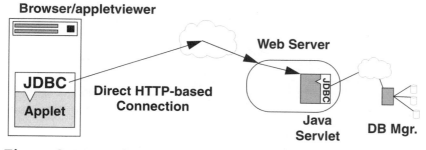

Figure 6-11 Applet POST Data through a Direct URL Connection to the Servlet

Java also provides a more flexible set of communication options over an HTML/JavaScript-based solution. Whereas the latter solution is restricted to HTTP communication to an HTTP server, a Java applet is able to make use of many input/output mechanisms, including sockets, RMI, HTTP, JDBC, and even files.

The main drawback is that the Java system will require substantially more system resources than a JavaScript interpreter embedded within a browser.

If Java is already being introduced in a system, and if the target client systems can afford the extra resource requirements implied by the combination of browser and Java interpreter, then it may make sense to standardize the development using a single language.

In the final choice, the decision to use Java may come down to:

- The resources available on the target client systems

- Whether or not Java is being used elsewhere in a project

The LMC's designers have developed a servlet Communicator class as described in Chapter 5, "Java-Based Clients" on page 55, and their code appears on the CD-ROM accompanying this book.

Applet with Direct JDBC Connection

This option may be preferable to the previous browser-based solutions for a couple of reasons:

- Whereas a forms-based solution is essentially limited to handling simply-structured data and interactions, the Java-based applet can deal with complex data structures and complex, transaction-oriented manipulations. Transactions that require visiting multiple "screens" of data before they are complete can be especially difficult to deal with using an HTML-based solution (regardless of whether JavaScript is also utilized).

- Allowing JDBC to transparently handle the mechanisms of data transfer and the protocol expected by the servlet or HTTP server results in a simpler programming task. Less programming effort typically means less code and thus greater reliability. This may also mean that the JDBC solution is slightly "thinner" than the alternative.

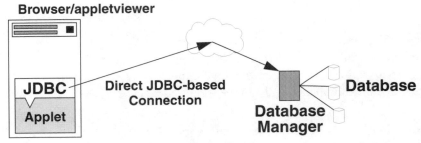

Figure 6–12 Applet Using the Facilities Provided by JDBC

The main fear associated with this method is that a JDBC driver for a specific database may not exist. This is a general concern with regard to JDBC and not specific to this implementation option.

This is examined in more detail in Chapter 8, "Java Servers Using JDBC" on page 123. The corresponding code appears on the CD-ROM supplied with this book.

Java Application Using JDBC Directly

For the design of the "main" Java module, the Patient Record display/edit application, the LMC's system designers faced a large number of choices. While all agreed that the complexity of the module required a fully-fledged application, there was disagreement regarding the communication mechanism to be employed. The designers decided to trial a number of alternatives, as they had done for the initial check-in module.

Having a Java application results in a rather less "thin" solution than those discussed so far and is thus more demanding of system resources. The use of Java allows the application to be more complex and to provide a sophisticated user interface. This is needed in this case.

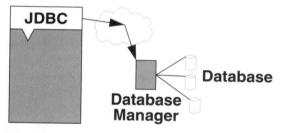

Figure 6–13 Application Using the Facilities Provided by JDBC

The actual application is described in Chapter 5, "Java-Based Clients" on page 55.

The first alternative communication mechanism trial utilized JDBC.

Although this configuration proved suitable from a technical point of view, the main drawback is related to the overall design of the LMC's systems, not directly to the JDBC technology. Many designers felt that instead of having the client access the database directly, a three-tier architecture would be more desirable, as discussed in Chapter 3, "Distributed Applications" on page 23.

A JDBC Communicator class is included on the CD-ROM that comes with this book.

Full Application Using Sockets

As a first step in introducing a three-tier system, the LMC's designers decided to implement a sockets-based Communicator module and an associated server.

Their design is examined in more detail in Chapter 9, "Java Servers and Socket Communication" on page 141.

For ease of implementation, the LMC designers decided that the server side should reuse the JDBC Communicator used in their earlier client-side trials.

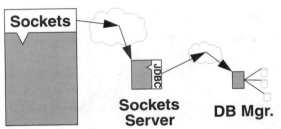

Figure 6–14 Application Using Sockets to Communicate with Its Server

The LMC's evaluation of this architecture produced a number of advantages and drawbacks.

Advantages include:

- Sockets are simple to understand.

- A system based on sockets can be quite efficient, both in terms of CPU and storage requirements.

- Sockets can be used in almost any situation, including those involving non-Java legacy systems.

There is one major disadvantage:

- Although initially simple, a complicated system using sockets can rapidly become very complex and force application designers to become protocol designers as well. Correct protocols are notoriously difficult to design.

The LMC's designers felt that this one disadvantage—the potential for scalability problems—was sufficient to force them to keep looking for alternative, better solutions.

A socket-based Communicator class is included on the CD-ROM that comes with this book for your reference.

Full Java Application Using Java RMI

Java's Remote Method Invocation (RMI) scheme overcomes most of the problems associated with sockets while remaining easy to use and providing an efficient communication mechanism.

RMI is probably the most powerful 100 percent pure Java solution currently available to the LMC's designers. It provides a simple and scalable networking mechanism. One of RMI's main aims is to make remote invocation of a method indistinguishable from that of a local method.

The LMC's network designers were happy with RMI, but noted one potential problem: the integration of legacy systems. This can be solved by *wrappering*, and this technique is discussed in Chapter 3, "Distributed Applications" on page 23.

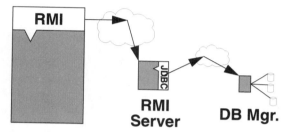

Figure 6–15 Application Using Java RMI to Communicate with Its Server

The combination of RMI and JDBC was considered to be the most effective solution for the LMC's Patient Record display/edit application.

The LMC's RMI implementation is examined in Chapter 10, "Java Servers and RMI Communication" on page 151.

In Summary

The LMC's designers have investigated many possible options for their distributed applications. The ease of use and safety of RMI, coupled with the flexibility and power of JDBC, offers the best solution for implementing the LMC's three-tier distributed architecture.

Java Servlets and HTTP Communication

Chapter 4 examined the implementation of very thin clients using HTML and JavaScript. Chapter 5 examined a Java Applet implementation of the same client application. This chapter examines the corresponding server application for the clients, which takes the syntactically valid data from the client, stores it to the chosen storage mechanism (either the filing system or a database), and provides some feedback to the browser.

There are many ways to code a server to achieve this functionality. Recall the browser and Web server architecture in Figure 4–3 on page 39. For Web-based client/server, it is possible to:

- Interface applications to the Web server using the Common Gateway Interface (CGI). With CGI, the Web server can invoke (upon request from the client) an external program coded in a language supported by the host system, pass client data to the program, and return the program's response back to the browser.

- Use an enhanced Web server with plug-ins, such as one allowing the Web server to interface directly with a database system.

- Interface Java applications to the Web server using Java servlets. Java servlets are platform-neutral components written to accept and respond to HTTP requests in much the same way as CGI applications, although there are fundamental differences in the underlying mechanisms. Servlets offer better performance than most legacy CGI applications because servlets are only loaded once and reused over and over by the server.

The vast majority of Web-based client/server applications utilize the HyperText Transfer Protocol as the underlying communication protocol. The clients submit their data to the server using one of a number of available submission methods. The HTTP protocol and submission methods will be examined in some detail.

Overview of the Hypertext Transfer Protocol and Request Methods

The Hypertext Transfer Protocol (HTTP) is an application-level protocol for distributed, collaborative, hypermedia information systems. The protocol is being developed as a standard by the Internet Engineering Task Force (IETF) of the W3C (see http://www.w3.org/Protocols/ for full details and specification of the HTTP protocol). It is a generic, stateless protocol that can be used for many tasks.

The HTTP protocol is a request/response protocol. Each client request and server response has three parts:

- Request or response line

- Header section

- Entity body

HTTP communications usually take place over TCP/IP connections, although this does not preclude HTTP being implemented on top of other communications protocols.

Under normal Web browsing conditions, the browser conducts HTTP communication with a Web server automatically—the user is not required to (and in most cases cannot) interact or interfere with the protocol. When you design HTTP-based client/server applications, you need to be cognizant of HTTP to correctly implement the connection, response and problem-handling mechanisms, and to fine-tune aspects of the protocol for best performance.

Protocol Steps

When a client initiates a transaction, several things occur:

1. The client contacts the server at a designated network port number (the default is port 80).

2. A document *request* is sent consisting of a single line of text which includes:
   - The request *method* (or purpose of the request)
   - The resource URI
   - The HTTP version number

3. Optional *header* information is sent to the server informing it of the client's configuration and supported data formats.

4. A blank line is sent to end the header.

5. Additional data (referred to as the client *entity body*) may be sent depending on the request method. The POST request method places its required data here.

In summary, a request message from a client to a server has the following general form:

```
Request = Method Request-URI HTTP-Version
              ( general-headers
              | request-headers
              | entity-headers )

              [ entity-body ]
```

Here is an example client request message generated by the patient check-in example from Figure 4–7 in Chapter 4:

```
POST /servlet/Process HTTP/1.0
User-Agent: Mozilla/4.04 [en] (WinNT; I)
Accept: image/gif, image/x-xbitmap, image/jpeg, image/pjpeg, */*
Host: www.moon.xyz
Content-type: application/x-www-form-urlencoded
Content-length: 102
Connection: Keep-Alive
Accept-Charset: iso-8859-1,*,utf-8
Referer: http://www.moon.xyz/medical.html

lastname=Smith&firstname=Jane&dobday=28&dobmonth=02&dobyear=1963
&ssec1=123&ssec2=AB&ssec3=789&gender=F
```

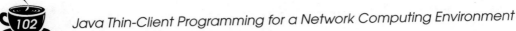

The server responds accordingly with:

1. A status line consisting of:

    - The HTTP version number

    - A three-digit status code in the range 100-599:

        - 100-199 is informational, indicating the client request was received and is being processed.

        - 200-299 means the client request was action was successfully received, understood, and accepted.

        - 300-399 means the client request was not performed and action must be taken in order to complete the request.

        - 400-499 means the client request contains bad syntax or cannot be fulfilled.

        - 500-599 means that the server failed to fulfill an apparently valid request.

    - A human-readable description of the status code

2. *Header* information that is sent to the client informing it of the server's configuration and the requested document.

3. A blank line is sent to end the header.

4. If the client's request was successful, the requested data is sent as the server *entity body*. This may be a copy of a file or the response from a server program (often as dynamically generated HTML).

5. In HTTP 1.0, once the server has finished sending its data, it disconnects from the client (unless otherwise directed by the `Connection: Keep Alive` header). The HTTP 1.1 default is a maintained connection until explicitly closed.

In summary, a response message from a server to a client has the following general form:

```
Request = HTTP-Version Status-Code Status-Description
              ( general-header
              | response-header
              | entity-header )

              [ entity-body ]
```

Here is an example server response message generated by a Web server:

```
HTTP/1.0 200 Document follows
Server: Domino-Go-Webserver/4.6
Date: Wed, 08 Apr 1998 20:09:26 GMT
Accept-Ranges: bytes
```

```
Content-Type: text/html
Content-Length: 254
Last-Modified: Wed, 8 Apr 1998 21:09:26 GMT
```

(rest of response in HTML form)

The useful things to know about HTTP are the available request and response header fields, the server response codes, and the differences between the request methods. Depending on which request method is used, the protocol described above may be slightly different.

In Java, the client request and server response *packets* are encapsulated in objects, with methods available to get and set the desired protocol properties (such as headers). Java provides a much more simplified and logical interface to the HTTP mechanism.

HTTP Headers and Server Status Codes

HTTP headers (see http://www.w3.org/Protocols/ for full details of the following header fields) are used to communicate various pieces of information between client and server applications. HTTP header fields include general, client request, server response, and entity header fields. General headers and entity headers are the same for both the client and server, although some may be more specific to either a client or server message. Each header field consists of a name:value line. Field names are case insensitive.

The order in which header fields are received is not significant. However, it is good practice to send general header fields first, followed by request header or response header fields, and ending with the entity header fields.

The entity body (if any) of an HTTP message is used to carry the main body of the request or response. When an entity body is included with a message, the data type of that body is determined through the header fields Content-Type and Content-Encoding. Content-Type specifies the media type of the underlying data. Content-Encoding may be used to indicate any additional content codings applied to the data, usually for the purpose of data compression, that are a property of the requested resource. There is no default encoding.

General Header Fields

There are a few header fields that apply to both request and response messages, but do not apply to the entity being transferred. These header fields apply only to the message being transmitted.

```
general header = Cache-Control
              | Connection
              | Date
              | Pragma
```

```
                        |  Transfer-Encoding
                        |  Upgrade
                        |  Trailer
                        |  Via
```

Client Request Header Fields

The client request header fields allow the client to pass to the server additional information about the request and about the client itself. These fields generally act as request modifiers.

```
    request header = Accept
                   | Accept-Charset
                   | Accept-Encoding
                   | Accept-Language
                   | Authorization
                   | Expect
                   | From
                   | Host
                   | If-Modified-Since
                   | If-Match
                   | If-None-Match
                   | If-Range
                   | If-Unmodified-Since
                   | Max-Forwards
                   | Proxy-Authorization
                   | Range
                   | Referer
                   | TE
                   | User-Agent
```

Server Response Header Fields

The server response header fields allow the server to pass additional information about the response which cannot be placed in the status line. These header fields give information about the server and about further access to the resource identified by the request URI.

```
    response header = Accept-Ranges
                    | Age
                    | ETag
                    | Location
                    | Proxy-Authenticate
                    | Retry-After
                    | Server
                    | Vary
                    | Warning
                    | WWW-Authenticate
```

Entity Header Fields

Entity header fields define optional metainformation about the entity body or, if no body is present, about the resource identified by the request.

```
entity header  = Allow
               | Content-Encoding
               | Content-Language
               | Content-Length
               | Content-Location
               | Content-MD5
               | Content-Range
               | Content-Type
               | Expires
               | Last-Modified
```

Server Response Status Codes

The status code in a server response message is a three-digit integer result code of the attempt to complete the request. An associated textual description is provided. The status code is intended for use by the system, and the description is intended for the user. The currently specified codes for HTTP 1.1 are:

```
Status Code    = "100"   ; Continue
               | "101"   ; Switching Protocols
               | "200"   ; OK
               | "201"   ; Created
               | "202"   ; Accepted
               | "203"   ; Non-Authoritative Information
               | "204"   ; No Content
               | "205"   ; Reset Content
               | "206"   ; Partial Content
               | "300"   ; Multiple Choices
               | "301"   ; Moved Permanently
               | "302"   ; Found
               | "303"   ; See Other
               | "304"   ; Not Modified
               | "305"   ; Use Proxy
               | "307"   ; Temporary Redirect
               | "400"   ; Bad Request
               | "401"   ; Unauthorized
               | "402"   ; Payment Required
               | "403"   ; Forbidden
               | "404"   ; Not Found
               | "405"   ; Method Not Allowed
               | "406"   ; Not Acceptable
               | "407"   ; Proxy Authentication Required
               | "408"   ; Request Time-out
               | "409"   ; Conflict
               | "410"   ; Gone
               | "411"   ; Length Required
```

```
|  "412"  ;  Precondition Failed
|  "413"  ;  Request Entity Too Large
|  "414"  ;  Request-URI Too Large
|  "415"  ;  Unsupported Media Type
|  "416"  ;  Requested range not satisfiable
|  "417"  ;  Expectation Failed
|  "500"  ;  Internal Server Error
|  "501"  ;  Not Implemented
|  "502"  ;  Bad Gateway
|  "503"  ;  Service Unavailable
|  "504"  ;  Gateway Time-out
|  "505"  ;  HTTP Version not supported
```

Client Request Methods

The HTTP client request method tells the server the purpose of the client request. Supported methods in HTTP 1.1 are:

```
Method = "GET"
       | "HEAD"
       | "POST"
       | "OPTIONS"
       | "PUT"
       | "DELETE"
       | "TRACE"
       | "CONNECT"
```

Each of the request methods result in different communication between the client and server. The choice of which method to use is based on the functional requirements of the application, security and performance needs, and other considerations. The three most commonly used methods are GET, HEAD and POST.

The GET Method

The GET method means retrieve whatever information (in the form of an entity) is identified by the request URI. The entity body portion of a GET request is always empty because any request data elements (such as the data submitted by an HTML form) are encapsulated in the request header URI, such as:

```
GET /servlet/Process?lastname=Smith&firstname=Jane HTTP/1.0
```

Since this information is encapsulated in the URI, one should not use the GET method for secure transactions because the request line (containing the URI) cannot be encoded and is often logged. Sensitive information submitted by the user is therefore potentially available to malicious entities. There is also a (system-dependent) physical limit to the amount of data submittable with GET. The method may not be appropriate for applications requiring submission of large data sets.

The semantics of the GET method change to a *conditional* GET if the request message includes an If-Modified-Since, If-Unmodified-Since, If-Match, If-None-Match, or If-Range header field. A conditional GET method requests that the entity be transferred only under the circumstances described by the conditional header field(s). The conditional GET method is intended to reduce unnecessary network usage by allowing cached entities to be refreshed without requiring multiple requests or transferring data already held by the client.

The semantics of the GET method change to a *partial* GET if the request message includes a Range header field. A partial GET requests that only part of the entity be transferred. The partial GET method is intended to reduce unnecessary network usage by allowing partially retrieved entities to be completed without transferring data already held by the client.

The response to a GET request is cachable.

The HEAD Method

The HEAD method is identical to GET except that the server does not return a message body in the response. This method can be used for obtaining metainformation about a requested document (such as modification time, size or type) without transferring the entity body itself. This method is often used for testing hypertext links for validity, accessibility and recent modification.

The POST Method

The POST method allows data to be sent to the server in a client request more securely than by using the GET method because the data is encapsulated (and optionally encoded) in the entity body of the request (recall the POST example mentioned previously). POST places no restrictions on the size of the entity-body; so applications with large data set submissions are supported. Generally speaking, POST should be the preferred method for data interaction between the client and server for applications like:

*   Database operations
*   Newsgroup, mailing list, or similar article submission
*   Submitting data to programs
*   Annotating resources on the server
*   ...and many others

Responses to POST are not cachable, unless the response includes appropriate Cache-Control or Expires header fields.

Other Methods

The following methods are also defined in HTTP 1.1 but not commonly used. Refer to the HTTP specification for more information:

- OPTIONS—This method represents a request for information about the communication options available on the request/response chain identified by the request URI.

- PUT—This method requests that the enclosed entity be stored under the supplied request URI. If the request URI refers to an already existing resource, the enclosed entity should be considered as a modified version of the one residing on the origin server.

- DELETE—This method requests that the server delete the resource identified by the request URI.

- TRACE—This method is used to invoke a remote, application-layer loop-back of the request message for debugging purposes.

- CONNECT—Reserved for future use in Secure Sockets Layer (SSL) tunneling.

Common Gateway Interface

The Common Gateway Interface (CGI) is the traditional mechanism for interfacing applications with information servers, such as HTTP or Web servers. A plain HTML document that a Web server retrieves is static, but a CGI program is executed in real-time, so that it can output dynamically generated information.

For example, it is possible to link a database to the World Wide Web by creating a CGI program that the Web server can execute and act as a *gateway* to the database (hence the name). The Web server passes the client information and data to the CGI program, which conducts some transaction with the database, receives and repackages the results, and passes them back to the Web server for transmission back to the client. Figure 7–1 shows this general process.

By placing an executable program on the Web, any user anywhere will be able to run the program on that system. Obviously, the Web server / CGI integration needs to be secure and well controlled, and caution is advised for the program design.

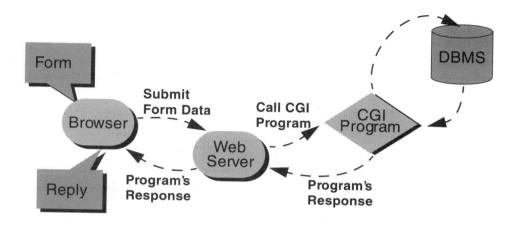

Figure 7–1 Simple Browser > Web Server > CGI Program > DBMS

Using CGI

CGI programs reside in a special directory whereby the Web server knows to execute the given resource as a program, rather than retrieve it as a file for display only. This directory is commonly named cgi-bin on the Web server's disk and is usually carefully controlled by the Web master with restrictions on deployment and execution. Once the CGI program is developed and saved by name in the CGI directory, it can be referenced by the client application using the program's URI. For example, a program called evaluate.sh (a UNIX shell script), saved in the cgi-bin directory of the Webserver www.moon.xyz, would be available to the client program through the URI:

```
http://www.moon.xyz/cgi-bin/evaluate.sh
```

A CGI program can be written in any supported language that allows it to be executed on the system, such as:

- C and C++
- UNIX Shell
- Batch Scripts
- Perl
- Visual Basic
- ... and many others

Different languages have different requirements. They have different levels of complexity, different performance characteristics, different system overheads, different features and facilities, different deployment steps, and so on. A C or Pascal program will require compilation and debugging prior to deployment in the CGI directory, whereas a script like UNIX Shell or Perl can be deployed immediately. Many people prefer to write CGI scripts instead of programs because they are easier to debug, modify, and maintain than a typical compiled program.

CGI programs obtain the client's data from the Web server as environment variables. One of the major environment variables used by a CGI program is QUERY_STRING, which is defined as anything which follows the first '?' in the request URI. The most common example is data submitted by an HTML form using the GET or HEAD method. QUERY_STRING is encoded in the standard URL format of changing spaces to '+', and encoding special characters with '%xx' hexadecimal encoding. QUERY_STRING must be decoded in the CGI program in order to use the data held in it.

Client data submitted using the POST method is passed to the CGI program by the Web server using standard input and must be dealt with accordingly.

CGI Headers

CGI programs can output any number of document types, such as regular text, HTML, image formats, and audio files. In doing so, the client must be advised what kind of document the program is returning in order to handle it appropriately. The first line of output from the CGI program must be a header of the form `Content-type: MIMEtype`, such as:

```
Content-type: text/html
```

Another CGI header allows referencing to another document for output, resulting in the server automatically outputting the referenced document as part of the program's response. This is commonly used to automatically redirect requests for Web documents using an old URI to the new location. This header takes the form `Location: URI`, such as:

```
Location: http://www.mars.xyz/realestate.html
```

Other headers are supported, as specified in the CGI specification (available at `http://hoohoo.ncsa.uiuc.edu/cgi/interface.html`).

Headers are ASCII text, consisting of lines separated by either line feeds or carriage returns (or both) followed by a single blank line. The output body then follows in whatever native format is appropriate, such as a page of dynamically created HTML or a file of binary image data.

Problems with CGI

Although CGI is a well-established mechanism for developing server applications, there are a number of important issues that must be considered:

- Controlling resource contention and consumption for CGI programs is complex. CGI applications create an entire system process (sometimes called *forking*) on their host machine every time they run. Under not-uncommon conditions, this can dramatically degrade server performance. The situation is worse if the CGI application requires an additional supporting system process to execute (for example, a Perl interpreter is required to execute each Perl script). Additionally, implementing proper fault detection and recovery with CGI is not for the faint-hearted.

- CGI program portability is difficult to achieve. Program code is highly platform dependent, and the codebase is tied to a specific programming language and version.

- Java servlets, although similar in concept to CGI programs, provide a superior solution for HTTP-based server applications. In terms of performance, management, portability, and ease of development, Java servlets are the tool of choice if supported by the Web server.

Java Servlets

In the race to provide complete solutions for developing and deploying distributed network computing applications, many products have emerged in the marketplace that address particular aspects of the problem. An enterprise's system environment, designed, for example, to support Internet-style network computing, will consist of a myriad of software and services with browsers, plug-ins and system extensions, Web servers with all manner of applications, gateways, and so on. Each of these components have a different codebase, deployment strategy, set of management requirements, and security regime. Java has emerged as one of the only complete single-technology-base solutions, to address client, server, and middleware requirements.

In the context of Internet-style network computing, while Java applets provide a way of dynamically extending the functionality of client-side browsers, Java *servlets* may also be implemented, allowing dynamic extension to the functionality of network servers. Java applets enable browsers to extend their behavior by supporting Java executable code (distributed from a central source) within the browser context. Similarly, Java servlets extend the functionality of Web servers

by supporting Java executable code in a similar fashion to CGI, but with much better performance and management characteristics. The client can ask for a live document generated by a servlet object.

Developers should consider servlets as server-side components. Servlets are to servers what applets are to browsers. Servlet code can be downloaded into a running server to extend its behavior to provide new or temporary services to network clients. There are many advantages in using servlets to provide dynamic content:

- Servlets are faster and cleaner than CGI scripts.

- Servlets use a standard API and language.

- Servlets support all the inherent advantages of Java.

- They are easily configured using a GUI-based administration facility.

- They can be loaded and invoked from a local disk or remotely across the network.

- Servlets can be linked together (chained) so that one servlet can call another servlet or several servlets in sequence.

- Servlets can be called dynamically from within HTML pages by using server-side include tags.

- The servlet API assumes nothing about the protocol being used for transmission, how the servlet is loaded, or the server environment it will be running in. This allows the servlet API to be embedded in many different kinds of servers in addition to HTTP-based Web servers.

- Servlets are extensible. Functionality can be inherited from the available base classes.

- Servlets are simple to implement and use.

Servlet Requirements and Usage

In order to *develop* Java servlets, the minimum requirements are the servlet API packages and classes—known as the Servlet Development Kit (SDK)—and a JDK 1.1.*x* compiler. They contain all the Java servlet packages and classes required to develop servlets as well as a small Java Web server called the *ServletRunner*. The Java servlet API is a Standard Java Extension API. The API is not part of the core Java 1.1.*x* framework; it is an extension that vendors implement as part of their Web server functionality. JDK 1.2 rolls the Java SDK into its core functionality.

Although all servlets are written in Java, their clients may be written in any language, the most common being Java applets and HTML forms.

In order to *use* Java servlets, the Web server must support the servlet mechanism. Servlets were initially supported in the Java Web Server from Sun, and since then a growing number of other Web servers have supported the API. Web server products currently supporting Java servlets include:

- Lotus Domino Go Webserver

- Netscape FastTrack and Enterprise Server

- Microsoft IIS

- Apache (and derived products)

Client/servlet interaction is based on the common request/response protocol used by many distributed system mechanisms, such as Remote Procedure Calls (RPCs) and HTTP.

Using servlets enables the Lunar Medical Center to connect their database to the Web because servlets can use Java Database Connectivity (JDBC) to interact with the data.

Servlet Interface

All Java servlets implement the Servlet interface within the javax.servlet package. This is typically achieved by subclassing either GenericServlet, which implements the Servlet interface, or (in the case of HTTP-based applications) by subclassing GenericServlet's descendent, HttpServlet. Only directly implement Servlet if the servlets cannot (or choose not to) inherit from GenericServlet or HttpServlet. For example, RMI or CORBA objects that act as servlets may directly implement this interface.

The Servlet interface defines methods to initialize a servlet, to receive and respond to client requests, and to destroy a servlet and its resources. These are known as *life-cycle methods* and are called by the network service in the following manner:

1. Servlet is created then initialized.

2. Zero or more service calls from clients are handled.

3. Servlet is destroyed then finalized and garbage collected.

GenericServlet Class

The GenericServlet abstract class greatly simplifies the writing of servlets. It provides simple versions of the Servlet lifecycle methods init() and destroy(), the methods in the ServletConfig interface, and an implementation of the log() method from the ServletContext interface.

Only the abstract `service()` method needs to be overridden. Though not required, the `getServletInfo()` method may be overridden, and the `init()` and `destroy()` methods may be specialized if expensive servlet-wide resources are to be managed.

HttpServlet Class

The `HttpServlet` abstract class extends the `GenericServlet` class and provides a simple framework for using the HTTP protocol. `HttpServlet` is an abstract class, so it must be subclassed with the appropriate method/s overridden, such as:

- `doGet()`: To support handling of HTTP GET request methods. Overriding `doGet()` automatically also provides support for the HEAD and conditional GET operations. Where practical, the `getLastModified()` method should also be overridden, to facilitate caching the HTTP response data. This improves performance by enabling smarter conditional GET support.

- `doPost()`: To support handling of HTTP POST request methods.

- `doPut()`: To support handling of HTTP PUT request methods.

- `doDelete()`: To support handling of HTTP DELETE request methods.

- `init()` and `destroy()`: To support management of resources that are held for the lifetime of the servlet. Servlets that do not manage resources do not need to specialize these methods.

- `getServletInfo()`: Provides descriptive information through a service's administrative interfaces.

The above methods are not abstract, but have minimal functionality unless overridden. For example, the `doXXX()` methods simply report an HTTP BAD_REQUEST error by default.

HTTP TRACE and OPTIONS request methods are supported, but the `doTrace()` and `doOptions()` methods are not typically overridden.

Servlets typically execute inside multithreaded servers; so they must be written to handle multiple service requests simultaneously. Access to shared servlet resources such as in-memory data (for example, instance or class variables of the servlet), files, database, and network connections must be synchronized.

Configuring the Web Server for Servlets

The typical series of tasks required to configure a Web server to support servlets includes:

- Specifying the directory where the JDK executables are located

- Specifying the directory where the JDK shared libraries are located

- Specifying the servlet JVM's CLASSPATH

- Specifying the maximum number of Java threads to allocate

- Defining the servlet message log

Every servlet deployed must be saved in the appropriate path, registered with the Web server and have any additional servlet initialization parameters defined. Any modifications to the servlet will require replacement of the servlet class file and the JVM restarted.

The majority of Web server products will provide a browser-based interface for these functions. Figure 7–2 shows a view of these administrative functions for the Lotus Domino Go Webserver product.

Figure 7–2 Typical Web Server Servlet Administration Interface

Identifying Servlets

Servlets can be loaded by the Web server from:

- A directory that is on the CLASSPATH.

- The `<web_root>/servlets/` directory (which does not need to be in the server's CLASSPATH).

- From a remote location. The servlet's class name must be prepended with its URI. Security implications may also need consideration if remote servlets are used.

Servlets are identified by either:

- A virtual name assigned to the servlet by using the administration tool or

- Its own class name if the servlet is deployed in the `/servlets/` directory. For example, the servlet `Validate.class`, placed in this directory, can be invoked using the following URI:

  `http://server.moon.xyz/servlet/Validate`

A `class_file.initArgs` file (for example `Validate.initArgs`) can be placed in the same directory as the servlet for passing initialization arguments to the servlet, such as system conditions and credentials. This file consists of `variable=value` pairs.

Invoking Servlets from HTML-Based Clients

In the case of HTML-based clients, servlets are used and invoked in two possible ways: for acting upon HTML form submissions and providing a dynamically created HTML response, and for providing dynamically created in-line HTML as part of a resource request.

Form Action Servlets

This option names the servlet as the responder to the ACTION defined for the HTML form, as in the Lunar Medical Center example:

`<FORM NAME=checkin METHOD=post ACTION=http://server.moon.xyz/servlet/Process>`

When the user submits the above form, the form's fields and data values are submitted to the servlet-enabled Web server using HTTP as discussed earlier in this chapter. The Web server invokes the indicated servlet, with the HTTP request available to the servlet code as a `HttpServletRequest` object instance. The servlet conducts its activity as required and provides its response to the Web server as a `HttpServletResponse` object.

This method is particularly useful for providing full client/server functionality for a browser/HTTP-based user environment.

Server Side Include (SSI) Servlets

In a similar fashion to invoking Java code in the browser using <APPLET> tags, <SERVLET> tags can be applied to HTML code to invoke Java code on the Web server. These tags are known as *Server Side Include* (SSI) tags. Files using SSI tags must be deployed using a particular file extension (<file>.shtml) which tells the Web server that the document contains SSI directives. The Web server executes the SSI code during its top-down processing of the HTML code, and the results are embedded in the response document before being returned to the client.

The <SERVLET> tags are very similar to the <APPLET> tags required for Java applet invocation. For example:

```
<SERVLET CODE=PatientData.class CODEBASE=http://server.mars.xyz/servlet/>
   <PARAM NAME=Use VALUE="Internal">
   <PARAM NAME=Language VALUE="Greek">
    :
</SERVLET>
```

The CODE tag attribute is the name of the class file that is to be loaded. The CODEBASE tag attribute is optional because the Web server knows by default to examine its assigned servlet directory. CODEBASE could be used to refer to a remote location for the servlet. Other optional tag attributes include initialization parameters for the servlet. The <PARAM> tags can provide any required parameters to the servlet.

This method is particularly useful for providing dynamic content for a Web page or site that does not require user input data.

The LMC's HTTP/Servlet Implementation

Let's examine the servlet required to register patients at the Lunar Medical Center. This code implements the service component of the design options described in Chapter 6. The source is created as Process.java, compiled to Process.class, deployed in the Web server's servlet directory, and registered through the administrative interface previously described.

```
import javax.servlet.*;
import javax.servlet.http.*;
import java.io.*;
import java.util.*;
import com.ibm.austin.itsc.javanc.Hospital.*;
import com.ibm.austin.itsc.javanc.Jdbc.*;

public class Process extends HttpServlet
   {
   public void doPost (HttpServletRequest request, HttpServletResponse response)
      throws ServletException, IOException
      {
      PatientRecord thisPatient = null;
      PrintStream out = new PrintStream (response.getOutputStream ());
      response.setContentType ("text/html");
```

```
// Try creating a PatientRecord based on data retrieved from the POST
try
  {
  thisPatient = new PatientRecord
    (
    request.getParameter("firstname"),
    request.getParameter("lastname"),
    request.getParameter("dobday"),
    request.getParameter("dobmonth"),
    request.getParameter("dobyear"),
    request.getParameter("gender").charAt(0),
    request.getParameter("ssec1"),
    request.getParameter("ssec2"),
    request.getParameter("ssec3")
    );
  }
catch (BadSSNFormatException b)
  {
  // code elided
  }
// Try writing the PatientRecord using the chosen Communicator class
try
  {
  Communicator.writePatientRecord(thisPatient);
  }
catch(Exception x)
  {
  // code elided
  }
out.close();
response.getOutputStream().close();
  }
}
```

Let's examine some interesting aspects of the Java code.

The Class

```
public class Process extends HttpServlet
```

The servlet is extending the HttpServlet abstract class; so all the features of the parent classes and interfaces in the servlet package are available, greatly simplifying the code necessary.

The Method

```
public void doPost (HttpServletRequest request, HttpServletResponse response)
    throws ServletException, IOException
```

The servlet is overriding the doPost() method to implement the requirements of client HTTP POST requests on the servlet. POST is utilized because it is the preferred method for conducting update-type transactions. The doPost() method's parameters provide the instances of the HttpServletRequest and HttpServletResponse objects. The former encapsulates the request data from the client; the latter encapsulates the response output.

HttpServletRequest

Note the use of the getParameter() method. This ServletRequest superclass method returns the values of the named request parameters. Recall that in a POST interaction, these parameters are passed down the wire in the entity-body of an HTTP request and correspond to the field values from the HTML form. There are many other useful methods available to examine and extract the request data. Here is a useful extension (in bold type) to the previous example for debugging purposes, showing some of the other methods available:

```
public void doPost (HttpServletRequest request, HttpServletResponse response
)
  throws ServletException, IOException
  {
  PatientRecord thisPatient = null;
  PrintStream out = new PrintStream (response.getOutputStream ());
  response.setContentType ("text/html");

// debugging code
out.println( "<BR>URI: " + request.getRequestURI ().toString ());
out.println( "<BR>Query String: " + request.getQueryString ());
out.println( "<BR>Method: " + request.getMethod ());
out.println( "<BR>Header Names: ");
String name,value;
for (Enumeration e = request.getHeaderNames (); e.hasMoreElements (); )
  {
  name = (String) e.nextElement ();
  value = (String) request.getHeader (name);
  out.println ( "<BR> " + name + "=" + value);
  }
// end of debugging code

// rest of code elided
```

HttpServletResponse

Note the use of this object's output stream (which will eventually be the newly created response page on the client). Messages that the servlet generates will be printed to this stream. The setContentType() method is used to indicate that the output will be handled as HTML by the client. The response stream is subsequently closed using the close() parent method.

Using the Communicator Class

```
Communicator.writePatientRecord(thisPatient);
```

The servlet has created a valid instance of a `PatientRecord` object and is calling the `writePatientRecord()` method, which saves the patient data to the chosen storage mechanism. In this case, the storage is a database because the JDBC version of the `Communicator` class is imported.

The output from the servlet of a successful submission from the client application (with debugging information) is shown in Figure 7–3. Naturally, one can now improve the quality of the feedback from the servlet by using any combination of HTML deemed appropriate.

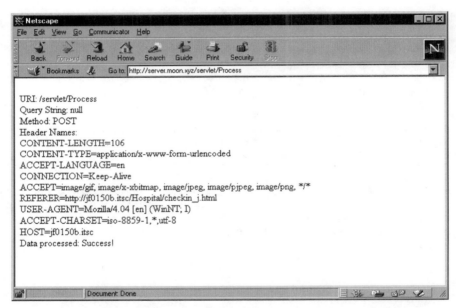

Figure 7–3 Output from the Servlet Shown in Client Browser

In Summary

HTTP has been in use since 1990, when it was first used as a simple protocol for raw data transfer across the Internet. It has subsequently been significantly extended and is in use by millions of users on millions of networks around the world.

You can see how much easier it is to implement the server component of an application using Java servlets. The Moonbase system designers can now easily extend the basic functionality of the Lunar Medical Center and quickly prototype the other Lunar facilities.

Bearing in mind the issues discussed in Chapter 6, the combination of HTTP and Java servlets provides a viable solution for unsophisticated client/server applications. The code is simple, highly portable, and the client application components are indeed thin!

Chapter 8

Java Servers Using JDBC

▼ OVERVIEW OF JDBC

▼ USING JDBC

▼ THE LMC'S JDBC IMPLEMENTATION

This chapter introduces Java Database Connectivity (JDBC), the Java API for standardized Structured Query Language (SQL) based database access. JDBC provides a uniform interface to a wide range of database systems and a common foundation on which higher-level tools and interfaces can be built. With JDBC, Java-based middleware services can be developed that utilize the powerful data storage and retrieval facilities of database systems. Using a database as the storage mechanism also supports other applications (for example, database forms) that work on the same data set.

The Lunar Medical Center application has several functions that require storage and retrieval of patient, history and other records from a database. The LMC designers have utilized a popular database system (DB2) and have developed a JDBC Communicator class (see Chapter 6) to support reusable code for different server application components.

Overview of JDBC

JDBC consists of two parts: The high-level API and multiple low-level drivers for connecting to different databases. Figure 8–1 shows the general architecture of JDBC.

The JDBC API specifies Java interfaces, classes, and exceptions to support database connections, SQL-based database query and update transactions, processing of data result sets, database metadata, and so on.

The drivers are managed by a JDBC driver manager, and there are a number of variations of driver architecture.

JDK 1.1 includes the high-level JDBC API in the *java.sql* package. It is a core feature of the language; so JDBC is valid for a 100 percent pure Java development initiative.

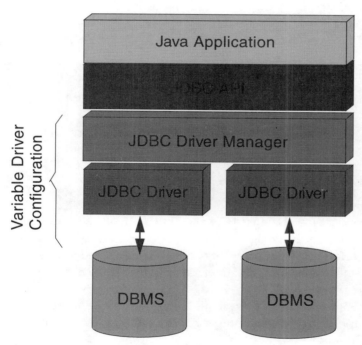

Figure 8–1 JDBC General Architecture

JDBC API

The important JDBC classes and interfaces are:

- java.sql.DriverManager
- java.sql.Connection
- java.sql.Statement
- java.sql.ResultSet

java.sql.DriverManager

The DriverManager class handles the loading of database drivers. As the management layer of JDBC, it works between the application and the drivers, to keep track of the drivers that are available and handling the establishment of a connection between a database and the appropriate driver. DriverManager also provides control over driver login time limits, logging and tracing, and other database system-specific features.

In most situations, only the getConnection() method is directly required. This method establishes a connection to a database, and the class manages the other details of establishing a connection.

java.sql.Connection

The Connection interface represents a session with a particular database. Within the context of a Connection, SQL query or update statements are executed (using a Statement object), and results are returned (as a ResultSet object).

A database's table information, supported grammar, stored procedures, connection capabilities, and other database metainformation may be obtained using the getMetaData() method.

java.sql.Statement

A Statement object is used as a container for executing an SQL statement string and obtaining the results produced by it as a ResultSet object.

There are in fact three types of Statement:

- Statement—which provides basic methods for executing simple SQL statements and retrieving results.

- PreparedStatement—which inherits from Statement, is used for executing a pre-compiled SQL statement and adds methods for dealing with IN parameters.

- CallableStatement—which inherits from PreparedStatement, is used for executing a call to a database stored procedure and adds methods for dealing with OUT parameters.

Only one `ResultSet` per `Statement` can be open at a time. If multiple `ResultSet` objects are being processed, they must have been generated using different `Statement` objects. Any open `ResultSet` objects are implicity closed if a new `Statement` is executed.

java.sql.ResultSet

The `ResultSet` object provides access to the resulting table of data generated upon execution of a given `Statement`. The rows in the `ResultSet` table are sequentially retrieved using the `next()` method, but the columns within a row can be accessed in any order (by name or number) through a set of `get` methods corresponding to the data type of the column (detailed below).

JDBC/SQL Data Type Mapping

Data is stored in a database according to the data type specified in the schema definition of that database. The data types in a database differ from those in Java, and we must therefore provide some form of mapping between the two. Luckily, the methods available with a `ResultSet` object, in combination with the format-handling characteristics of the JDBC database driver, allow this potentially troublesome issue to be dealt with transparently. You simply need to be aware of which `ResultSet` `get` method to use for which column.

For example, if the `get` method is `getString()`, the data type of the corresponding column in the database is VARCHAR, the JDBC driver will convert the VARCHAR data and return a Java `String` object.

Table 1 indicates the `get` methods recommended for retrieving the given SQL data type (in dark shade) and those which may otherwise be legally used but must be handled appropriately (in light shade). The `getObject()` method will return any data type as a Java `Object` and is useful when the underlying data type is a database-specific abstract type or when a generic application needs to be able to accept any data type.

Table 8-1 JDBC ResultSet getXX Method / SQL Data Type Matrix

Legend: R = recommended (dark cell), S = supported (gray cell)

ResultSet getXX method ↓ \ SQL data type →	TINYINT	SMALLINT	INTEGER	BIGINT	REAL	FLOAT	DOUBLE	DECIMAL	NUMERIC	BIT	CHAR	VARCHAR	LONGVARCHAR	BINARY	VARBINARY	LONGVARBINARY	DATE	TIME	TIMESTAMP
getByte()	R	S	S	S	S	S	S	S	S	S	S	S	S						
getShort()	S	R	S	S	S	S	S	S	S	S	S	S	S						
getInt()	S	S	R	S	S	S	S	S	S	S	S	S	S						
getLong()	S	S	S	R	S	S	S	S	S	S	S	S	S						
getFloat()	S	S	S	S	R	S	S	S	S	S	S	S	S						
getDouble()	S	S	S	S	S	R	R	S	S	S	S	S	S						
getBigDecimal()	S	S	S	S	S	S	S	R	R	S	S	S	S						
getBoolean()	S	S	S	S	S	S	S	S	S	R	S	S	S						
getString()	S	S	S	S	S	S	S	S	S	S	R	S	S	S	S	S	S	S	S
getBytes()														R	R	S			
getDate()											S	S	S				R		S
getTime()											S	S	S					R	S
getTimestamp()											S	S	S				S	S	R
getAsciiStream()											S	S	R						
getUnicodeStream()											S	S	R						
getBinaryStream()														S	S	R			
getObject()	S	S	S	S	S	S	S	S	S	S	S	S	S	S	S	S	S	S	S

JDBC Database Drivers

All JDBC calls are passed to a JDBC driver manager. The driver manager in turn passes the request to the JDBC driver that can handle the request. JDBC drivers fit into one of four categories as shown in Figure 8–2 on page 128.

JDBC-Net Pure-Java Driver

This driver translates JDBC calls into a database-independent network protocol which is then translated to a database protocol by a server. In general, this is the most flexible JDBC alternative, although not the most widely available option at this time.

JDBC-ODBC Bridge plus ODBC Driver

There are a number of products that provide JDBC access through Open Database Connectivity (ODBC) drivers. The ODBC binary code, and in many cases database client code, must be loaded on each client machine that uses this driver.

Native-API Partly-Java Driver

This kind of driver converts JDBC calls into database product-specific API calls on the client (such as OCI for Oracle and CLI for DB2). This style of driver also typically requires some product-specific code to be installed on each client machine. Because this driver uses proprietary features, it is generally obtained from the database vendor.

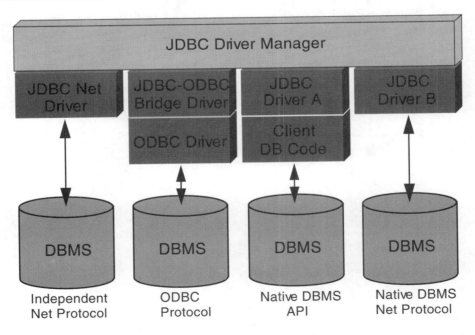

Figure 8–2 JDBC Driver Categories

Native-Protocol Pure-Java Driver

This kind of driver converts JDBC calls into a database product-specific network protocol used by that database system (such as SQL*Net for Oracle), thereby supporting direct connection from the Java client to that database. Because this driver also uses proprietary features, it too must generally be obtained from the database vendor.

The first and last of these driver categories are the preferred way to access databases from JDBC. The second and third are considered interim solutions, where direct pure-Java drivers are not available.

Case Study—IBM DB2 JDBC Driver

The DB2 JDBC driver supports both the JDBC-Net pure-Java (referred to by IBM as *applet driver* support) and native-API partly-Java techniques.

Figure 8–3 illustrates how the DB2 JDBC applet driver works. The driver consists of a JDBC client and a JDBC server. The JDBC client driver is loaded along with the applet (or indeed *servlet*).

> ### Note
>
> In the case of the Lunar Medical Center HTML/servlet/JDBC implementation, there is no client-side requirement on the browser. The servlet acts as the JDBC client and therefore requires the JDBC driver.

When a connection to a DB2 database is requested by the applet, the driver opens a TCP/IP socket to the JDBC server on the Web server machine. After a connection is set up, the client sends each of the subsequent database access requests from the applet to the JDBC server though the TCP/IP connection. The JDBC server then makes corresponding Call Level Interface (CLI) requests to perform the task. Upon completion, the JDBC server sends the results back to the client through the connection.

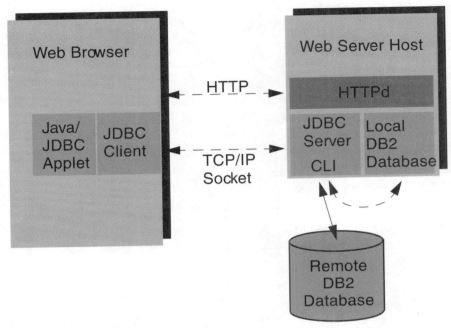

Figure 8–3 DB2's JDBC "Applet Driver" Architecture

Figure 8–4 illustrates how a DB2-based JDBC application works. Calls to JDBC are translated to DB2 CLI calls (through Java native methods). This dependency requires that the DB2 Client Application Enabler (CAE) component be installed at the client. A JDBC request flows through DB2 CLI to the DB2 server through the normal CAE communication flow.

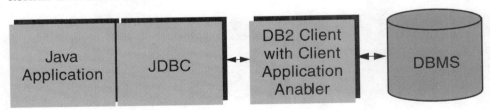

Figure 8–4 DB2's JDBC Application Architecture

Using JDBC

The typical steps to connection and manipulation of a database using JDBC are quite straightforward:

1. Import the Java JDBC package:
   ```
   import java.sql.*;
   ```

2. Set some useful static class variables in your code. In connecting to a database, you will require the appropriate JDBC driver, the URI of the database instance, and the authentication credentials. The URI takes the modified URL form `protocol:subprotocol://host:port/database`. For example:

```
private static final String DRIVER = "COM.ibm.db2.jdbc.net.DB2Driver",
                            URL = "jdbc:db2://server.moon.xyz:8888/sample",
                            USER = "db2admin",
                            PASSWORD = "password";
```

3. Register the appropriate JDBC driver with the `DriverManager` class. `DriverManager` maintains a list of `Driver` classes that have registered themselves by calling the method `registerDriver()`, although you would not normally call this method directly. The method is called automatically by a driver when it is loaded. A useful technique to achieve this uses a static initialiser block at the head of your class, as in:

```
static
  {
  try
    {
    Class.forName (DRIVER);
    }
  catch (ClassNotFoundException x)
    {
    x.printStackTrace (System.out);
    }
  }
```

4. Set the connection `Properties`. Typically, the connection credentials are the only properties you need to set manually. For example:

```
Properties info = new Properties ();
info.put ("user", USER);
info.put ("password", PASSWORD);
```

5. Make the connection to the database. For example:

```
Connection connection = DriverManager.getConnection (URL, info);
```

6. Create your SQL statement string/s and create a `Statement` object for your connection. For example:

```
selectStmt = "SELECT first_name,last_name FROM patient";
insertStmt = "INSERT INTO ssn VALUES (1,222,'AB',333)";
Statement statement = connection.createStatement ();
```

7. Execute the statement in the database using an execution method of the `Statement` object. If your statement contains an SQL query (`SELECT`), you use the `executeQuery()` method, and receive a `ResultSet` object. If your statement contains an SQL INSERT, UPDATE, DELETE or DDL (such as CREATE TABLE or DROP TABLE) statement, you use the executeUpdate() method and receive an integer value indicating the resulting row count of the command. For example:

```
ResultSet result = statement.executeQuery(selectStmt);
int rowCount = statement.executeUpdate(insertStmt);
```

8. If execution of the statement results in an SQL error, an SQLException will be thrown.

    Note that the Connection automatically commits changes to the database after executing each statement. If automatic commit has been disabled on your database, an explicit COMMIT command must be executed, or database changes will not be saved.

9. Process the ResultSet. Columns in your ResultSet are numbered from 1. For example:

```
system.out.println ("Patient Records (Firstname, Lastname):");
while (result.next ())
    {
    system.out.println(result.getString(1) + ", " + result.getString(2))
    }
```

10. Close the ResultSet and Statement objects.

```
result.close();
statement.close();
```

11. Cycle back to step 6 for further transactions, or

12. Close the database Connection.

```
connection.close();
```

    If you will be conducting multiple transactions, it is better to predefine your Statement and ResultSet objects with null values, and then set them as required, as in:

```
    :
ResultSet result = null;
Statement selectStmt = null;
    :
selectStmt = "SELECT first_name,last_name FROM patient";
statement = connection.createStatement ();
result = statement.executeQuery (selectStmt);
    :
result.close ();
statement.close ();
    :
selectStmt = "SELECT title,description FROM history";
statement = connection.createStatement ();
result = statement.executeQuery (selectStmt);
    :
result.close ();
statement.close ();
    :
```

The LMC's JDBC Implementation

Let's examine the Java code required to implement the Lunar Medical Center JDBC Communicator class used by various server components (the servlet for example). The class stores and retrieves data using the set of database tables defined below. This table schema corresponds to the object model shown in Figure 8–5, previously discussed in Chapter 6.

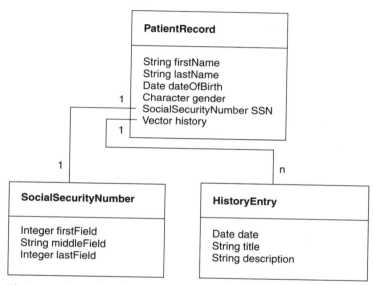

Figure 8–5 Simple Object Model for the LMC's Systems

Table 8-2 SSN - Social Security Number

Column	Type	Length
SSN_ID	INTEGER	4
PART1	SMALLINT	2
PART2	CHARACTER	2
PART3	SMALLINT	2

Table 8-3 Patient - Patient Data

Column	Type	Length
PATIENT_ID	INTEGER	4
FIRST_NAME	VARCHAR	40
LAST_NAME	VARCHAR	40
BIRTH_DAY	INTEGER	4
BIRTH_MONTH	INTEGER	4
BIRTH_YEAR	INTEGER	4
GENDER	VARCHAR	1

Table 8-4 History - Patient History Data

Column	Type	Length
ENTRY_ID	INTEGER	4
PATIENT_ID	INTEGER	4
DAY	INTEGER	4
MONTH	INTEGER	4
YEAR	INTEGER	4
TITLE	VARCHAR	80
DESCRIPTION	VARCHAR	1024

The ssn table holds unique Social Security Numbers that are used as the primary key of the patient table and also act as a foreign key of the patient history table. It should be noted that data held in Java objects is being stored to a relational database system (and vice versa); so the code needs to implement the necessary flattening mechanism.

It is useful to present the bulk of the class' source code to examine how some of the JDBC methods are used in practice. The Java class file has two methods (with the definitions shown in bold type in the source):

- readPatientRecord()—which retrieves data from the database in order to create and return a PatientRecord object that corresponds to a given SocialSecurityNumber object

- writePatientRecord()—for storing a PatientRecord object's data to the database

```
import java.io.*;
import java.sql.*;
import java.util.*;
import com.ibm.austin.itsc.javanc.Hospital.*;

public class Communicator implements Serializable
  {
  private static final String DRIVER = "COM.ibm.db2.jdbc.net.DB2Driver",
                              URL = "jdbc:db2://server.moon.xyz:8888/sample",
                              USER = "db2admin",
                              PASSWORD = "password";

  static
    {
    try
      {
      Class.forName (DRIVER);
      }
    catch (ClassNotFoundException x )
      {
      x.printStackTrace (System.out);
      }
    }

  public static PatientRecord readPatientRecord (SocialSecurityNumber SSN)
    throws PatientRecordException
    {

    Connection connection = null;
    Statement statement = null;

    try
      {
```

Extract the Social Security Number strings from the provided object:

```
      String sSNFirst = SSN.getFirstField () + "",
             sSNMiddle = SSN.getMiddleField (),
             sSNLast = SSN.getLastField () + "";

      String selectStmt;
      java.sql.Date dateOfBirth = null;
      boolean patientFound;
```

```
Properties info = new Properties ();
info.put ("user", USER);
info.put ("password", PASSWORD);
```

The database connection is actually made:

```
connection = DriverManager.getConnection (URL, info);
```

Dynamically create an SQL SELECT (query) statement to search the PATIENT and SSN tables, linked on the key ID fields, to obtain the single patient record corresponding to the provided Social Security Number:

```
selectStmt = "SELECT first_name,last_name,birth_day,birth_month,birth_year," +
             "gender FROM patient,ssn" +
             " WHERE patient_id=ssn_id" +
             " AND part1=" + sSNFirst +
             " AND part2='" + sSNMiddle + "'" +
             " AND part3=" + sSNLast;
```

Create a Statement object on the connection and execute the query:

```
statement = connection.createStatement ();
ResultSet result = statement.executeQuery (selectStmt);
```

If there are no records in the ResultSet, throw an exception:

```
if (!result.next ())
    throw new PatientRecordException ("PatientRecord not found in " + URL);
```

Instantiate a new PatientRecord object using data extracted from the ResultSet:

```
PatientRecord thisPatient = new PatientRecord
    (
    result.getString (1), result.getString (2),
    result.getInt (3) + "", result.getInt (4) + "", result.getInt (5) + "",
    result.getString (6).charAt (0),
    sSNFirst, sSNMiddle, sSNLast
    );
```

Close these ResultSet and Statement objects:

```
result.close ();
statement.close ();
```

Dynamically create another query statement to search the HISTORY and SSN tables, linked on the key ID fields, to obtain all history records associated with the patient as identified by the Social Security Number:

```
selectStmt = "SELECT entry_id,day,month,year,title,description FROM history,ssn" +
             " WHERE patient_id=ssn_id" +
             " AND part1=" + sSNFirst +
             " AND part2='" + sSNMiddle + "'" +
             " AND part3=" + sSNLast +
             " ORDER BY entry_id";

statement = connection.createStatement ();
result = statement.executeQuery (selectStmt);

Vector thisHistory = new Vector ();
HistoryEntry thisEntry = null;
```

Moving through the `ResultSet` rows, populate a vector of `HistoryEntry` objects using the data extracted from the current `ResultSet` row (note that we have to do some minor manipulation of date values to satisfy the requirements of the Java `Date` object):

```
while (result.next ())
   {
   thisEntry = new HistoryEntry
      (
     new java.util.Date (result.getInt (4) - 1900, result.getInt (3) - 1,
                           result.getInt (2)),
     result.getString (5),
     result.getString (6)
     );
   thisHistory.addElement(thisEntry);
   }

result.close();
statement.close();
```

Add the vector of `HistoryEntry` objects to the `PatientRecord` object and return:

```
thisPatient.setHistory(thisHistory);
return thisPatient;
   }

catch (Exception x)
   { /* code elided */ }
finally
   {
   // Clean up connection
   try
      {
```

Close the Connection object:

```
connection.close();
      }
   catch (Exception x)
      { /* code elided */ }
   }
}

public static void writePatientRecord (PatientRecord patientRecord)
   throws PatientRecordException
   {
   String sSNFirst = patientRecord.getSSN ().getFirstField () + "",
          sSNMiddle = patientRecord.getSSN ().getMiddleField (),
          sSNLast = patientRecord.getSSN ().getLastField () + "";

   Connection connection = null;
   Statement statement = null;
   ResultSet result = null;

   try
```

```
{
Properties info = new Properties ();
info.put ("user", USER);
info.put ("password", PASSWORD);
connection = DriverManager.getConnection (URL, info);
int thisSsnId,
    temp,
    rowInserted;
```

Dynamically create a query statement to search the SSN table to try and obtain a record corresponding to the provided Social Security Number, thereby indicating that the patient record already exists in the database:

```
String selectStmt = "SELECT ssn_id FROM ssn" +
                    " WHERE part1=" + sSNFirst +
                    " AND part2='" + sSNMiddle + "'" +
                    " AND part3=" + sSNLast;

statement = connection.createStatement ();
result = statement.executeQuery (selectStmt);
```

If no record was found, new records need to be inserted:

```
if (!result.next ())
    {
    result.close ();
    statement.close ();
```

Dynamically create another query statement to obtain the current maximum identifier from the SSN table. This will be used as the basis for the ID value of the to-be-inserted, new Social Security Number record (note that this is not the ideal way of doing this. If your database system supports a protected automatic incrementing facility, use that):

```
String select_max_ssn_stmt = "SELECT MAX(ssn_id) FROM ssn";

statement = connection.createStatement ();
result = statement.executeQuery (select_max_ssn_stmt);
```

Add 1 to the maximum value found, or start with a new value of 1 if not found:

```
if (!result.next ())
    thisSsnId = 1;
else
    {
    temp = result.getInt (1) + 1;
    if ( ! result.wasNull ())
        thisSsnId = temp;
    else
        thisSsnId = 1;
    }

result.close();
statement.close();
```

Dynamically create an SQL INSERT statement to insert a new Social Security Number record into the SSN table:

```
String insertSsnStmt = "INSERT INTO ssn VALUES (" +
                       thisSsnId + "," +
                       sSNFirst + ",'" +
                       sSNMiddle + "'," +
                       sSNLast + ")";

statement = connection.createStatement ();
```

Execute the statement and return the number of rows inserted (will not be 1 if there was a problem):

```
rowInserted = statement.executeUpdate (insertSsnStmt);
statement.close ();

if (rowInserted != 1)
   throw new PatientRecordException ("Could not insert SSN: ID=" +
                               thisSsnId + " in " + URL);
```

Dynamically create another SQL INSERT statement to insert a new patient record into the PATIENT table:

```
String insertPatientStmt = "INSERT INTO patient VALUES (" +
      thisSsnId + ",'" +
      patientRecord.getFirstName () + "','" +
      patientRecord.getLastName () + "'," +
      patientRecord.getDateOfBirth ().getDate () + "," +
      (patientRecord.getDateOfBirth ().getMonth () + 1) + "," +
      (patientRecord.getDateOfBirth ().getYear () + 1900) + ",'" +
      patientRecord.getGender () + "')";

statement = connection.createStatement ();
rowInserted = statement.executeUpdate (insertPatientStmt);
statement.close ();

if ( rowInserted != 1)
   throw new PatientRecordException ("Could not insert Patient: ID=" +
                               thisSsnId + " in " + URL);

}
else
{
```

A Social Security Number was previously found, extract the value:

```
thisSsnId = result.getInt (1);
result.close ();
statement.close ();
}
```

Dynamically create an SQL DELETE statement to delete all records from the HISTORY table for the associated patient:

```
String deleteHistoryStmt = "DELETE FROM history" +
                           " WHERE patient_id=" + thisSsnId;

statement = connection.createStatement ();
rowInserted = statement.executeUpdate (deleteHistoryStmt);
statement.close ();
```

```
Vector thisHistory = patientRecord.getHistory ();
HistoryEntry thisEntry=null;
String insertEntryStmt;
int thisEntryIndex = 0;
```

Moving through the `PatientRecord` vector of `HistoryEntry` objects, dynamically create an SQL INSERT statement to insert the current history entry as a record in the HISTORY table (note that we have to do some minor manipulation of date values to deal with the contents of Java `Date` objects):

```
for (Enumeration e = thisHistory.elements (); e.hasMoreElements () ;)
  {
   thisEntryIndex++;
   thisEntry = (HistoryEntry) e.nextElement ();

   insertEntryStmt = "INSERT INTO history VALUES (" +
                     thisEntryIndex + "," +
                     thisSsnId + "," +
                     thisEntry.getDate ().getDate () + "," +
                     (thisEntry.getDate ().getMonth () + 1) + "," +
                     (thisEntry.getDate ().getYear () + 1900) + ",'" +
                     thisEntry.getTitle () + "','" +
                     thisEntry.getDescription () + "')";

   statement = connection.createStatement ();
   rowInserted = statement.executeUpdate (insertEntryStmt);
   statement.close();

   if (rowInserted != 1)
     throw new PatientRecordException ("Could not insert History Entry: ID=" +
               thisEntryIndex + "/" + thisSsnId + " in " + URL);
   }
  }

catch( Exception x )
  { /* code elided */ }
finally
  {
   // Clean up connection
   try
    {
    connection.close ();
    }
   catch (Exception x)
    {
     throw new PatientRecordException ("Problem cleaning up " + URL +
                                       "\n" + x.getMessage());
    }
   }
 }
}
```

Chapter 9

Java Servers and Socket Communication

▼ INTRODUCTION TO TCP/IP SOCKETS

▼ SOCKETS WITH JAVA

▼ THE LMC'S SOCKET IMPLEMENTATION

▼ IN SUMMARY

This chapter deals with methods available in Java to slice monolithic applications into functional units that communicate through a network, thus making it a distributed application. The chapter introduces the Internet Protocol (IP) and its API-using sockets. Sockets provide the functionality to transport data blocks or data streams over the network and provide a very elementary facility for the creation of distributed components.

At the Lunar Medical Center (LMC), the receptionist enters the patient's data at check-in time. LMC doctors can access this data and attach further information about diagnosis and treatments. As with any hospital, the LMC has many doctors and can have more than one receptionist. To let them work in parallel and share a common set of data, they must access a centrally-managed (but distributable) data facility.

How can the hospital applications be designed or extended to meet these needs? The LMC designers are interested in a solution that supports their Java-based network computing vision, and one of the options is to base the infrastructure on non-proprietary TCP/IP (Transmission Control Protocol/Internet Protocol) and UDP/IP (User Datagram Protocol/Internet Protocol) communications.

Introduction to TCP/IP sockets

To establish a network connection between two parties, it is first necessary to agree on a protocol for the communication. The most widely used, standardized and non-proprietary protocol for computer networking is TCP/IP.

The basic procedure to set up a TCP/IP connection is to create a *socket* at each communication endpoint—the server and the client.

Sockets represent the API to TCP/IP and UDP/IP. Their purpose is to hide the details of the network from the programmer. There are three types of sockets:

- Stream

- Datagram

- Raw

Stream and datagram sockets interface to TCP and UDP protocols respectively and are positioned above the IP network layer. The raw socket makes use of the lower-layer IP and Internet Control Message Protocol (ICMP). Raw and datagram sockets provide a fast service, but do not guarantee correct and complete delivery of the data packets. Such functionality needs to be implemented in the application. Raw and datagram sockets also operate on single data packets rather than on continuous data streams. The most appropriate option for the LCM designers is the stream socket mechanism.

A socket consists of an IP address and a port number.

- An IP address is a 32-bit number. It can be represented numerically or symbolically, such as 137.138.131.253 or www.cern.ch. The symbolic representation (www.cern.ch) is converted to the four-byte representation by the Domain Name Service (DNS). In a network domain, an IP address represents exactly one host. It is possible, however, for a given host to be a member of more than one network domain, and in this case, the host may possess multiple IP addresses.

- A port number is a 16-bit number. Ports are required to distinguish the different connections which might be established with one host. There are *well-known ports* that are reserved for specific services like Telnet (port 23) or WWW/HTTP (port 80). Servers must register the port number that will be used for accessing their service. Clients must know this port address and specify it when trying to establish a connection. The client does not have to register its port number before the connection is made, to allow data transfer from the server to the client, but communicates its port to the server using the initial unidirectional connection from the client to the server. The client port number is usually chosen by the client operating system from a list of available ports during run time.

The following sequence of operations (shown graphically in Figure 9–1 on page 143) set up a bidirectional client/server communication with a multithreaded server:

1. The server registers the port number it wishes to use for the communication.
2. The server listens on the specified port for client requests.
3. The client initiates a connection to the server using the specified port.
4. The server accepts the connection.
5. The server starts a separate thread to service the request (necessary to allow concurrent access).
6. The connection is established, and the two applications can perform their data exchange.
7. The client and the server both terminate the connection.

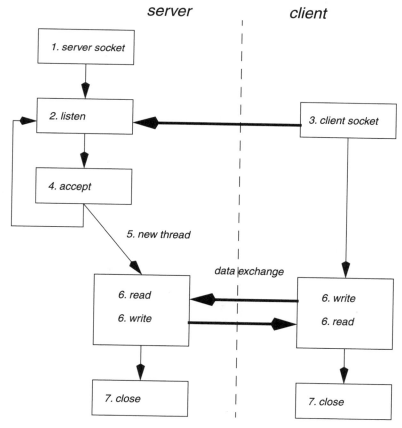

Figure 9–1 Sequence of Interactions in Client/Server Socket Communication

For complex applications, it is a challenge to make sure that the system does not enter a "deadlock" situation (where both the client and the server wait for input at the same time). Establishing a complete, robust protocol between the parties requires a significant effort.

Sockets with Java

Java provides access to sockets through the `java.net` package. The classes and methods necessary to implement a typical socket-based client/server application are:

- `ServerSocket`: This class implements server-side sockets. A server waits for requests to come in over the network, performs some activity, and may return a result to the requester. Important methods are:

  - `accept()`: accept the client request
  - `read()`: read data from the client through a stream
  - `write()`: write data to the client through a stream
  - `close()`: close the stream and terminate the connection
  - `getInputStream()`: return the input stream associated with the socket
  - `getOutputStream()`: return the output stream associated with the socket

- `Socket`: This class implements the client-side socket. Important methods are:

  - `read()`: read data from the server through a stream
  - `write()`: write data to the server through a stream
  - `close()`: close the stream and terminate the connection
  - `getInputStream()`: return the input stream associated with the socket
  - `getOutputStream()`: return the output stream associated with the socket

Compatibility of Different Socket Implementations

The JVM definition provides a standardized run-time environment, including the representation of data types. Because of this, exchanging data between two Java applications is relatively painless.

Exchanging data with an application written, for example, in C through a TCP/IP stream may be a different proposition.

C (for instance) does not define a representation for integers or floating point numbers or other structured data types. The byte sequence of an integer in a TCP/IP stream may consequently differ between *little-endian* and *big-endian* machines. To overcome this problem, the idea of a defined *net order* for transmission was introduced. Since Java obeys net orders, as long as the communication partner also obeys net orders, interoperability is assured.

> ### Note
>
> Little-endian machines store the least significant byte first. Big-endian machines start with the most significant byte.

The LMC's Socket Implementation

The LMC's socket Communicator class is found within the com.ibm.austin.itsc.javanc.Socket package, which also encapsulates additional server functionality in two new classes: PatientRecordServer and PatientRecordServerThread. These two additional classes are required to provide support for concurrent access to the server resources, because new requests will need to be accepted while still servicing a client request. To achieve this, the PatientRecordServer class creates a new thread from the PatientRecordServerThread class upon acceptance of each request. Figure 9–2 on page 145 shows all the classes and methods in the LMC com.ibm.austin.itsc.javanc.Socket package (as viewed within VisualAge for Java).

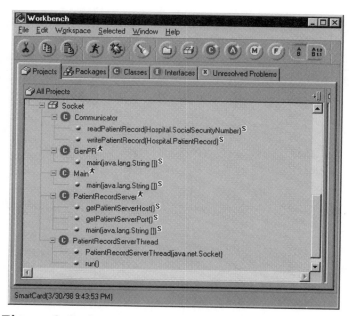

Figure 9–2 Overview of the Socket Package

Implementing the Socket Client

The com.ibm.austin.itsc.javanc.Socket.Communicator class provides the readPatientRecord() and writePatientRecord() methods for patient record retrieval and storage, as do all other Communicator classes developed at the LMC:

- The methods first create a client socket utilizing the appropriate server configuration (the server host name and the port number the server listens to).

- Using the Socket methods getInputStream() and getOutputStream(), object input and output streams are created.

- The raw input and output streams are "wrapped" to allow for object serialization.

- The objects can now be transferred using read() and write().

- The client issues the close() command.

```
public static PatientRecord readPatientRecord(SocialSecurityNumber SSN)
  throws PatientRecordException
  {
  Socket sock = null;
  ObjectOutputStream remoteOut = null;
  ObjectInputStream remoteIn = null;
  try
    {
    sock = new Socket (PatientRecordServer.getPatientServerHost (),
                       PatientRecordServer.getPatientServerPort ());
    remoteOut = new ObjectOutputStream (sock.getOutputStream ());
    remoteOut.writeObject (SSN);
    remoteIn = new ObjectInputStream (sock.getInputStream ());
    PatientRecord patientRecord = (PatientRecord) remoteIn.readObject ();
    return (patientRecord);
    }
  catch (Exception e)
    {
    throw new PatientRecordException (e.getMessage ());
    }
  finally
    {
    try
      {
      sock.close ();
      remoteIn.close ();
      remoteOut.close ();
      }
    catch (Exception e)
      { /* SQUELCH! */ }
    }
  }

public static void writePatientRecord (PatientRecord patientRecord)
```

```
throws PatientRecordException
{
Socket sock = null;
ObjectOutputStream remoteOut = null;
try
  {
  sock = new Socket(PatientRecordServer.getPatientServerHost (),
    PatientRecordServer.getPatientServerPort ());
  remoteOut = new ObjectOutputStream (sock.getOutputStream ());
  remoteOut.writeObject (patientRecord);
  }
catch (Exception e)
  {
  throw new PatientRecordException (e.getMessage ());
  }
finally
  {
  try
    {
    sock.close ();
    remoteOut.close ();
    }
  catch (Exception e)
    { /* SQUELCH! */ }
  }
}
```

Implementing the Socket Server

The PatientRecordServer class consists of a main() method and methods to allow main() to safely obtain the server host name and port number. The main() method creates a server socket with the server port number it should listen to. An infinite loop is used to listen for and accept client requests and to create and start a new thread for servicing a request before returning to the beginning of the loop.

The server makes use of multithreading and thus provides the ability to service concurrent client requests. After the server accepts a request and a bidirectional connection is established, both parties agree to change the port on the server side in order not to block further requests. The new port number is chosen by the server operating system from a list of currently unused ports. This is the same mechanism used by the client socket to obtain a port number. All these details are fortunately hidden in the java.net package and the host operating system; so they are transparent to the Java programmer.

```
import java.io.*;
import java.net.*;
import com.ibm.austin.itsc.javanc.Hospital.*;
import com.ibm.austin.itsc.javanc.File.*;

public class PatientRecordServer
  {
```

```
private static final int patientServerPort = 5432;
private static final String patientServerHost = "127.0.0.1"; // localhost

public static String getPatientServerHost ()
  {
  return patientServerHost;
  }

public static int getPatientServerPort ()
  {
  return patientServerPort;
  }

public static void main (String [] args)
  throws IOException, ClassNotFoundException
  {
  ServerSocket servSock = new ServerSocket (getPatientServerPort ());
  for ( ; ; )
    {
    try
      {
      Socket sock = servSock.accept ();
      Thread serverThread = new Thread (new PatientRecordServerThread (sock));
      serverThread.start ();
      }
    catch (Exception e)
      {
      // code elided
      }
    }
  }
```

The last component required to service the client request is the server class. This implements the `java.lang.Runnable` interface and receives the socket reference as an argument when instantiated. The important aspect of the class is its `run()` method, which is triggered by the `serverThread.start` method call in `PatientRecordServer`. As both client read and write requests are utilized, the request must be distinguished in the method:

- Because the server in both cases will first receive an object, an input stream is opened from the socket (similar to the client code).

- Upon reception of the client object, the `instanceof` operator provides the decision mechanism for acting on the client request:

  - If the object is an instance of `SocialSecurityNumber`, then the server should read the corresponding PatientRecord object.

  - If a `PatientRecord` object is received, then the object must be stored.

- Ports are a precious host-operating-system resource. Therefore, the client and server close the connection and release their respective ports after the exchange of data is completed.

```
public void run ()
   {
   ObjectInputStream remoteIn = null;
   ObjectOutputStream remoteOut = null;
   try
      {
      remoteIn  = new ObjectInputStream (socket.getInputStream ());
      Object obj = remoteIn.readObject ();
      if (obj instanceof SocialSecurityNumber)
         {
         SocialSecurityNumber SSN = (SocialSecurityNumber) obj;
         PatientRecord patientRecord =
           com.ibm.austin.itsc.javanc.File.Communicator.readPatientRecord (SSN);
         remoteOut = new ObjectOutputStream (socket.getOutputStream ());
         remoteOut.writeObject (patientRecord);
         }
      else if (obj instanceof PatientRecord)
         {
         PatientRecord patientRecord = (PatientRecord) obj;
         com.ibm.austin.itsc.javanc.File.Communicator.writePatientRecord (patientRecord);
         }
      }
   catch (Exception e)
      {
      // code elided
      }
   finally
      {
      try
         {
         remoteIn.close ();
         remoteOut.close ();
         }
      catch (Exception e)
         { /* exceptions from cleaning up are ignored */ }
      }
   }
```

Prior to starting the LMC client application, the server process must be running on the server host. This is accomplished by starting the `PatientRecordServer` class on the host that is specified by the `patientServerHost` final variable in the `com.ibm.austin.itsc.javanc.Socket.Communicator` class.

In Summary

This chapter introduced the basic concepts of the Java socket API for network data exchange. The LMC application has been extended to a client/server architecture using sockets for communication. Sockets are a powerful and capable communication mechanism. Java greatly simplifies the use of sockets for the programmer.

Using sockets for applications that deal with serializable data streams is appropriate. The effort necessary to map the LMC application objects to a single I/O stream was quite small. In addition, no big effort to synchronize the operations on client and server was necessary

Chapter **10**

Java Servers and RMI Communication

▼ RMI: AN EASY WAY TO IMPLEMENT JAVA CLIENT/SERVER APPLICATIONS

▼ THE RMI ARCHITECTURE

▼ THE LMC'S RMI IMPLEMENTATION

This chapter introduces Remote Method Invocation (RMI). As its name suggests, this standard Java facility makes it possible to invoke Java methods remotely. RMI makes it easy to develop distributed applications with components that communicate across multiple systems in a network.

Although RMI requires more infrastructural support from the host computer than sockets (see Chapter 9, "Java Servers and Socket Communication" on page 141), it nevertheless offers a more effective and efficient mechanism for developing applications requiring complex interactions between components.

RMI: An Easy Way to Implement Java Client/Server Applications

RMI allows for 100 percent pure Java solutions. With RMI, invoking methods remotely and passing arguments and objects across the network is as easy as for a local application. The creation of a complete distributed Java application requires only a little more extra effort than the development of a simple, nondistributed component.

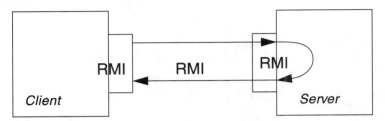

Figure 10–1 An RMI-Based System

RMI allows you to:

- Invoke a method on a remote object in the same manner as a local object
- Use a remote object without giving regard to its location
- Pass and return objects as arguments

Although actually made available under Java 1.02, RMI was formally introduced in Java Version 1.1.

The RMI Architecture

RMI has a three-layer architecture (see Figure 10–2 on page 152) consisting of:

- The transport layer
- The remote reference layer
- The stub and skeleton layer

Because each of these layers has its own API, it is easy to augment RMI with new or improved implementations, and it is anticipated that this will indeed happen. As technologies such as CORBA's IIOP (the Internet InterOperability Protocol) become more widespread, RMI will be updated to incorporate new capabilities.

Client		Server
Stub	Stub & Skeleton Layer	Skeleton
Remote Reference Layer		
Transport Layer		

Figure 10–2 Remote Method Invocation Architecture

Stub and Skeleton Layer

This layer is the interface between the application and the RMI system proper.

The *Stub* acts as a client-side *proxy* (in this case, an object that operates on behalf of the remote server object). It implements all the interfaces available on the remote object and during remote invocation is responsible for:

- Asking the remote reference layer for the location of the remote server object
- Serialization of the arguments to the output stream (a process called *marshalling*)
- Informing the remote reference layer that all parameter data has been sent and thus the actual call can be performed by the server
- Unmarshalling the serialized return value
- Informing the remote reference layer that the call is complete

The *Skeleton* is a server-side proxy. Its responsibilities mirror those of the stub. The skeleton is responsible for:

- Unmarshalling arguments
- Sending the call to the actual server object
- Marshalling the return value or exception back to the client-side stub

The relationship between client, server, stub, and skeleton is illustrated in Figure 10–3 on page 153.

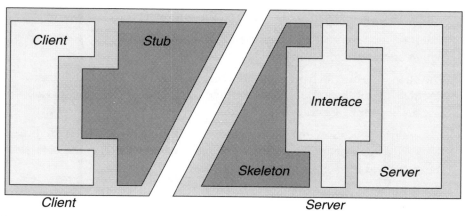

Figure 10–3 RMI Implementation

Remote Reference Layer

This layer sits between the stub and skeleton layer and the transport layer. It is potentially responsible for a number of activities, including:

- Finding the location of the remote object

- Making a point-to-point invocation (and handling automatic reconnection)

- Activation of a new server process if not done earlier

- Maintaining replication if required

The last two of these functions are not implemented in the Java 1.1 Version of RMI, but will be offered quickly as the technology becomes more established.

Transport Layer

This layer is the lowest of the three layers and is responsible for:

- Maintaining a table of objects in the local JVM

- Establishing and maintaining the connection between two Java Virtual Machines

- Listening for and responding to invocations

- Locating the dispatcher object for the target of the remote invocation and passing the connection to this dispatcher

The RMI transport interfaces only exist at the virtual machine level and are not available directly to the application.

RMI Method Invocation Mechanism

The RMI invocation mechanism is based on the following major steps:

1. The RMI server object registers itself to a separate *RMIRegistry* server, which operates at the transport layer.

2. The client object searches for and finds the remote server through the *RMIRegistry* at the remote reference layer level and receives the server's corresponding stub object.

3. The client application invokes methods on a remote object. These invocations are actually handled by the stub object, which is interposed between the client and the server's skeleton object.

4. The arguments are marshalled and sent across the network.

5. The remote call is initiated through the client stub.

6. The call is dispatched to the relevant object at the transport-layer level.

7. The arguments are unmarshalled at the server's end.

8. The method specified in the call is invoked locally.

9. Return values are marshalled by the server's skeleton object.

10. Return values are transmitted to the stub on the client side.

11. Return values are unmarshalled by the stub and passed upwards to the caller.

RMI from a Programmer's Perspective

To the RMI programmer, the only visible parts of RMI are the client, the server and the server's advertised interface; most of the underlying mechanism is hidden (see Figure 10–4 on page 155). One aspect of the implementation is visible; however, since the transportation mechanism uses serialized object streams, all the objects transmitted between client and server—either as parameters or as return values—must implement the `java.io.Serializable` interface.

Server Side

The server must implement an interface (which must extend the standard `java.rmi.Remote` interface) describing all the public methods available within it that are being advertised to the clients.

In addition, the server-side class must extend `java.rmi.Server.UnicastRemoteObject`.

To advertise itself to clients on the network, a server must execute either the `java.rmi.Naming.bind()` or `java.rmi.Naming.rebind()` methods, which associate a server object with a new name or reset the value of an existing name, respectively.

Client Side

From the client side, a remote method made available to the network through the server's advertised interface can be invoked just as if it were a local method within the same JVM (as shown in Figure 10–4 on page 155).

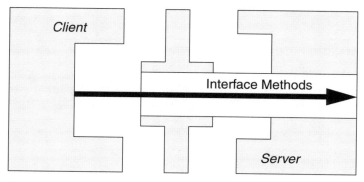

Figure 10–4 RMI Programmer Viewpoint

Prior to making a remote invocation, the client is required to determine the location of the server advertising the remote method to use. To do this, the client makes use of the `java.rmi.Naming.lookup()` method. This will return a stub object implementing the server's advertised interface. Stub methods called on this object will cause the actual implementations to be invoked at the server object.

Establishing Callbacks Using RMI

It is possible to arrange for a server to call a method of the client. This technique is called a *callback* and is typically used when it is necessary for the server object to let the client know when it has completed a requested operation or has to inform its client of the occurrence of some other event.

Figure 10–5 on page 156 shows the sequence of events involved in using callbacks:

1. Clients register a notification method with the server that will be invoked ("called back") when a noteworthy event occurs.

2. A client triggers an event for which clients are registered.

3. The server calls back to the registered client through the supplied method.

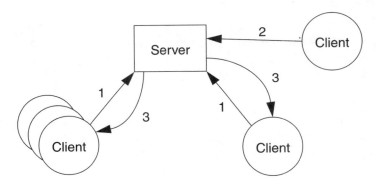

Figure 10–5 Using Callbacks

Establishing callbacks in RMI is relatively easy. To allow the server to call a method of a client object, the client must also become a simple server.

It is necessary for the client to implement an interface describing the method that the server should use when performing the callback. A simple example is:

```
import java.rmi.*;
public interface Notifiable extends Remote
    {
    void notify (Integer reason) throws RemoteException;
    }
```

Since the callback is purely for use between client and server, the client does not need to bind a name in the registry. It is also not required for the client object to extend `java.rmi.Server.UnicastRemoteObject`. This means that any arbitrary object can register itself for an RMI callback:

```
public class Client extends Frame
                    implements Notifiable
   {
```

The client can become a server by executing the following, perhaps in it's constructor:

```
try
   {
   UnicastRemoteObject.exportObject ();
   }
catch (RemoteException re)
   {
   // code elided
   }
```

Since the client class is now acting as a server, it is necessary to execute the `rmic` tool on the client code to generate the requisite stub and skeleton classes.

To install a callback, the real server object needs to provide a remotely callable method that is able to save a reference to the client's remote interface. In the following example, this method is called `registerForNotification()`.

```
try
   {
   ServerI s = (ServerI) Naming.lookup ("Server");
   Client c = new Client (s);
   s.registerForNotification (c);
   }
catch (Exception e)
   {
   // code elided
   }
```

The server's `registerForNotification()` would resemble:

```
private Notifiable thingToNotify;
public void registerForNotification (Notifiable n) throws RemoteException
   {
   this.thingToNotify = n;
   }
```

When the server determines that a notification is needed, it executes code similar to the following:

```
Integer HEART_ATTACK = new Integer (911);
try
  {
  this.thingToNotify.notify (HEART_ATTACK);
  }
catch (Exception e)
  {
  // code elided
  }
```

Callbacks are a simple and powerful tool for building object-based distributed systems.

RMI Security Manager

To run an RMI application, it is first necessary to download a stub corresponding to the server object's advertised interface. While the downloading will be automatically handled by the RMI mechanism, a minimum level of security is required to be in place before commencing.

RMI provides a default RMISecurityManager class that disables all functions except class definition and access. In case a security manager is not established, stub loading at the client is disabled, effectively preventing RMI from working.

"The RMI Server Class" on page 162 shows how a new RMISecurityManager can be instantiated and installed.

RMI Registry

Java's RMIRegistry application provides a simple URL-based "white pages" service for clients and servers. When a server starts, it ensures that its URL is advertised in the registry. When a client needs to locate a server, it performs a lookup on the URL to locate the server object on the network.

Major RMI Classes

To facilitate development using RMI, three packages are provided in Java Version 1.1:

- java.rmi contains the classes used on the client side to access remote objects.

    This following list describes the main constituents of the package that are required to build a client/server application with RMI.

    java.rmi.Remote interface

    java.rmi.RemoteException

    java.rmi.Naming defines interfaces to the URL-based RMIRegistry

- `bind()`, `rebind()` register a remote server object in the registry
- `lookup()` search in the registry for a remote server object

`java.rmi.RMISecurityManager` defines a default security policy for RMI

`java.rmi.server.UnicastRemoteObject` base functionality for the server object

- `java.rmi.server` contains the class and interface framework required to define and implement remote server objects.

- `java.rmi.registry` contains the classes and interfaces necessary to define a registry service.

For a complete description, refer to the RMI documentation.

Developing with RMI

Developing with RMI requires the following major steps:

1. Create the requisite interface containing the necessary public methods.
2. Create the server-side with the remote class implementing and advertising the appropriate interface.
3. Create a client to invoke the remote methods.
4. Generate the requisite stub and skeleton classes using the `rmic` tool.

Stub and skeleton are generated by running the JDK's `rmic` tool over the remote object class.

```
rmic RMIServer
```

Two new classes, with _Stub and _Skel appended to the class names, are created.

The `rmic` tool also replaces a client's normal methods calls (generated by the `javac` compiler without regard to whether RMI is involved or not) with corresponding calls to the methods in the stub class.

In the LMC's system, the remote object class is named `RMIserver`. The generated stub and skeleton classes are:

```
RMIserver_Stub
```

```
RMIServer_Skel
```

IBM VisualAge for Java does this slightly differently, using the Tools/Remote Method Invocation/Generates Proxies menu entry. Figure 10–6 on page 160 shows this menu entry.

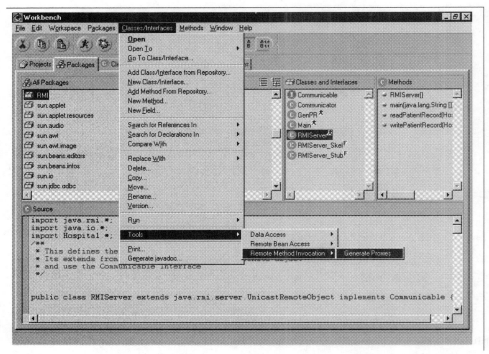

Figure 10–6 Generating Stub and Skeleton with IBM VisualAge for Java

To execute an RMI-based system:

1. Start the RMIRegistry server.

2. Ensure that the server has registered its remote interface with the RMIRegistry at startup.

3. On the client side, look up the appropriate remote server.

4. Invoke the remote server object's methods as if they were local methods.

The RMIRegistry is typically started from the command line. In Windows NT, for instance, the appropriate command to start the registry looking at port 1099 is:

```
start /min rmiregistry 1099
```

The VisualAge for Java Integrated Development Environment (IDE) provides a specific dialog for this purpose, accessible through Workspace—Options—RMI as shown in Figure 10–7.

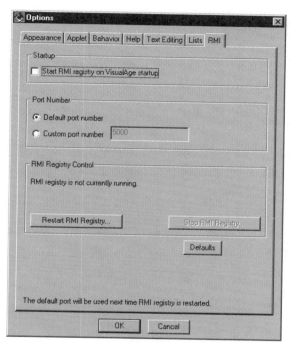

Figure 10–7 Starting the RMI Registry within IBM VisualAge for Java

The LMC's RMI Implementation

This section discusses the RMI Communicator class and the associated RMI server application created by the LMC's developers to support their network computing application suite.

The following code is all found in a package with the name com.ibm.austin.itsc.javanc.RMI and is found on the CD-ROM accompanying this book.

The RMI Server Interface

An RMI server object advertises the subset of methods for which it is prepared to accept remote invocations through an interface that extends the standard java.rmi.Remote interface.

For the LMC's RMI-based server, the interface is:

```
import java.rmi.*;
import com.ibm.austin.itsc.javanc.Hospital.*;

public interface Communicable extends Remote
   {
  public  PatientRecord readPatientRecord (SocialSecurityNumber SSN)
    throws PatientRecordException, RemoteException;
  public void writePatientRecord (PatientRecord patientRecord)
    throws PatientRecordException, RemoteException;
   }
```

Since RMI assumes that a network error can affect any operation, it is obligatory that each method advertised in the interface must be declared to throw a java.rmi.RemoteException.

The RMI Server Class

The LMC's RMI server runs as an application that advertises the Communicable interface to client classes.

This section will step through the server's code and describe various important points and features.

```
import java.rmi.*;
import java.io.*;
import com.ibm.austin.itsc.javanc.Hospital.*;

public class RMIServer
   extends java.rmi.server.UnicastRemoteObject
   implements Communicable
   {
   private static final String DATADIR = "C:\\WINNT\\System32\\",
                                SUFFIX = ".LOG";
```

The URL string is exported to ensure that the client and server both have knowledge of the server's advertised name.

```
  public static final String URL =
    "JF0150A.itsc.austin.ibm.com:1099/PatientRecordRemote";
```

An unusual feature of this code is the presence of a distinct no-arguments constructor that simply calls super() (it is not normal to supply such a constructor, since this is typically regarded as the default behavior). In this case, RMI requires an explicit call to super() to account for the situation where a RemoteException could be thrown.

```
  public RMIServer () throws RemoteException
     {
     super();
     }
```

The main() method is called to start the server and register it to the RMIRegistry.

The main method first registers an RMISecurityManager instance to allow the download of the appropriate stub objects to the client side. The method then creates an instance of its encapsulating class, which is then registered with the RMIRegistry. The Naming.rebind() method used will first remove any preexisting value associated with the URL being registered, before giving it a new value.

```
public static void main (String [] args) throws RemoteException
   {
   System.setSecurityManager (new RMISecurityManager ());
   try
      {
      Communicable comm = new RMIServer ();
      Naming.rebind(URL, comm);
      }
   catch (Exception e)
      { /* code elided */ }
   }
```

In the following method, the PatientRecord object is directly serialized to a file. An equivalent mechanism would utilize the com.ibm.austin.itsc.javanc.File Communicator class developed for use elsewhere.

Note the way that any exception thrown by the code is propagated. To simplify exception handling in the client code, all exceptions are converted into a PatientRecordException containing the message obtained from the real exception to make it possible to determine the reason why the exception is being thrown.

```
public  PatientRecord readPatientRecord (SocialSecurityNumber SSN)
   throws PatientRecordException, RemoteException
   {
   ObjectInputStream ois = null;
   FileInputStream fis = null;
   try
      {
      fis = new FileInputStream (DATADIR +
                          SSN.getFirstField () + SSN.getMiddleField () +
                          SSN.getLastField () + SUFFIX);
      ois = new ObjectInputStream (fis);
      return ((PatientRecord) ois.readObject ());
      }
   catch (Exception e)
      {
      throw new PatientRecordException (e.getMessage ());
      }
   finally
      {
      try { ois.close (); fis.close (); } catch (Exception e) {}
      }
   }
```

```
public void writePatientRecord (PatientRecord patientRecord)
   throws PatientRecordException, RemoteException
   {
   // code to write a PatientRecord elided...
   }
}
```

The RMI Client Class

The straightforward class com.ibm.austin.itsc.javanc.RMI.Communicator
implements the two methods used by application code to retrieve and update a
PatientRecord object. For RMI, these two methods simply invoke the remote
methods advertised by a RMI server object.

The class is established as a client of the RMI server within the class constructor.

```
import java.io.*;
import com.ibm.austin.itsc.javanc.Hospital.*;
import com.ibm.austin.itsc.javanc.RMI.*;
import java.rmi.*;
import java.rmi.server.*;
import java.rmi.registry.*;

public class Communicator
   {
   private static Communicable server = null;
   public Communicator () throws RemoteException
      {
      super();
      System.setSecurityManager (new RMISecurityManager ());
      try
         {
         server = (Communicable) Naming.lookup (RMIServer.URL);
         }
      catch (Exception e)
         {
         throw new RemoteException (e.getMessage ());
         }
      }

   public static PatientRecord readPatientRecord (SocialSecurityNumber SSN)
      throws PatientRecordException, RemoteException
      {
      PatientRecord patientRecord = null;
      try
         {
         patientRecord = server.readPatientRecord (SSN);
         }
      catch (Exception e)
         { /* code elided */ }
      return (patientRecord);
      }
```

```
public static void writePatientRecord (PatientRecord patientRecord)
   throws PatientRecordException, RemoteException
   {
   // code elided
   }
}
```

This class provides a thin wrapper to ensure that the RMI server's advertised methods can be treated in exactly the same fashion as any other variety of Communicator class.

In Summary

From a programmer's point of view, the minimum coding required to implement RMI is detailed in the following list:

RMI Programming

1. The remote class must be a subclass of `java.rmi.server.UnicastRemoteObject`.
2. The class must also implement an interface that describes the public methods that are being advertised for clients to invoke.
3. The interface must be a subclass of the standard `java.rmi.Remote` interface.
4. Each method in the remote interface must throw a `java.rmi.RemoteException`.
5. An `RMIRegistry` server must run on the machine hosting the server object.
6. An instance of the server class must register with the `RMIRegistry`.
7. Both client and server must know the server's URL.
8. Generate Stub and Skeleton classes using `rmic`.

Detailed information on RMI is available on the World Wide Web at:
```
http://www.javasoft.com/products/jdk/rmi/index.html
http://java.sun.com/products/jdk/1.1/docs/guide/rmi/spec/rmiTOC.doc.html
```

Chapter 11

Client Diets

▼ Looking at the Options

▼ In Summary

The LMC's developers know that when they finish their trial implementations and come to introduce production-quality systems, they will need to use a number of techniques to improve and optimize their code.

This chapter looks at some of the techniques and issues the LMC's developers had to be aware of to produce optimized code—both in terms of speed and size—to maximize the "thinness" of their solutions and to ensure that they make best use of the available resources.

Optimization is a tricky task, to be carried out only when needed and with care. The optimizer must be careful to bear in mind the following aphorism:

"We should forget about small efficiencies, say about 97% of the time: premature optimization is the root of all evil."

— *Donald Knuth*

Looking at the Options

The LMC's developers have examined many of the possible options for optimization, including:

Table 11-1 Possibilities for Optimization

Speed	Thinness	Subject
+		Compiler facilities
+	+	Pre-initialization
+	+	Re-initialization
+	+	Garbage collection
+		Memory access
+		Error checking
	+	Packaging
	+	Class loading

In Table 11–1 on page 168, shaded cells indicate show which aspect (speed or size) is primarily affected by the subject being examined.

It is clear that some optimizations being considered will have an effect on both the memory usage pattern of the application and its run-time performance. Others will primarily affect either speed or memory.

There are certain principles that apply to optimization in any computer language, and Java is no exception. The LMC developers applied the following very sensible rules to their optimization activities:

- Don't optimize as you go:

  Write your program *completely without regard* to possible optimizations. Clean, correct, and understandable code is more valuable in the long run. If the code is too big or too slow when finished, *then* consider adjustments and tweaks.

- The 80 percent/20 percent rule:

  80 percent of a piece of code's execution time is expended in 20 percent of the code.

- The 80 percent/20 percent rule (2):

  You can get 80 percent of the result with 20 percent of the effort.

- Don't pre-guess nature:

  Use profiling to find out where that 80 percent of execution time is going, so you know where to concentrate your effort.

- Always run "before" and "after" benchmarks:

  How else will you know that your optimizations actually made a difference? If your optimized code turns out to be only slightly faster or smaller than the original version, undo your changes and go back to the original, clear code.

- Use the right algorithms and data structures:

  Don't sequentially search through a thousand items stored in an array (an $O(n)$ technique) when you could use an $O(1)$ Java hash table with no extra effort.

These rules ensure that development effort is directed appropriately, with certainty.

The Compiler and Tools

The Sun Microsystems `javac` compiler is capable of optimizing the bytecodes that it produces. In addition, the `java` interpreter is capable of producing simple profiling information for code that it executes.

Optimization

To optimize code for execution speed, the `javac` compiler accepts the switch -O. This causes the compiler to "inline" (replace all method calls with copies of the appropriate bodies) all the static, final and private methods in a class. The usual time/space trade-off considerations apply here, of course. While the code may execute faster, it will almost certainly be substantially larger than unoptimized code; so optimization must be carefully considered and not used in a "blanket" fashion.

Profiling

Profiling is a valuable technique for estimating the relative importance of blocks of code (typically methods) in a class.

If the `java` interpreter is invoked with the -prof switch, it will create a file with the name `java.prof` in the invocation directory. At execution's end, this file can be examined. This information can provide information to help when deciding which methods should be further optimized.

Several other profilers exist, including:

- IBM's own *Jinsight* tool (http://www.alphaWorks.ibm.com/formula/jinsight)

- OptimizeIt (http://www.optimizeit.com/)

  OptimizeIt is a profiling tool that allows developers to understand and solve performance issues in their Java programs. The tool provides "hot spot detectors" and method call graphs to make it easy to detect excessive object allocations or time-consuming algorithms.

Other useful tools include:

- DashO-Pro™ (http://www.preemptive.com/DashO/index.html)

- Jshrink (http://www.e-t.com/jshrinkdoc.html)

Both of these tools remove unused code and data and replace symbolic names with shortened ones, resulting in smaller files that load faster and that yield less information when decompiled.

Packaging, Class Loading and Pre-Initialization

Java 1.1 introduced the Java archive (JAR file): a packaging and performance enhancing mechanism. The JAR format allows a Java applet and its requisite components (all the associated class files, images, sounds, and so forth) to be downloaded by a browser in a single HTTP transaction, rather than by a new connection as each is needed. This greatly improves the speed with which an applet can be loaded onto a Web page and begin executing.

The JAR format also supports compression, which reduces the size of the file and improves download time still further.

This mechanism should be used judiciously, however. Recall the 80 percent/20 percent rule: 80 percent of a piece of code's execution time is expended in 20 percent of the code. In a typical application, there are large chunks of code that do not get touched in any given execution. Downloading this code is wasteful and time-consuming.

Instead of packaging all the code for an applet into a single JAR, the download time can be optimized by creating a JAR file for the most frequently used 20 percent only.

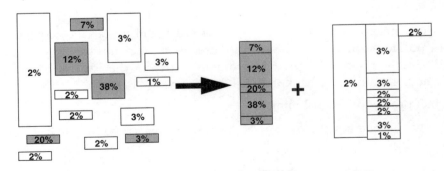

Figure 11–1 Packaging an Applet for Efficient Download

The other 80 percent of the code can be split into second-tier packages (if other appropriate groupings can be identified).

JAR files are specified as part of the <APPLET> tag embedded in the HTML file, as this example shows:

```
<APPLET ARCHIVE = "TH.jar, TH1.jar" CODE = "Thing.class" WIDTH = 350
HEIGHT = 100>
<PARAM NAME = "theSound" VALUE = "playme.au">
</APPLET>
```

Note the way multiple archive files are specified in a comma-separated list. If archives are used, all needed resources must be packaged in archives. This is the case in practice, but it is different to the documentation, which says that if a resource cannot be found in an archive, it is retrieved "in the normal fashion."

It is important to bear in mind that JAR files are completely loaded into memory when referenced. This can cause problems in low-memory situations.

One technique that the LMC's designers evaluated was that of preloading classes before they were needed. This is used to improve the apparent interactive performance of an applet or application. Without preloading, whenever the user calls up a new type of window or makes use of some functionality for the first time, the user can experience a long delay as the JVM loads classes (perhaps across the network).

To ensure that the class preloading doesn't adversely affect the execution of the main application, it is common to perform the loading in a separate thread. One easy way of initiating the loading is to use the java.lang.Class.forName() method, which will cause a class to be loaded by the JVM but which will not instantiate an object or call any method of the class.

```
public class PreLoad implements Runnable
  {
  String [] classes;
  public PreLoad (String [] classes)
    {
    this.classes = classes;
    }
  public void run ()
    {
    try
      {
      for (int i = 0; i < classes.length; i ++)
        Class.forName (classes [i]);    // perform the preload
      }
    catch (ClassNotFoundException cnfe)
      {
      // do something...
      }
    }
```

To use this facility requires code like:

```
void doThePreLoad1 ()
  {
  final String [] list = {
                          "java.awt.Button",
                          "java.util.Vector",
                          // more...
                          "org.moon.LMC.Thing",
                          };
  new Thread (new PreLoad (list)).start ();
  }
```

The major drawback of this technique is the necessity to pepper calls to the doThePreLoad1(), doThePreLoad2()..., doThePreLoadX() methods through an application's code. Determining precisely when to initiate a preload is an art.

One obvious memory saving technique would be to unload classes when they can be determined by the application to be no longer needed. With the current JVM, this is not possible. The decision regarding when to unload a class is made by the virtual machine and cannot be influenced at the application level. This is unfortunate.

Unloading classes is not strictly the same as unloading objects. The garbage collector will unload an object instance when it determines that the instance can no longer be used by the application code. The JVM will not unload a class until it considers that no more objects are going to be made from it "for a while." Objects are unloaded to reclaim application space, whereas classes are (nominally, at least) part of the system space and are thus something slightly different.

Object Recycling

Object creation and destruction in Java are extremely time-consuming operations. To reduce the number of objects created and destroyed, the LMC's developers introduced two guidelines:

- When a single object instance is allocated repeatedly (by a particular method for example), declare a static variable to store the object between successive method invocations. Within the method, call a `reinitialize` method on the stored object to ensure that it behaves as if newly allocated.

  Using this scheme, the following method:

```
class NoRecycle
  {
  public void doLotsOfWork ()
    {
    for (int i = 10; i >= 0; i --)
      theMethod (i);
    }
  private void theMethod (int i)
    {
```

```
    Thing usedOnce = new Thing (i);
    // code elided
    }
  }
```

Becomes:

```
class Recycle
  {
  private static Thing usedRepeatedly = new Thing (-1);
  public void doLotsOfWork ()
    {
    for (int i = 10; i >= 0; i --)
      theMethod (i);
    }
  private void theMethod (int i)
    {
    // instead of: usedRepeatedly = new Thing (i);
    usedRepeatedly.reinitialize (i);
    // code elided
    }
  }
```

Note that the variable usedRepeatedly should not be considered as part of the instance data for the class. It is effectively a "cache" for a variable.

This scheme can be described by the phrase "recycle, don't generate garbage."

• When multiple instances of the object are active simultaneously and their lifetimes cannot be localized to a single part of the application, use a Vector to implement a *free instance repository*. When an object is no longer needed, a static method adds it to the free object pool (static methods are more efficient to invoke than instance methods, and this reduces the overhead associated with this technique). Similarly, to obtain a new instance of the class, another static method releases an available instance from the repository and invokes the reinitialize method on it. The constructors of pooled classes should be declared private so that the application cannot allocate new instances directly.

Both techniques rely upon a reinitialize method in the optimized class. These techniques can also be used where objects are aggregated into other objects, but the actual programming of such situations can be involved.

Garbage Collection

Armed with Java's built-in garbage collection, the LMC's developers originally assumed that they no longer needed to worry about how memory for their objects is allocated and when (or indeed, whether) it is released after being used.

Although it simplifies the task of object-oriented development, garbage collection can also cause significant performance problems. The developers tended to create objects liberally because they perceived that they were relatively cheap to create: The Java Virtual Machine masks the costs of memory allocation and deallocation for objects.

On compute-intensive applications, such as servers, object creation has significant effects. The garbage collector is supposed to only execute when no other application threads are executing (it runs in its own low-priority thread), thus minimally impacting an application's performance. High-performance applications may not offer such idle periods, however; so the garbage collector must steal time from the application, and this lowers execution efficiency.

Garbage collection can be invoked manually, through:

```
System.gc ();
```

If this method is invoked explicitly from time to time, when the load on the application allows, it may be possible to lessen the undesirable "cycle stealing" effect to some degree.

The amount of free memory available to an application can also be measured:

```
long getAvailableMemory (boolean collect)
  {
  if (collect)
    System.gc();
  return (Runtime.getRuntime().freeMemory());
  }
```

To assist in the efficient reclamation of memory, it is always good to explicitly set a reference to null after use. This allows the collection algorithm to more quickly decide to reclaim an object instance. If all references to the object were not explicitly "lost," the decision to reclaim an object would be a lot more involved and time-consuming.

Before an object is reclaimed by the garbage collector, its finalize method (if one is explicitly provided) is called. At first sight, this seems to provide an effective means of cleaning up an object. This can cause problems. When the collector determines that an object is ripe for reclamation, it is first placed in a finalization queue, ready to be properly reclaimed at a later date. Because the collector can take an unspecified amount of time before calling the finalize method, all resources associated with the yet-to-be finalized object are held. Performance can actually be worse when explicit finalization is used.

The java command accepts a flag –verbosegc, which causes the garbage collector to announce its actions when it runs. This can be very helpful to developers involved in tuning and optimizing. Additional flags include:

- −noasyncgc

  Turns off asynchronous garbage collection. When activated, no garbage collection takes place unless it is explicitly called or the program runs out of memory. Garbage collection normally runs as an asynchronous thread in parallel with other threads.

- −noclassgc

  Turns off garbage collection of Java classes. By default, the Java interpreter reclaims space for unused Java classes during garbage collection.

Optimizing Memory Accesses

Developers of high-performance applications are acutely aware of the increasing divergence between processor speeds and memory access times and the associated need to minimize memory access when possible.

In contrast to a compiled language such as C++, application performance in Java is noticeably affected by what types of variables are accessed and how they are accessed. For example, while stack variables are directly addressable (and may even be placed in registers), instance variables typically require an extra level of indirection to be accessed.

This implies the potential value of *data location shifting*, changing the storage location of data based on the access patterns. For example, a data-intensive operation would benefit from first copying instance variables into stack variables, operating on the stack variables, and, finally, copying the stack variables back to the permanent instance variables.

This technique is particularly useful when a method variable is accessed repeatedly within a loop. For example, the common loop construct:

```
for (int i = 0; ++ i <= limit; )
```

can be improved by 25 percent (5 percent with a JIT compiler) by rewriting it as

```
for (int i = limit; -- i >= 0; )
```

to reduce the number of accesses to the `limit` variable.

When optimizing memory access, it is important to be aware that the JVM requires "scratch" memory above that explicitly used by the Java application. In memory-constrained situations, this can become important. For instance, to deal with a 1 MB GIF-format image file, the JVM will require about 2 MB of extra working memory. This hidden requirement can cause a developer to grossly underestimate the memory needs of his or her code.

The `java` command accepts a number of options that can be used to "tune" its memory performance:

- `-mx x`

  Sets the maximum size of the garbage collected heap

- `-ms x`

  Sets the startup size of the heap

- `-ss x`

  Each Java thread has two stacks: one for Java code and one for C code (used by the JVM, rather than the Java code directly). The `-ss` option sets the maximum stack size that can be used by C code in a thread.

- `-oss x`

  Sets the maximum stack size that can be used by Java code in a thread

These options allow a developer to explicitly set the memory requirements of the JVM and can make a substantial change to Java's performance. These options also make it easy to "stress test" an application to investigate its behavior under low-memory conditions.

Synchronization Overheads

In Java, methods and code blocks may be marked with the `synchronized` keyword. Multiple threads cannot simultaneously execute within any of the synchronized methods on the same class instance, and a synchronized code block is treated like a synchronized method on the object that is provided as an argument to the synchronized keyword. To support this capability, the Java Virtual Machine links a monitor to each object having synchronized methods. A monitor is a high-level thread synchronization mechanism. Whenever a thread enters a synchronized block, it must first obtain a lock on the monitor for the associated object.

In tests, the LMC's developers found that adding synchronization to a method degrades performance by between 8 and 11 times, even if the application is only executing a single thread (so that the thread could never block on the monitor). This result indicates that the synchronization overhead is primarily incurred in checking for the lock, rather than in actually obtaining it.

They also found that a JIT compiler cannot improve the lock access and contention overhead at all because it has no information about the application's structure. The performance overhead of the JIT compiler actually slows the program execution. In contrast, the JIT compiler improves performance slightly when the calls are unsynchronized.

Synchronization impacts application performance in subtle ways. For example, the memory allocator is synchronized, meaning that object creation incurs a synchronization penalty.

Many common functions in the Java class library are designed to be thread-safe and are, therefore, synchronized. For example, accessing an indexed element in a Vector requires a synchronized method call, as does calling the nextItem method on an associated enumeration.

In the LMC's applications, collections are only accessed by a single thread; so this synchronization imposes considerable overhead for little benefit.

To allow the application to selectively disable this synchronization, for example, the LMC's designers subclassed the Java Vector class to provide unsynchronized access methods:

```
import java.util.*;
public class EVector extends Vector
  {
  public Object getElementAt (int index)
    {
    if ((index < 0) || (index >= elementCount))
      return (null);
    return (elementData [index]);
    }
  // code elided
  }
```

Similar issues arise in the I/O stream library, where approximately 90 percent of the overhead of writing formatted data through a DataOutputStream is attributable to the underlying synchronized calls to OutputStream methods.

Where the developers could not eliminate synchronization, they found that they could occasionally improve performance by placing a series of synchronized calls inside a single synchronization block. For example, replacing:

```
for (i = 0; i < count; i ++)
  x.f(); // synchronized on x
```

with:

```
synchronized (x)
  {
  for (i = 0; i < count; i ++)
    x.f (); // synchronized on x
  }
```

The replacement code allows the Java Virtual Machine to short-circuit the method synchronization. It should only be used if the synchronization is short-lived (because it will otherwise block other threads) or if no thread contention exists.

Error Handling

The Java Virtual Machine provides native instructions to support exception handling, in contrast to C++ which relies on compiler-generated code.

These native instructions mean that exception handling in Java is relatively fast.

The near-zero cost of entering a try clause allows the widespread use of exception handling (there is a larger penalty associated with actually executing a catch clause, however) instead of explicitly error-checking when errors are expected to be rare (the exception would rarely be thrown). Consider the task of indexing into an array, for example:

```
if ((idx >= 0) && (idx < array.length))
  x = array[idx];
else
  // error
```

An exception-oriented approach leads to rewriting the above code block in the following form:

```
try
  {
  x = array [idx];
  }
catch (ArrayOutOfBoundsException e)
  {
  // error
  }
```

The exception-oriented approach is 50 percent faster than the traditional approach in the (common) case where the index is within range. As long as the common case occurs sufficiently often relative to the exception condition, there is a performance improvement—eliminating the error check on each execution. This is particularly true in loops. Similar situations arise with type casting using the instanceof operator versus catching ClassCastException.

The performance characteristics of try-catch clauses make it possible for developers to re-define how exceptions are used in high-performance applications. Instead of simply using exceptions to signal errors, it becomes possible to use exceptions to signal uncommon occurrences, even if those occurrences do not represent actual error conditions.

This is consistent with the idea of "making the common case fast."

Other Issues and Optimizations

As with any programming language, many other intricate optimizations are possible. For instance, the String concatenation operator + looks innocent, but involves a lot of behind-the-scenes work: a new StringBuffer is created, the two arguments are added to it with append, and the final result is converted back by the toString() method. This is expensive both in terms of space and time. In particular, when appending more than one String, consider using a StringBuffer directly instead.

A much-overlooked issue is to explicitly close files after use. A file is always closed during finalization before garbage collection, but the potentially long delay before collection may mean that an application prematurely runs out of available file handles.

A thread has a minimum memory requirement, even though it may be very small. Creating many small threads may lead to inefficient memory use and fragmentation. To minimize problems, it is better to create large-grain threads where possible. It is also possible to use options to the JVM adjust its requirements.

The LMC's developers explored many optimizations that are beyond the scope of this book. The developers found a wealth of material to guide their activities on the Internet, particularly at:

java.sun.com
www.javaworld.com

and:

http://www.cs.cmu.edu/~jch/java/optimization.html

In Summary

These optimizations reveal that, with care, Java can be used to implement high-performance applications.

Although future versions of the Java Virtual Machine may change the need for the specific optimizations, many situations cannot easily be optimized without human intervention. For example, static analysis of multithreaded applications is still not possible; so optimizing structures to account for the precise access patterns of a number of threads is a task that cannot be left to a compiler.

Chapter 12

Tasty Additions

This chapter introduces Java programming for accessing SmartCards and serial ports on a Network Computer, using the IBM Network Station 1000 as an example.

At the Lunar Medical Center, doctors authenticate themselves with their SmartCards and can see information regarding their patient on their Network Computer. They can add information manually or through automatic data retrieval from monitoring devices through the serial port available on the Network Computer.

Introduction to SmartCards

SmartCards store the card holder's personal information on a chip which is embedded in a plastic carrier. Their compact and handy size together with their robustness and resistance to harsh environments make them the medium of choice for many applications. Figure 12–1 on page 182 shows the physical properties of a SmartCard.

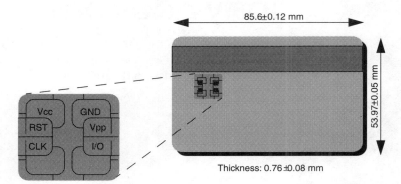

Figure 12–1 Physical Properties of an ISO 7816 SmartCard

In contrast to simple magnetic stripe cards or memory cards, SmartCards provide a highly secure mechanism to protect stored data from external access. Smart-Cards contain a micro processor which can be used to hide data (for example, secret keys used for encryption).

Figure 12–2 on page 183 depicts the internal structure of the micro-computer inside a SmartCard. It consists of a Central Processing Unit (CPU), Read Only Memory (ROM)—which contains the Card Operating System (COS), Random Access Memory (RAM) to store temporary data, an Electrically Erasable Programmable Read Only Memory (EEPROM)—which can store data persistently without the need for permanent external power supply, and a serial I/O interface—which allows the communication with the outside world.

No direct access from the outside world to the EEPROM is possible. An exchange of data is only possible through the protocol implemented by the COS. During the initialization and personalization phase of the card, the privileges for accessing certain data in the EEPROM are defined.

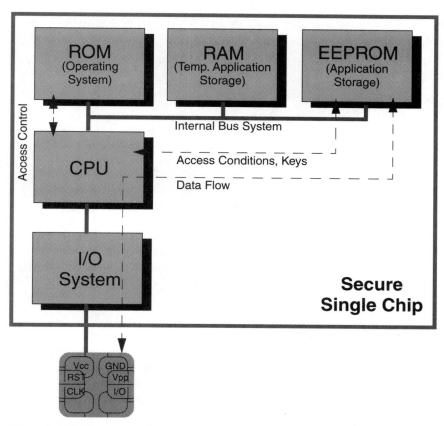

Figure 12–2 Internal Structure of a SmartCard

The life cycle of a SmartCard can be subdivided into three phases:

1. Manufacturing process: printing process, chip embedding

2. Initialization and personalization phase: file creation and data updating, thermal printing

3. Customer usage phase: use of SmartCard for particular application

Step 1 is conducted at the card factory. Step 2 is security-critical and can either be carried out by the manufacturer or by the card provider. Under most circumstances, some proprietary software (from the card manufacturer) is used for the initialization.

SmartCards differ substantially from manufacturer to manufacturer. Therefore, it is important that standards exist for their interoperability. There are three different kinds of interoperability.

Physical Interoperability: This includes the ability to establish a communication with the SmartCard and necessitates the standardization of the mechanical and electrical properties. The mechanical properties include the card dimensions and tolerances and the mechanical stability of the card.

> *Note*
>
> These properties are defined by the International Standards Organization in the de-jure standard ISO 7816-1. The positions of the electrical contacts are defined in ISO 7816-2. The electronic specifications define, for example, operating voltages and the low-level communication protocol, and are standardized in ISO 7816-3.

Syntactic Interoperability: This addresses the ability to use different SmartCards from different manufacturers for the same functionality during the customer usage phase. The requirement can be realized by a framework, which provides the application developer a set of high-level card operations and allows the card manufacturer to implement low-level functions which encapsulate the proprietary elements. "The OpenCard Framework" on page 186 introduces such a framework. Physical interoperability is a prerequisite for syntactic interoperability.

Semantic Interoperability: It refers to the ability of different applications to use information stored in different formats. It is necessary to agree on a common interpretation of the data objects. In addition, a common set of rules for manipulating the objects is required. Guidelines for the handling of certificate and public-key representations are an example. Syntactic interoperability is a prerequisite for semantic interoperability.

While physical interoperability is ensured by standards conformance, syntactic interoperability needs to be provided by a framework. The responsibility of this framework is to bring together SmartCard and card terminal manufacturers on one side and application developers on the other. The OpenCard Framework does this by placing a high-level programmatic interface at the disposal of the developer while defining the low-level interface for implementation by the manufacturers. It supports ISO 7816-compliant cards as well as others. Furthermore, OpenCard coexists with operating system and hardware-specific specifications, like Microsoft's SmartCard specification for personal computers.

The SmartCard File System

Access to a file system is a functionality that most SmartCards provide. It has been standardized by the ISO 7816-4 specification and involves three different file types:

- Master File (MF): corresponds to the root directory

- Dedicated File (DF): corresponds to a directory

- Elementary File (EF): corresponds to a standard file

Figure 12–3 on page 185 shows an example of an ISO 7816-4 SmartCard file system. Each file is identified by a logical identifier, which is represented by four-digit hexadecimal numbers. Elementary files can be specified to be transparent (unformatted), have fixed or variable record size, or to be cyclic, with fixed record size.

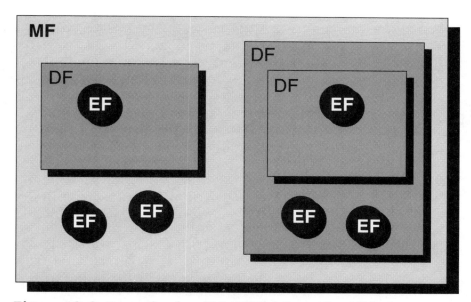

Figure 12–3 Example of an ISO 7816-4 SmartCard File System

Access control can be assigned to each file individually. Different access modes like *read*, *update* or *administer* can be combined with access conditions like *always*, *never*, *protected*, or *encrypted*. The file system layout is defined during the initialization phase of the SmartCard.

The OpenCard Framework

To provide application developers with a common platform, IBM Corp., Netscape Communications Corporation, Oracle's NCI, and Sun Microsystems Inc. together developed the OpenCard Framework, the first SmartCard standard enabling access to personalized data and services from any Network Computer. OpenCard provides a framework for applications that use SmartCards, and with the first reference implementation written in Java, OpenCard provides the most portable basis possible in the emerging Network Computer industry

Figure 12–4 on page 186 shows the OpenCard Framework architecture.

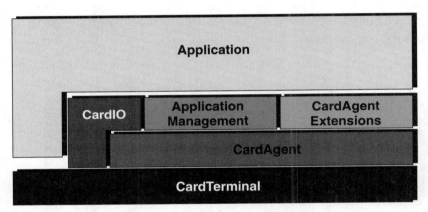

Figure 12–4 Architecture of the OpenCard Framework

CardTerminal

The CardTerminal component encapsulates the access to the card terminal. This functionality is provided by the Java classes CardTerminal, Slot, and CardID. CardTerminal is an abstract super class which is extended individually for the different card terminals. For the IBM Network Station, this is done in the package com.ibm.zurich.smartcard.

The class has one or more Slot objects, each representing a physical card slot of the terminal. From the perspective of the terminal, an actual SmartCard is represented by the CardID object, which simply contains the card's response to an Answer-To-Reset (ATR) operation. CardID has static information about the card's abilities. Card resources are accessed using the CardIO component of the SmartCard object.

Card terminals can be dynamically added and removed by the CardTerminalFactory class, which is implemented by the card terminal manufacturer. The CardTerminalRegistry class keeps track of the installed card terminals and provides methods to register, unregister, and list all installed terminals. Figure 12–5 on page 187 gives an overview on the hierarchy of the main CardTerminal classes.

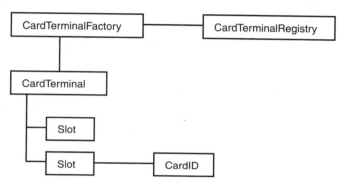

Figure 12–5 Class Hierarchy for the CardTerminal Component

CardAgent

The CardAgent component encapsulates details about the card operating system. Its central class is the abstract CardAgent class, which is responsible for communication with the Card Operating System (COS).

The messages exchanged in the card protocol are called Application Protocol Data Unit (APDU) and are defined in the ISO 7816-4 specification. This protocol is not stateless, and therefore the CardAgent class has to keep track of the card state. CardAgent also takes care of the optional authentication procedure.

As with the CardTerminal component, the central class is controlled by a factory and a registry class. The factory class is provided by the card operating system supplier. For a CardID object, CardAgentFactoryRegistry will return the appropriate CardAgentFactory. Figure 12–6 on page 187 shows the hierarchy of the main CardAgent classes.

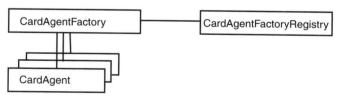

Figure 12–6 Class Hierarchy for the Main CardAgent Objects

CardIO

The CardIO component provides the main functionality for the application-visible side of the framework. All access to the SmartCard must make use of CardIO classes. The central class is the SmartCard class, which represents the physical SmartCard with its resources (and in particular the file system).

Accessing the file system is done by mounting the Master File (MF) to the Smart-Card object. The mounting method returns a CardFile object, representing the MF. All other SmartCard files can be accessed from the MF CardFile object by creating new CardFile objects, which then are used to create input/output streams or random access files.

The CardIO component provides the classes CardFileInputStream, CardFileOutput-Stream and CardRandomAccessFile, which are implementations of the abstract classes InputStream, OutputStream and the interfaces DataInput and DataOuput from the java.io package.

Because access to the files on the SmartCard can be restricted during the initialization process, it may be necessary for the application to authenticate. The KeyBag and KeyStore objects contain this information and are optionally associated with the CardFile object which needs authentication. A link to the CardTerminal component can be made from the SmartCard object to the Slot object.

The hierarchy of the main classes in the CardIO component, for a typical application file system, are shown in Figure 12–7 on page 188.

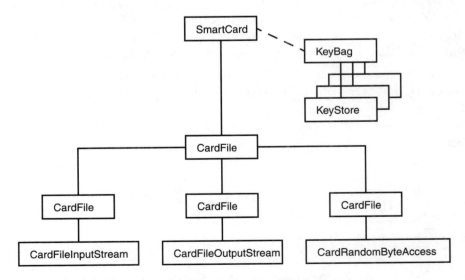

Figure 12–7 Class Hierarchy of the CardIO Component

CardAgentExtension

The CardAgentExtension component takes care of individual card functionalities (such as cryptographic or electronic purse functions) in addition to file access.

The central class CardAgentExtension communicates with a CardAgent to obtain the necessary data. CardAgentExtension components are supplied by the COS supplier. The component is not needed when solely accessing the SmartCard file system.

ApplicationManagement

The ApplicationManagement component was added to the OpenCard Framework, since modern SmartCard (due to their higher capacities) offer the possibility to implement several applications on the same card.

The responsibility of the ApplicationManagement component is to load and iden-tify the list of supplied applications provided by the SmartCard and pass the information to the appropriate applications. It may also be used to supply appli-cations with symbolic file names.

The component makes use of the ISO 7816-5 application identifiers for unambigu-ous referencing of card-resident applications. The class hierarchy of the CardAp-plication component follows the same design pattern as the CardTerminal or CardAgent component in that it provides an implemented, system-wide Applica-tionManagerFactoryRegistry and abstract ApplicationManagerFactory and Appli-cationManager classes, which have to be implemented by the card issuers.

Sample SmartCard Application

At this stage, programming to support SmartCards may seem a daunting task, but in practice, using the OpenCard Framework results in compact, logical code.

For this sample application:

- During the initialization phase of the card, a file with a fixed record size of 64 bytes with the identifier C009 has been created in the MF of a SmartCard, for example an IBM Multi Function Card (MFC).
- Assume that this file does not require authentication for access. This means that cryptography key management is not required, including the CardAgentExtention and ApplicationManagement components.
- Before accessing the SmartCard file system, a card request must be issued by creating a CardRequest object.
- A time-out must be granted for the request (for example, 2 minutes).
- A particular card type is not required.

```
// Create Card Request for new or already inserted card
CardRequest cardRequest = new CardRequest ();
cardRequest.timeout (120);
cardRequest.waitBehavior (CardRequest.ANYCARD);
```

Next is the central part of the sample application—access to the SmartCard file system:

- First, obtain a `SmartCard` object from the card terminal registry.

- Mount the card and define `BLOCKING`—which means that no concurrent accesses to the card are allowed from other processes.

- The mounting procedure returns a `CardFile` object pointing to the master file.

- To select the file with the identifier C009, generate a new `CardFile` from the former one pointing to the master file.

- Instantiate a file input stream, which is implemented by the `CardFileInput-Stream` class.

- The SmartCard data can now be accessed as if it were on a disk.

```
    // Wait for the smart card
SmartCard card = CardTerminalRegistry.registry ().waitForCard
    (cardRequest);

// Access the root of the smart card file system,
// wait until card becomes available.
CardFile file = card.mount (CardFileOpenMode.BLOCKING);

// Open file
file = new CardFile (file, ":C009");

// Create a CardFileInputStream for file and read data
dis = new DataInputStream (new CardFileInputStream (file));

    // code elided
```

Upon completion of the SmartCard data exchange and application, the terminal session must be closed to allow further access to other processes. For the sample application, the following `com.ibm.*` command is issued:

```
((PHANTOMCardTerminal) CardTerminalRegistry.registry ().
    cardTerminalForName ("PHANTOM")).close ();
```

The complete application is:

```
import java.io.*;

import opencard.io.*;
import opencard.terminal.*;
import opencard.util.*;
import com.ibm.zurich.smartcard.terminal.phantom.*;

public static void main (java.lang.String [] args)
```

```
{
DataInputStream dis = null;
SmartCard card = null;
CardFile root = null;
CardFile file = null;
try
   {
   // Create Card Request for new or already inserted card
   CardRequest cardRequest = new CardRequest (120);
   cardRequest.waitBehavior (CardRequest.ANYCARD);

   // Wait for the smart card
   card = CardTerminalRegistry.registry ().waitForCard (cardRequest);

   // Access the root of the smart card file system,
   // wait until card becomes available.
   root = card.mount (CardFileOpenMode.BLOCKING);

   // Get user file
   file = new CardFile (root, ":C009");
   dis = new DataInputStream (new CardFileInputStream (file));
   // Read in data
   int len = (int) file.length ();
   byte [] array = new byte [len];
   dis.read (array, 0, len);
   dis.close ();
   // Print out file
   System.out.println ("The user file has a length of " + len + " bytes.");
   for (int i = 0; i < len; i ++)
     System.out.println ("Data[" + i + "] = " + array [i]);
   }
catch (Exception e)
   { /* code elided */ }
finally
   {
   try
      {
      ((PHANTOMCardTerminal)
        CardTerminalRegistry.registry ().
          cardTerminalForName ("PHANTOM")).close ();
      }
   catch (Exception e)
      { /* code elided */ }
   }
}
```

Thoroughly amazed, the LMC designers can now extend the hospital application. For example, the data in the C009 file can store basic patient or hospital employee data and can be used to avoid reentering this constant information, or could be used (in the case of an employee) to authorize use of particular applications.

Accessing a Serial Port

> ### Note
>
> Unfortunately, no medical monitoring devices were available to the authors for data acquisition or control; so it was decided to use the popular X-10 control system (used to switch power supplies) as the testbed for Java-based serial port access. We have chosen to connect and control an Espresso Coffee Maker, because doctors need coffee too!
>
> The X-10 controller sends commands to the power switches by modulating the AC power line. It can be connected to a Network Computer (NC) through a serial interface. The architecture of the connection is shown in Figure 12–8 on page 192.

How is specific hardware attached to a generic virtual machine without undermining the concept of portability? The Network Station (as an example of an NC) has solved the problem by *wrapping* the serial interface and providing access to it using a TCP/IP connection on a predefined port. Recall Chapter 9, "Java Servers and Socket Communication" on page 141, which discusses the socket facility for programming for such an architecture.

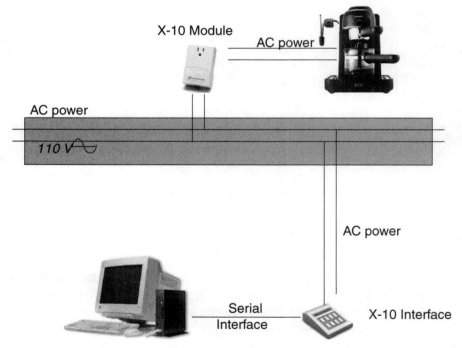

Figure 12–8 External Device Controlled by NC Using Serial Port and X-10

X-10 Architecture and Protocols

X-10 communicates between transmitters and receivers using digital information signals over existing power line wiring. A complete description on how the information is passed on the wire is available at the following Web address: `http://www.x10.com/technology1.htm`

Some controllers provide a timer function that can be programmed by a computer through a serial port. When they have received a set of instructions, they can be disconnected from the computer. In this case, the NC will not be used to program timer capabilities, but for sending direct commands (for example ON or OFF) to the receiver.

Programming the X-10 CP290 Home Control Interface

The X-10 CP290 Home Contral Interface (see `http://smarthome.com`) connects to a computer through an RS-232 interface. The characteristics of this serial interface are:

- Baud rate: 600

- Data bits: 8

- Parity: none

- Stop bits: one

The transport layer for the transmitter/receiver hardware is managed by the X-10 system, and the CP290 provides the means for controlling an X-10 environment from a computer. What is needed is the signal/stream protocol between devices. Such a protocol for interaction between the NC and the CP290 can be easily implemented in Java.

The interface and units are addressed and controlled using a sequence of hexadecimal bytes sent on the AC wires. For example:

- Each command begins with a synchronization stream.

- The command byte is sent. Eight commands are available for the X-10 controller. The important command type for the LMC espresso machine is the *Direct Command*, which supports simple ON/OFF functionality.

- X-10 organizes devices to be switched by numbering the units (from 1 to 16) and by *House Code* (A to P). Bytes are sent representing the House Code and unit number of the required device. Using one bit for each unit allows the X-10 to send the same command to multiple units at the same time.

- A variable number of bytes may be sent as data required by the command.

- A checksum byte is sent.

Upon receipt of a request sequence, a response acknowledgment is sent.

For full details on the byte representations and protocol of the CP290 device, refer to:

`http://smarthome.com/manuals/MAN-1130_31p.pdf`

The Java Espresso Machine Example

To operate the X-10 appliance unit with Java, a class (for example X10Device) must be defined that represents the units and their behavior. Two public methods `on()` and `off()` will be called from a Java application to start and stop the coffee maker.

The LMC coffee maker is plugged into appliance socket A3; so the necessary steps are:

- Instantiate unit 3 for house code A.

- Start the coffee maker by changing the unit status to ON with the `on()` method.

- After five minutes, stop the coffee maker by changing the unit status to OFF with the `off()` method

```
package NetworkStation;
public class MakeJava {
/**
 * This method makes a good pot of Java.
 */
public static void main(String args[]) {
        try {
                /* create X-10 device for the coffee machine in
                "house" A, unit 3 */
                X10Device dev = new X10Device('A', 3);
                /* switch on coffee machine */
                dev.on();
                /* wait for 5 min */
                Thread.sleep(5*60*1000);
                /* switch off coffee machine */
                dev.off();
        }
        catch (Exception e) {}
    }
    }
```

The `on()` and `off()` method must send a sequence of bytes to the serial port. On an NC, the serial port is addressed using the TCP/IP loopback address (127.0.0.1). The TCP/IP port that is used must be specified (for example, port 87), and since the serial port is viewed as a TCP/IP address, sending and receiving data will be done using sockets programming.

See "Accessing the Serial Port" on page 221 for more details on using the NC serial port.

The x10Device class execute() method sends the array of bytes to the socket and receives the return bytes from the CP290.

```
/**
 * This method sends a sequence of bytes to the serial interface.
 * @param sequence byte array to be sent
 */
private synchronized void execute ( byte[] sequence ) {
        try
            {
                /* initialize the socket and the I/O streams */
                Socket sock = new Socket(server, serverPort);
                DataOutputStream serialOut = new
            DataOutputStream(sock.getOutputStream());
                DataInputStream serialIn = new DataInputStream(
            sock.getInputStream());
                /* Let the X-10 controller synchronize */
                sync(serialOut);
                /* write the command sequence to the serial interface */
                for (int i = 0; i < sequence.length; i++)
                 serialOut.writeByte(sequence[i]);
                /* read in 12 bytes of response */
                serialIn.read(response, 0, 12);
                /* close streams and socket */
                serialIn.close();
                serialOut.close();
                sock.close();
            }
        catch (Exception e) {}
        return;
    }
```

The private method assemble() prepares the whole sequence of bytes for the command and asks the execute() method to send the data to the serial port.

The total sequence is achieved by:

- Generating the synchronization data (16 bytes of 0xFF) with the sync() method

- Generating the direct command (0x01), which is hard-coded in the assemble() method

- Generating the hex codes for the unit and house codes in the class constructor

- Generating the necessary checksum in the crc() method

The full code of the x10Device class is available on the enclosed CD-ROM.

Running the LMC Java Espresso Machine

Before the application is run on the NC, the NC's serial port must be configured to the characteristics indicated earlier. Refer to "Accessing a Serial Port" on page 192 to set the Network Computer serial port.

A simple way to access the Java application is to implement a button on the desktop of the NC. Refer to "Running Java Programs in the IBM Network Station" on page 229.

The following steps are also required:

- Plug in the CP290 controller and the appliance module to AC power.

- Connect the LMC doctors' espresso machine to the appliance module.

- Connect the CP290 to the serial port of the Network Computer.

Remember

The Java Garbage Collector has nothing to do with dirty coffee cups!

Chapter 13

NC Deployment: Using IBM Network Stations

The purpose of this chapter is to give an overview of an existing Network Computer solution and its configuration: The *IBM Network Station 1000*. Because this area of IT development is highly dynamic, this chapter should not be used as a reference for the setup and use of the IBM Network Station, but instead should give a feeling what the current status for this technology looks like.

For any case where a reference for the IBM Network Station is needed, the appropriate documentation for the used system levels should be used. Actual publications for the IBM Network Station can be found at:

`http://www.as400.ibm.com/networkstation/rs6000`

In case this or all the following URLs in this chapter regarding the IBM Network Station are changed, the generic entry point should be the IBM NC Website at: `http://www.ibm.com/nc`

In addition, this chapter provides some tips and techniques to improve the Network Station's performance.

Introduction

One of the key characteristics of the network computing world is that most system resources reside on the server instead of on the client in order to achieve centralized administration, but parts of data processing are left on the client.

While on one hand the administration of a classical "dumb" terminal is very easy and therefore cheap, on the other hand, in today's world, it lacks functionality and flexibility, usability and user acceptance. At the same time, a personal workstation such as a PC provides a high level of functionality and flexibility, but the administrative costs are often unacceptably high.

A Network Computer, such as the IBM Network Station, tries to get the best of both worlds by offering minimum administration for the client and enhancements that enable you to run leading-edge applications.

With its capability to run as an X-Windows server and as a 3270 or 5250 emulator, it is able to be a front-end for RS/6000 and UNIX systems as well as for S/390 and AS/400 mainframes. And with WinCenter (from Network Computing Devices, Inc.) it is even capable of running Windows NT applications as a kind of Windows terminal.

In addition, Internet and intranet applications reachable through a Web browser are supported as are Java applets and applications.

Software Requirements

The software requirements for our sample scenario are based on AIX running on an RS/6000 platform consisting of either:

- AIX, Version 4.1.5, plus the IBM Network Station PTF update, or
- AIX Version 4.2.1 with the IBM Network Station Manager, or
- AIX Version 4.3.0 with the IBM Network Station Manager

This software includes native code for terminal support for 3270, 5250 and X-Windows servers and the Navio Browser for the IBM Network Station as well as a native Java Virtual Machine (JVM 1.1.2 in the current release).

All screenshots and descriptions for the IBM Network Station in this and in the next chapter are based on the current release, 2.5, of the IBM Network Station Manager software and on Version 2.9.7 of the Network Station's Boot Monitor. Actual and updated code for the Network Station can be found at
`http://service.boulder.ibm.com/nc/rs6000/index.html`

The Initialization Process

The IBM Network Station, as a thin client, needs a server to boot from. This server acts as a repository for the system and configuration files that are needed to start the Network Station and its user applications. The initial file, called the *boot file* or *kernel*, contains the kernel required by the Network Station to control devices such as network and input devices as well as the software required to support applications.

The first task of the boot file after it has been successfully downloaded from the server is to read the configuration files and set up the defined environment. These configuration files contain all the information about which initial applications have to be loaded and started and about which resources are required.

The initialization process shown in Figure 13–1 on page 200 involves several tasks. These tasks are performed automatically after the IBM Network Station has been turned on. The administrator has to configure and modify the client only once, the first time the Network Station is turned on, in order to point it to a specific boot server and configuration profile. Other modifications can be performed as desired.

The four basic tasks described in the following sections are:

- Power-On Self-Test
- Locating the boot server
- Loading the kernel
- Initialization of the environment

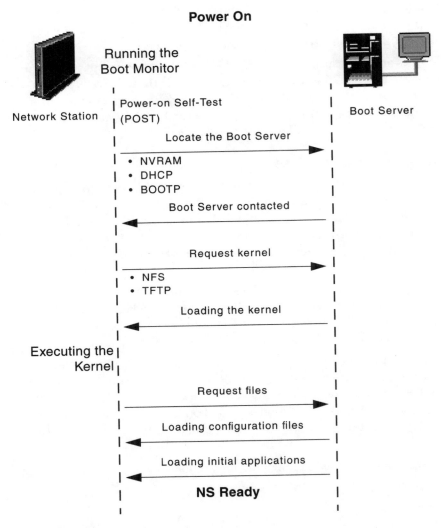

Figure 13-1 Initialization Process

The Power-On Self-Test

When the Network Station is powered up, it runs a special program stored in its Non-Volatile Random Access Memory (EPROM - Erasable Programmable ROM). This program is called the *Boot Monitor*, and its first task is to perform the Power-On Self-Test (POST), as shown in Figure 13–1. This test verifies that all hardware components (such as video adapter, RAM, keyboard or mouse, I/O ports or network adapter) are working OK.

Locating the Boot Server

After the self-check, the IBM Network Station must locate the boot server to load the boot configuration files (see Figure 13–2). The boot server can be found in different ways:

- The Network Station is configured using the DHCP protocol. When using DHCP, the IBM Network Station has no valid IP address at boot time; therefore, it has to send an IP broadcast to identify a DHCP server. Upon obtaining a valid IP configuration from the DHCP server, the DHCP server can also provide information about the boot server to be used.

- The Network Station keeps its IP configuration in its Non-Volatile Random Access Memory (NVRAM). In this case, the IP configuration consists of up to three different boot server IP addresses from which the Network Station tries to boot sequentially.

Both methods can be configured in the *Boot Menu Panel*, which is explained in more detail in "Set Network Parameters Panel" on page 205.

Figure 13–2 IBM Network Station Boot Panel

Loading the Kernel

When the IBM Network Station has determined and contacted the server from where it will boot, the next step is to load the boot file called the *kernel* and the configuration files from the server, as is shown in Figure 13–3 on page 203. In its current release, the Network Station can access the boot data in two different ways across the network: either using the Trivial File Transfer Protocol (TFTP) or the Network File System (NFS).

Even with the choice of these two protocols, the recommendation is clearly to go for NFS. TFTP has only two advantages:

- It is very easy to configure.
- It is available on many platforms (presumably more than NFS).

Because of the ease of configuration, it is a good idea to configure the Network Station first to use TFTP, but for a productional environment, NFS has so many advantages over TFTP that the usage of NFS becomes almost mandatory:

- NFS is much faster than TFTP because it uses a much bigger package size than TFTP (8192 bytes versus 512 bytes), and it does not use a handshake protocol after every transmitted IP package.
- NFS provides security options, but TFTP is an absolutely unsecured protocol.
- NFS provides a real file system, but TFTP can just get complete files. This becomes a deciding factor when deciding whether Java should be used on the Network Station. In Java, it is very popular and powerful to bundle several class files together in a ZIP file. When a class is loaded, it gets extracted out of this ZIP file and transferred across the network. This technique is not possible when using TFTP because TFTP does not provide access to particular parts of a file. In this case, all class files must exist as separate files on the server—a very unsatisfactory solution.

For more details about how to configure the boot file access protocol, please refer to "Set the Boot Parameters Panel" on page 208.

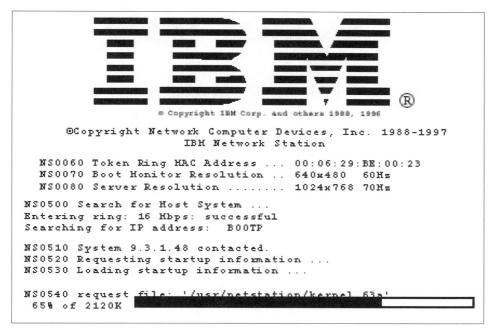

Figure 13-3 IBM Network Station, Loading the Kernel

Initiate the Environment

If the kernel has been downloaded successfully, it attempts to initialize the environment, such as configuring the background color, the mouse speed, setting the configured options, and starting the default applications in the following order:

- Read the initial configuration file (standard.nsm or as specified in the NVRAM setup) which works as a link to other configuration files.

- Set the operating characteristics of the IBM Network Station stored in the configuration files, such the background pattern, the keyboard definition file, and the colors name file (rgb.txt).

- Load the initial applications configured by the administrator.

After these automatically performed steps, the IBM Network Station is ready to be used.

IBM Network Station Set Up

As described earlier, the IBM Network Station attempts to determine the boot server after it has successfully performed the Power-On Self-Test (POST). While the message

NS0500 Search for Host System ...

appears in the Boot Panel, the Setup Utility Panel can be entered by pressing the **Esc** key.

The NVRAM Setup Utility Panel

In order to prevent unauthorized access to the NVRAM Setup Utility Panel, the IBM Network Station can be protected by a password (called the *Administrator password*). By default, this password is not set, but in case it is, a logon screen will appear as shown in Figure 13–4 on page 204. The Administrator password is stored in the Non-Volatile Random Access Memory (NVRAM) and is also encrypted in the configuration file, default.nsm.

In case the password is not known, it is possible to bypass the password query by pressing **F12**. In this situation, it is only possible to display the boot options, not modify them.

```
SCRN01                    IBM Network Station
                          Administrator Password

   Password .........................











                Type Administrator password and press Enter.



 Enter=Continue   F12=Cancel
```

Figure 13–4 IBM Network Station Password Panel

If the password is entered correctly, the IBM Network Station gives the full choice of displaying and modifying the boot parameters shown in Figure 13–5 on page 205.

```
SCRN02                        IBM Network Station
                                 Setup Utility

F2 = View Network Parameters
F3 = View Boot Parameters
F4 = View Hardware Configuration

F5 = Set Network Parameters
F6 = Set Boot Parameters
F7 = Set Monitor Parameters
F8 = Set Language Parameters

F9 = Verbose Diagnostic Messages Enabled




Enter=Reboot
```

Figure 13–5 IBM Network Station Administrator Setup Utility Panel

Set Network Parameters Panel

The prior section, "Locating the Boot Server" on page 201, discussed the way used by the IBM Network Station to locate the boot server in order to load the boot and the configuration files. As mentioned earlier, there are two possible ways to perform this task:

- Obtaining the IP Address from the boot server using DHCP or BOOTP protocol
- Using the configuration recorded in the NVRAM

The desired option can be set by using the *IP Addressed from* option in the Set Network Parameters panel, as shown in Figure 13–6 and Figure 13–7.

Obtaining the IP Address from the Network

The panel shown in Figure 13–6 allows you to change the type of protocol used to obtain an IP configuration (DHCP, BOOTP or RARP). The server must have at least one of these protocols configured: DHCP or BOOTP. These protocols assume that the IBM Network Station only knows its own MAC address. When the Network Station starts looking for an IP configuration server, these servers receive the IBM Network Stations MAC address. Depending on this unique data, they can look in their configuration file (for BOOTP or DHCP) and return a predefined configuration back to the IBM Network Station.

```
SCRN04                    IBM Network Station
                        Set Network Parameters


    IP Addressed from ...............  Network   NVRAM

    DHCP IP Addressing Order:........  Disabled
    BOOTP IP Addressing Order:.......  1
    RARP IP Addressing Order:........  Disabled

















                Use cursor keys to select option



    Enter=Save   F12=Cancel   F11=Restore Parameter
```

Figure 13–6 Set Network Parameters Panel with Network Option Selected

Using NVRAM

When using DHCP or BOOTP to acquire a valid IP address for the Network Station, the configuration server is discovered through a broadcast. In case there are multiple BOOTP or DHCP servers in the network that are providing IP configurations to any requesting MAC address, or multiple servers having different configurations for the same MAC address, the Network Station can have different states after any boot process. In order to be sure that the Network Station is booting up with the same state each time, the network must either be administered very strictly, not allowing any "wild" BOOTP or DHCP servers, or you assign your Network Station a valid IP configuration from the beginning.

Knowing that most networks are not administered with an ironed fist, the most suitable way for most environments is to go for individually assigned IP configurations. This configuration is stored in the NVRAM (Non-Volatile Random Access

Memory). With the IP configuration, it is also necessary to specify the IP address of at least one boot server. In case the first boot server is not responding (because it is overloaded or down), it is possible to define two more boot servers that can be contacted instead. The specified boot servers should provide the same boot image in order to provide the Network Station with redundant failback servers.

```
SCRN05                     IBM Network Station
                          Set Network Parameters

    IP Addressed from ............... Network   NVRAM

    Network Station IP Address ...... 9.3.1.121
    First Boot Host IP Address ...... 9.3.1.48
    Second Boot Host IP Address ..... 0.0.0.0
    Third Boot Host IP Address ...... 0.0.0.0
    Gateway IP Address .............. 9.3.1.74
    Subnet Mask ..................... 255.255.255.0
    Broadcast IP Address ............ 9.3.1.255







              Use cursor keys to select option


    Enter=Save  F12=Cancel  F11=Restore Parameter
```

Figure 13–7 Set Network Parameter Panel with NVRAM Option Selected

Each field of the Set Network Parameter panel shown in Figure 13–7 is described as follows:

Network Station IP Address: The IP address assigned to the IBM Network Station by the administrator.

First Boot Host IP Address: The IP address of your first boot server. This address is provided by the administrator.

Second Boot Host IP Address: If the environment consists of several boot servers, this field is pointing to a backup server in case the first boot server is unavailable.

Third Boot Host IP Address: In case the first and second boot server are unavailable, this field points to the last boot server.

Gateway IP Address: The default router of the network in which the IBM Network Station is installed.

Subnet Mask: The mask of the subnet in which the IBM Network Station is installed.

Broadcast IP Address: The broadcast IP address of the network in which your IBM Network Station is installed.

The upcoming new release of the IBM Network Station software includes more configuration fields, as described in "Coming Soon: IBM Software Release 3" on page 224.

Set the Boot Parameters Panel

As previously discussed in "Loading the Kernel" on page 202, the IBM Network Station is able to use two different file services: TFTP and NFS. Figure 13–8 shows the panel in which the order of use for those protocols can be defined and where the base configuration for the protocols is done.

```
SCRN06                    IBM Network Station
                          Set Boot Parameters


   Boot File ...................... kernel

   TFTP Boot Directory .............

   NFS Boot Directory ............. /usr/netstation/

   Configuration File ............. standard.nsm

   Configuration Directory ........ /usr/netstation/configs/

   TFTP Order ..................... Disabled
   NFS Order ...................... 1
   MOP Order ...................... Disabled
   LOCAL Order .................... Disabled



            Field help messages are displayed here



   Enter=Save   F12=Cancel   F11=Restore Parameter
```

Figure 13–8 Set Boot Parameters Panel

The parameters for using TFTP or NFS are described as follows:

Boot File: The name of the boot file. The default for the IBM Network Station 1000 is kernel.63a.

TFTP Boot Directory: The name of the directory from which the boot file can be loaded. This option is only used if TFTP is enabled. If TFTP is not enabled, this field can remain empty.

NFS Boot Directory: The name of the directory from which the boot file can be loaded. As with TFTP, this option is only used if NFS has been enabled.

Configuration File: As shown in "System-Level Configuration Files" on page 213, this file has the required links to load other configuration files in order to set up the environment. By default, the name of the file is *standard.nsm*, but can be changed.

Configuration Directory: The name of the directory on which the configuration file is stored.

> **Note**
>
> Directories require a tailing slash ("/"), because the Boot Monitor is just concatenating the entry for the directory with the file names. Not specifying the tailing slash results in invalid file names.

The following options can be set either to be disabled or to a value between one and four. All values (except of "disabled") can only be assigned to one protocol. In order to use NFS as first choice and TFTP as backup protocol, assign "1" to NFS and "2" to TFTP, and disable all other protocols.

The following shows the preferred configuration with just NFS enabled:

TFTP Order: Leave as Disabled

NFS Order: Leave as 1. This is the preferred service, please refer to "Loading the Kernel" on page 202 for more information.

MOP Order: Leave as Disabled.

LOCAL Order: Leave as Disabled.

The new release of the IBM Network Station software modifies the fields in the Set Boot Parameters Panel. Please refer to "Coming Soon: IBM Software Release 3" on page 224.

The IBM Network Station Manager

The IBM Network Station Manager (NSM) is a browser-based, user-friendly tool that is used to configure some parameters of the IBM Network Station. A requirement for using NSM is a graphical browser with JavaScript capabilities.

All changes made using NSM are stored in the configuration files on the server, as well as in the startup files. It is strongly recommended to use NSM to perform all changes to the configuration files because NSM performs some context checking and changes the configuration file with constant accuracy. However, it is also possible and sometimes necessary to modify the configuration files manually. This should only be done by an experienced administrator using all possible precautions (if at all).

"The Configuration Files" on page 212 discusses the configuration files and some of the parameters. It will show that the use of NSM is safer and also much more convenient than modifying the configuration files manually with an editor.

In the current release of the IBM Network Station Manager, it is accessible on the boot server through the following URL:

```
http://hostname/NetworkStation/en_US/nsmgr.htm
```

where `hostname` is the name of the boot server. If a hostname is not provided on the DNS, it is also possible to use the boot server's IP address—as is customary for URLs.

When you enter the URL in the browser, NSM asks for a *user name* and *password*. After entering a valid information for the boot server, the NSM graphics interface appears in the browser, as shown in Figure 13–9 on page 211.

Levels of Configuration

NSM manages three levels of configuration:

- System defaults: these settings affect all users
- Workstation defaults: these settings affect one IBM Network Station
- User defaults: these settings affect a specific user

These three levels are shown in the main right side frame of NSM when the Setup option has been selected.

Only the administrator has the access to all the options, a specific user is allowed to modify the information pertinent to himself.

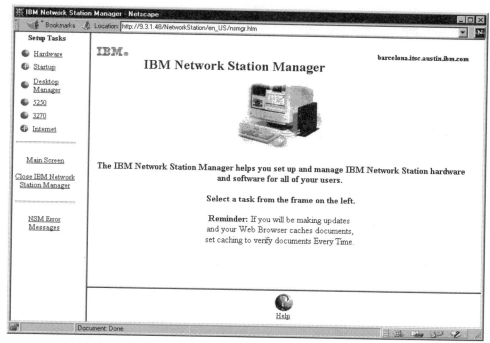

Figure 13–9 The Network Station Manager

At the left side of the frame is the *Setup Task* list, which contains the following six options:

- Hardware

  This option provides the possibility to modify some hardware defaults, such as the mouse, keyboard and monitor settings, on the Network Station as well as the administrator password and more.

- Startup

  This option is used to modify the user's work space. It provides the possibility to configure the applications offered in the menu bar, the applications that are automatically started after logon, and to define some environment variables.

- Desktop Manager

  This option provides the possibility to modify the screen properties, such as screen color, font size, icon position, and more.

- 5250

  This option is used to modify the default environment and the options available for the 5250 sessions.

- 3270

  This option is used to modify the default behavior and the options available for the 3270 sessions.

- Internet

  This section groups the options related with the Internet access, such as the configuration of the proxies and the behavior of the browsers packed with the IBM Network Station code.

  - Network: Used to add the personal data of the user who is using the Internet access and the configuration to establish a secure connection.

  - IBM Browser: Set the preferences of the browser

  - Navio NC Navigator: Set the preferences of the browser

  - Applet Viewer: Used to set the options used to run the applet viewer (for example, the verbose mode, the heap size, and so forth).

The Configuration Files

When the IBM Network Station has loaded the kernel during the boot process, it is ready to load the configuration files containing all the necessary information to start the work session for any user.

There are three levels of configuration files:

- System-level
- Workstation-level
- User-level

The Configuration File Syntax

Although the files are in text format and can therefore easily be modified, they should only be modified through NSM or through any of the other GUI applications developed for this purpose. However, it can be useful to have a look at this file; therefore it makes sense to know about the syntax used in these files.

- Comments are indicated with a "#" character as the first nonspace character in a line. These lines are ignored.

- Parameter statements are used to assign values to system parameters. If the parameter can hold more than one entry, brackets are needed as shown below:

```
set exec-disabled-commands = {
#   { login }
#   { logout }
  { serial }
  { dialer }
```

```
#    { quicksetup }
#    { setup }
#    { pref }
}
```

In this sample, the `exec-disable-command` parameter can have multiple values, but only `serial` and `dialer` are active, the others are commented out.

- The adding index `-1` used to add a value to an existing parameter, for example:

```
exec-disabled-commands[-1] = { "setup" }
```

is adding `setup` to the existing values of the parameter. Note that the set command can be omitted.

System-Level Configuration Files

These files belong to the first level of customization. They are independent of the user and hostname and are used to set the default behavior of the IBM Network Station. This file resides in the /usr/netstation/configs directory.

> ### Note
>
> The order of the files is important because one parameter can be set many times, but only the last value is retained. This means that the last set statement overrides the previous one.

The files are:

standard.nsm: The default initial configuration file. Its role is to call other configuration files. Because the syntax is simple, it can easily be modified by the user.

required.nsm: This file contains settings for the IBM Network Station hardware and kernel, such as the serial and parallel port, the autostarting applications, the modules, environment variables, and more. If changes are required, use the **Setup Parameters** option located in the **User Services** window (see "The IBM Network Station User Services" on page 216). Changes are not stored in this file, but in defaults.dft.

control.nsm: This file contains some default values to configure the IBM Network Station hardware and kernel preference. If any changes are needed, they can be done by the IBM Network Station Manager, which inserts statements in the default.nsm file.

defaults.nsm: Contains the modified values of control.nsm and is modified by NSM.

defaults.dft: Contains the modified values of required.nsm and is modified by NSM.

local.nsm: Same purpose as default.dft.

> ### Note
>
> There is a file called configd.doc located in the /usr/netstation/configs/ directory. This file contains a brief description of any parameter and value in order to understand the configuration files.

Workstation-Level Configuration Files

These files are directly related to the IBM Network Station unit. They reside in the /usr/netstation/configs directory. These three files are workstation dependent and are created by the administrator using NSM to modify any workstation setting. Suppose the workstation name is *stationname*; the files should be:

stationname: This file loads other configurations files much like standard.nsm. This file and the next two are created by NSM when the administrator attempts to make changes using the **Workstation defaults** button in the **Hardware** option.

stationname.nst: This file contains the changes made by the administrator when choosing the **Workstation defaults** button in the **Hardware** option.

stationname.trm: As with the previous file, this file is created by NSM and initially is empty. This file should be used by the administrator to manually override the values in the stationname.nst file.

> ### Note
>
> To activate this workstation-dependent configuration, add the following statement in default.dft:
>
> ```
> set unit-query-for-name-at-boot = tcpip
> ```
>
> After this change, the default configuration file that the IBM Network Station attempts to read first in the boot process is the stationname file.

User-Level Configuration Files

These files contain characteristics of a specific user. They are processed after the user has successfully logged in. These files resides in the /usr/netstation/nsm/username/ directory, where *username* is the identification of the user. These files are:

username.nsu: This file contains values to configure the work environment of the user and is created or modified by the administrator or the user using NSM.

username.usr: As with the previous file, it is created by NSM and initially is empty. It can be used to manually override the values in the username.nsu file.

The Startup Files

These files, called by startup.nsm, contain information about which menu option and which environment variables are set in order to have a useful work space. They are separated into three levels:

* IBM-level

  Located in the /usr/netstation/SysDefaults/ directory the startup.nsm file contains the IBM-supplied values and should not be manually modified. This file contains menu items to the default applications of the IBM Network Station, such as the 5250 session, the Navio Browser, and so forth, and the default settings for the task bar. The content of startup.nsm is shown below:

```
SET TRACE ON
SET NSM_HTTP_PORT 80
SET NSM_LOGOUT YES
SET NSM_HIDE YES
SET NSM_TOPBOTTOM YES
SET NSM_LOCK YES
SET NSM_TASKBAR YES
MENUITEM "NSterm" term -ctype telnet -xrm "NCDterm.showLocal:False" -n NSterm
MENUITEM "5250" ns5250
MENUITEM "3270" ns3270
MENUITEM "IBM Browser" loadb nsb
MENUITEM "Navio Browser" loadb navio
RUN wm
```

* System-level

  Located in the /usr/netstation/nsm/SysDefaults/ directory, the startup.nsm file contains the configuration common to all users and is configured by the administrator using NSM. An application that should be available to any corporate user (such as mail or calendaring) could be added to this level.

- User-level

  Located in the /usr/netstation/nsm/username/nsm/ directory, where *username* is the identification of the user, the startup.nsm file contains specific configuration for each user. It is modified by the administrator using NSM.

Note

"Running Java Programs in the IBM Network Station" on page 229 describes the steps to add items to the task bar, such as Java applications and applets.

The IBM Network Station User Services

The User Services window, also known as the Console window, is an application used to access services available only from the workstation screen. These services involve statistics information and provide the ability to log on to other servers and to modify some configuration parameters.

It is toggled on and off using the Pause/Break key. By default, it shows the Console window, which is used to access the message log as shown in Figure 13–10.

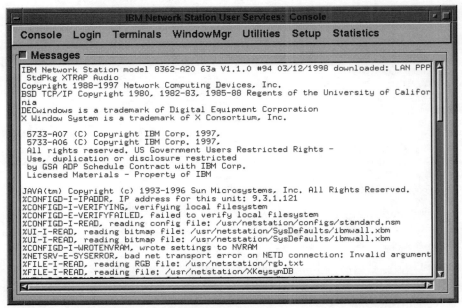

Figure 13–10 The Console Window

Most available options are very intuitive; therefore only the Setup Parameters option in the Setup menu is discussed here.

The Setup Parameters option is used to view or to modify many setup parameters, such as Access Control, Java Environment, Boot Configuration and so forth. Figure 13–11 shows the configuration window with different configuration topics (the list is actually longer than shown in the window).

IBM Network Station User Services: Setup Parameters

File   Sections

- Access Control
- ARP
- Booting
- Commands and Startup
- Configuration
- Diagnostics
- File Manager
- File Service

Messages:

Auto Save File

| Apply | Restart | Defaults | Cancel |

Figure 13–11 Setup Parameters Window

The changes made in this window are not permanent until you click on the **Apply** button, and some of them will take effect after the next reboot (the messages box shows it). The options most used by us in this window were:

Access Control: This option is used to restrict the access. For example, it is possible to limit the access to the message log, limit the local and remote access to the serial port, configure the global password, and more. See "Allowing Remote Telnet Session" on page 219 for an example.

Booting: Used to set the network and boot parameters of the IBM Network Station. This option can be used as an alternative to the Setup Utility Panel. See "IBM Network Station Set Up" on page 204.

Java: Used to set the directory where the Java run-time resides and to set the command to invoke the applet viewer.

Serial: Is necessary when any application uses the serial port. See "Allowing Access to the Serial Port" on page 222 for an example.

The IBM Network Station Message Log

The Console Window shown in Figure 13–10 is used to access the message log. It can be brought to the screen by pressing the **Pause/Break** key.

This window shows all messages generated by the IBM Network Station and any applications running in it. These messages are useful when applications do not work properly because they provide an idea about what's happening. Even so, the Console Window shows only the latest messages.

There are several ways to access the message log:

- The Console Window shown in Figure 13–10 on page 216
- Starting a local session in the IBM Network Station
- Starting a Telnet session to the IP address of the IBM Network Station, port 5998 (remote Telnet has to be enabled; see "Allowing Remote Telnet Session" on page 219).

Local Session

A local session is a command shell running on the Network Station. To start a local session, follow these steps:

1. Toggle on the **Console** window from the **Terminals** menu.
2. Click on the **New Terminal** option.
3. Choose the **Diag** terminal as in Figure 13–12.
4. Press the **OK** button to finish.

Figure 13–12 The Terminal Chooser

The window shown in Figure 13–13 is the Local Diagnostic Manager. It provides the possibility to modify the size of the fonts, print the message log, and more.

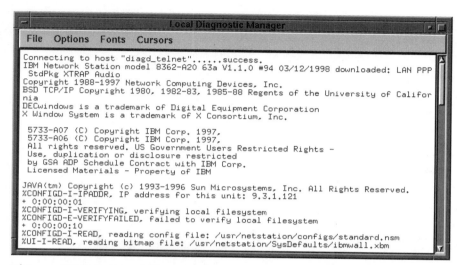

Figure 13–13 Local Terminal

Allowing Remote Telnet Session

This is the best way to access the message log, but it is possible that the administrator has the option disabled for security reasons.

The administrator can give free access to the message log or only give access to a group of users.

If only a few users should have access to the message log, they can be added to a control list by following these steps:

1. Go to the **Console** window, select **Setup -> Setup Parameters -> Access Control** to arrive at the Diagnostic Daemon section. The result is shown in Figure 13–14 on page 220.

2. Select the **Enable Diagnostic Access Control** checkbox.

3. Add the IP address of the authorized station in the **Diagnostic Access Control List**.

4. Click on **Apply** to save your changes.

To give free access, the administrator only needs to select the **Enable Diagnostic Access Control** checkbox.

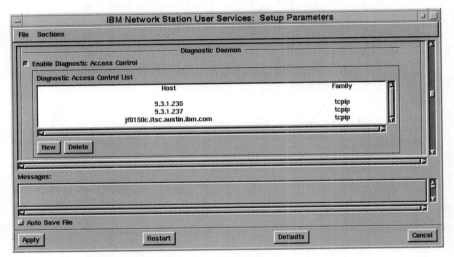

Figure 13–14 Allowing Access to the Message Log

Remote Telnet Session

This option is recommended when you want to closely review the messages, maybe to print and read them later, or to look for entries that identify problems.

Assume that the IP address of the Network Station is 9.3.1.121. In order to start a remote session, open a Telnet session to this IP address and to port 5998. Using Windows NT, this command looks like this:

```
Telnet 9.3.1.121 5998
```

The result of this command is shown in Figure 13–15.

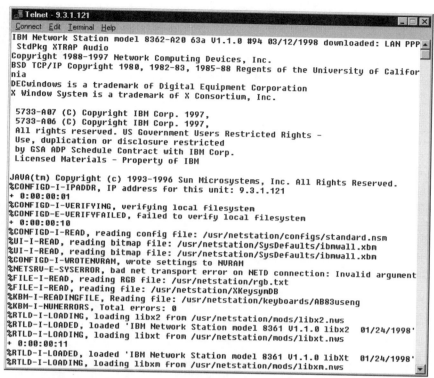

Figure 13-15 Windows NT Telnet Session

Accessing the Serial Port

Whenever any device attached to the serial port of the IBM Network Station has to be accessed, the serial port has to be configured, and access has to be given to a group of users.

The access to the serial port is realized by an IP daemon listening by default, on port 87.

Allowing Access to the Serial Port

If only a group of users are allowed to access the serial port, the IP address of their systems needs to be specified as follows:

1. Go into the **Console** window and choose **Setup -> Setup Parameters -> Access Control** to reach the Serial and Parallel Daemon section.

2. Select the **Enable Serial and Parallel Access Control** checkbox.

3. Add a new item in the **Serial and Parallel Control List** with the IP address of the **Host** that should have access, and leave the family as **tcpip**.

4. Click **Apply** to save and apply the changes.

If free access to the serial port is desired, enable the **Enable Serial and Parallel Access Control** checkbox.

> *Note*
>
> Applications running on the Network Station can access the serial port either by their IP address or—more generically—through the loopback address, 127.0.0.1.

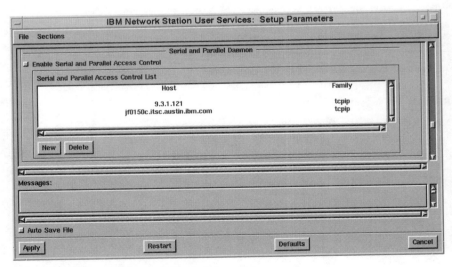

Figure 13–16 Allowing Serial Access

Initializing the Serial Port

If serial port is needed to access a device attached to it, the IBM Network Station has to initialize the port to the appropriate settings by following these steps:

1. In the **Console** Window, select **Setup -> Setup Parameters -> Serial** to reach the configuration panel shown in Figure 13–17 on page 223.

2. The Serial Interfaces Table has these options:

Port Number	In the used release, port 1 is the only port supported.
Port Use at Boot	Leave as printer.
Current Port Use	Leave as printer.
Baud Rate	Depends or your application and must be between 50 and 115200 bauds.
Data Bits	Depends on your application and must be 7 or 8 bits.
Stop Bits	Default is 1; modify if necessary.
Parity	Default is none; modify if necessary.
Handshake	Default is XON/XOFF, modify if necessary.
Hangup	Leave it as none.

3. Click **Apply** to save and apply your changes.

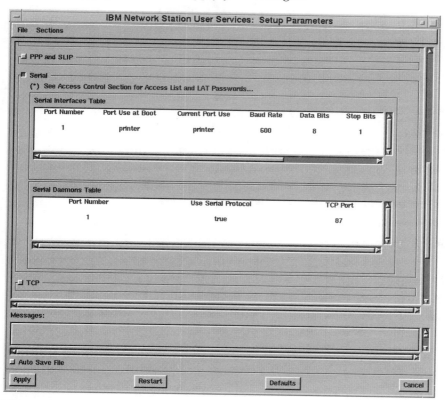

Figure 13–17 Configuring the Serial Port

Coming Soon: IBM Software Release 3

When this book was written, a lot of upcoming changes and improvements were planned and should be available before the release of this book. Some of the improvements are discussed in this section.

The Setup Utility Panel

The new version allows you to load the configuration files from a server that is not the boot server. The options have been modified to create new groups.

In the Set Network Parameters panel, add information to the following fields:

- First Configuration Host IP Address is used to indicate the IP address of the server which has the configuration files. If this is the boot server, the field can be left empty; if not, the IP address of the boot server has to be entered.

- Second Configuration Host IP Address is used in the case that the first configuration server is not available. If such a server does not exist, leave this field empty.

The Set Boot Parameters panel only includes the first three fields of the last version: Boot File, TFTP Boot Directory and NFS Boot Directory options.

The remaining options are in the Configuration Parameters panel. New options that are found in the Setup Utility panel include a Second Configuration Directory field.

IBM Network Station Manager

The following list describes the IBM Network Station Manager.

New level of Configuration: In addition to the three levels of configuration described in the box labeled "Levels of Configuration" on page 213, this release adds the *group defaults* level. This gives the administrator the possibility to set the environment to a specific group of users.

NC Navigator: This browser replaces both the IBM browser and the Navio browser. It is a compatible subset of the Netscape Navigator Release 3 browser.

Lotus eSuite WorkPlace Administrator: Lotus eSuite is a set of productivity applications that includes a spreadsheet, a word processor and calendar functions. eSuite is written in Java and was designed to run on a thin-client environment, such as the IBM Network Station. For best performance, eSuite should be run on a Series 1000 Network Station with 64 MB of RAM. eSuite is already generally available.

Java Support

This section describes the enhancements in the IBM Network Stations Java support.

Java Virtual Machine: Includes the 1.1.4 version of the JVM.

Java Just-In-Time Compiler: Allows you to compile the byte-codes when it is downloaded in the IBM Network Station; this improves the performance in the execution of the Java applications and applets.

## Chapter 14

Java in the IBM Network Station

▼ INTRODUCTION

▼ JAVA SETTINGS

▼ RUNNING JAVA PROGRAMS IN THE IBM NETWORK STATION

▼ TROUBLESHOOTING JAVA EXECUTION PROBLEMS

▼ THE eSUITE

This chapter focuses on the use of Java in the IBM Network Station. It will discuss how to successfully run Java applications and applets on the IBM Network Station and provide some tips and techniques to avoid common errors.

Introduction

The IBM Network Station is a typical workstation in the Network Computing environment. Compared to a PC, it simplifies the system administration by moving the desktop and application configuration from the desktop to the server. However, it is possible to have individual configurations for each user. This means, wherever users log on to a system, they'll get their customized configuration that gives them desktop access to everything they need.

Java programs are part of this customized environment. Compared to the build in 3270 or 5250 emulators or to the build in an X server, which are used to get a view of applications running on the server, the Java application has to run on the IBM

Network Station itself. This provides the possibility to have a sophisticated GUI, thus reducing the network traffic and reducing the CPU load on the server itself— provided that a good application design was implemented.

IBM Network Station Series 1000 is used because of its robust support of business-critical applications and personal productivity tools that take advantage of Java. In addition, this model is able to work with SmartCards and access them with Java.

Java Virtual Machine

The Java Virtual Machine (JVM) is in charge of controlling the Java execution environment and obtaining resources from the kernel. These are used by the Java applications, as opposed to Java applets. Currently, the Network Station can only run one Java application at a time, but it can start several Java applets at the same time.

Memory Requirements

Because the IBM Network Station has no other local storage except its real memory, it has no virtual memory capabilities. When an application runs on the Network Station, all its code is loaded in real memory until the application ends. Therefore, calculating the real memory requirements becomes more important than on a PC, because if the limit on real memory is reached, the system will stop.

Table 1 provides an overview of how much memory is used by the default Network Station components.

Table 14-1 IBM Network Station Software Memory Requirements

Software	Memory Requirements (RAM)
Base System	5.35 MB
Java Virtual Machine	5 MB
Navio NC Navigator Browser	5 MB

This means that the footprint for having the Network Station up and running is around 5-10 MB. In order to run Java applications or Java applets using the Navio Browser, a minimum of 32 MB is recommended. This is the minimum amount of memory delivered with the IBM Network Station.

Java Settings

In order to use Java applications in the IBM Network Station, the Java directory statement must be set. This can be done by using the **User Services** window's **Setup Parameters** option, as shown in Figure 14–1, and by following these steps:

1. Scroll down to the **Java** section.

2. In the **Java directory** field, write `/usr/netstation/java` (default).

3. In the **AppletViewer Command,** write `java ncd.applet.NCDAppletViewer` (default).

4. Click on **Apply** to activate the settings.

It is possible to set the applet viewer parameters using the NSM. This is shown in Chapter 13, subsection "The IBM Network Station Manager."

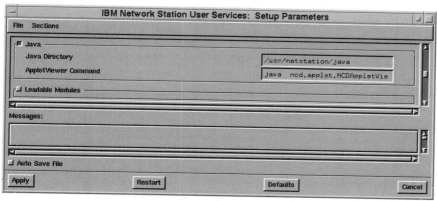

Figure 14–1 Java Configuration

Running Java Programs in the IBM Network Station

Setting up Java applications or applets for use on the IBM Network Station can be done with the IBM Network Station Manager (NSM). Java applications or applets can either be defined to start automatically after a user has logged on successfully to the Network Station, or they can be added as menu items to the taskbar for easy access.

Adding a Java Applet Item to the Taskbar

The following describes the way to configure a Java applet to be launched from the taskbar. As an example, we use the TicTacToe demo applet from the Java Development Kit.

When using NSM with administration privileges from any browser with Java Script support (such as Navio shown in Figure 14–2), the steps are:

1. In the **Setup** tasks, select **Startup -> Menus -> System defaults** to reach the Java Applet menu section.

2. Add an item and label it `TicTacToe`.

3. In the Applet URL field, add the path to the HTML document starting the applet: `/usr/netstation/java/TicTacToe/example1.html`

4. Finally, click on the **Finish** button to save all changes.

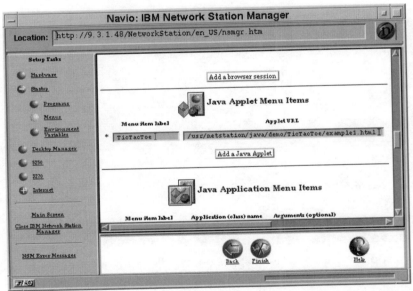

Figure 14–2 Adding a Java Applet

The changes result in an entry in the startup.nsm file as shown below:

```
MENUITEM "TicTacToe" appletviewer /usr/netstation/java/TicTacToe/example1.html
```

Figure 14–3 shows the result of this modification after the user logs on. In the taskbar, the TicTacToe menu item appears. As the figure also shows, it is possible to run multiple Java applets concurrently.

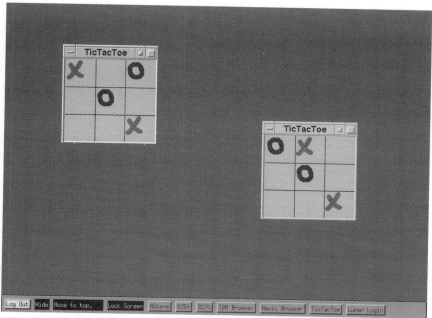

Figure 14–3 Multiple Applets Running on the IBM Network Station

Adding a Java Application Item to the Taskbar

Similar to Java applets, it is also possible to configure Java applications to be started from the taskbar. This time, the example uses this book's sample code for the Lunar Medical Center login application.

When using NSM with administration privileges from any browser with Java Script support, such as Netscape (shown in Figure 14–4), follow these steps:

1. In the **Setup** tasks, select **Startup -> Menus -> System defaults** to reach the Java Application menu section.

2. Add an item and label it Lunar Login.

3. Specify the class name, in this case Main.

4. Add the base path where is your application is located to the CLASSPATH, in this case:

`/usr/netstation/java/applications/MedCenter`

5. Click on the **Finish** button to save the changes.

The result of this operation is shown in Figure 14–5 on page 233.

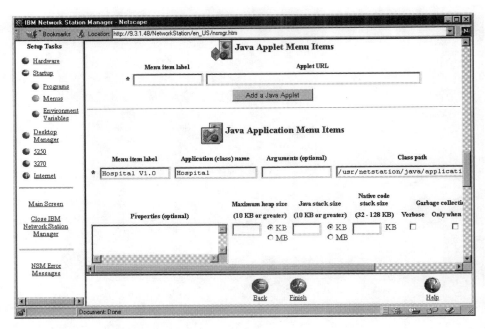

Figure 14–4 Adding a Java Application

The modifications using NSM result in a new entry in the startup.nsm file. For the example just shown, the new statement would look like following:

```
MENUITEM "Lunar Login" java -classpath
/usr/netstation/java/classes.zip:/usr/netstation/java/applications
/MedCenter Main
```

> **Note**
>
> When an application is not launched, it is possible to trace the problem by turning on the verbose mode located in the same section in NSM where the application is defined. See Troubleshooting Java Execution Problems, for an explanation of some common problems.

Figure 14–5 shows the logon screen of the Lunar Medical Center Java application.

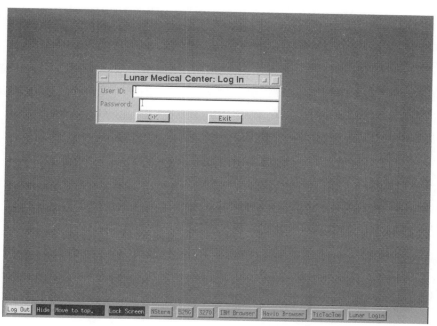

Figure 14–5 The Lunar Login Application in the Network Station

> *Note*
>
> Unusual for Java, the path to classes.zip (on the Network Station by default /usr/netsta-
> tion/java/classes.zip) must not be part of the CLASSPATH, because it is defined in the envi-
> ronment variable called NCDCLASSES. The Java run-time on the Network Station
> automatically adds this variable to the CLASSPATH whenever a Java application gets
> started.

Autostarting Java Programs and Applets

As in the previous sections, using the NSM is a comfortable way to modify the
user environment. This section shows the necessary steps to add a Java program
or applet to the autostarting list. This Java code gets executed after the user logs
on to the system.

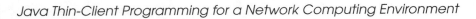

When starting the NSM with administrator privileges in any browser with Java Script support, follow these steps:

1. In the **Setup** tasks, select **Startup -> Programs -> System defaults** selection. Instead of selecting System defaults, it is also possible to select **User defaults**, depending on whether the changes are for a specific user or for all users.

2. Scroll down to the **Java Applets to AutoStart** section or to the **Java Applications to Autostart** section, depending on whether a Java application or applet has to be added.

The options shown at this point are similar to the options reviewed in the sections "Adding a Java Applet Item to the Taskbar," and "Adding a Java Application Item to the Taskbar." The configuration panel here can be configured in the same way it was done on the panels in these sections.

Troubleshooting Java Execution Problems

If the configured Java application or applet does not work properly, it is useful to activate the **Console** window (pressing the **Pause/Break** key) and open the messages by selecting the **Messages** checkbox. The messages provide information about the problems found by the JVM.

Cannot find class or class not found

The problem that causes this message is simple: the classloader used in the application tries to load a class referenced in the application, which is not found in the CLASSPATH. This can either happen if the class really does not exist, or more often, when the CLASSPATH is not set correctly. Inexperienced administrators often refer directly to the class file, forgetting that the class itself is part of a package.

For example, a class file, `aTool.class`, located in `/usr/netstation/java/com/ibm/austin/itsc/tools`, which is part of the package `com.ibm.austin.itsc.tools`, can only be started as `com.ibm.austin.itsc.tools.aTool.class` out of the `/usr/netstation/java` directory, and not at as `aTool.class` out of the `/usr/netstation/java/com/ibm/austin/itsc/tools` directory.

Another common problem is that the missing class is part of a ZIP or JAR archive file and this archive file has not been specified in the CLASSPATH environment variable.

For the sample above, if the class `aTool.class` from the package `com.ibm.austin.itsc.tools` has been provided in a ZIP file called `AUSTOOLS.ZIP` located in the `/usr/netstation/java` directory, the CLASSPATH must contain the entry `/usr/netstation/java/AUSTOOLS.ZIP` in order to find the class file.

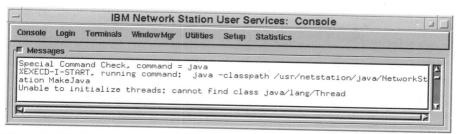

Figure 14–6 Java Error

Out of memory

This happens because either the Network Station is really running out of physical memory, or the Java stack is consumed and therefore must be adjusted for the specific needs of the application environment. The Java stack size can be modified with administrator rights using the IBM Network Station Manager.

Error reading ZIP file

One possible reason for this error message is that the IBM Network Station was configured to use TFTP instead of NFS in order to access files from the server. TFTP does not allow access to particular parts of a file, and therefore it cannot be used to extract single class files out of an archive. If TFTP has to be used for whatever reason, the ZIP files have to be extracted (with the stored directory structure) to the server's file system in the correct CLASSPATH.

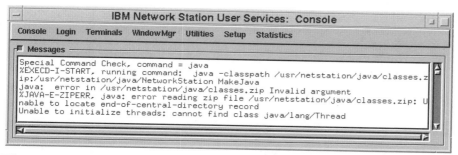

Figure 14–7 Java Error

Too many copies already running

One limitation of the current release is that it can only run one Java Virtual Machine. This makes it impossible to run Java applets and Java applications or two Java applications at the same time. Also when using the Navio browser to run Java applets, the only JVM available is used and therefore blocks any attempt to use the JVM for a Java application. However, it is possible to run multiple Java applets at the same time by using one JVM.

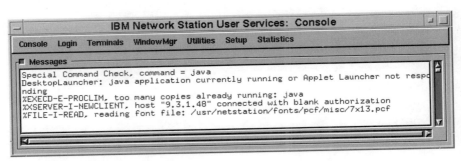

Figure 14–8 Java Error

Others

If no other messages in the message log explain the problem, it is useful to turn on the verbose mode, using NSM. Please refer to Running Java Programs in the IBM Network Station for details.

The eSuite

The eSuite is a Java application developed by Lotus which provides a user friendly interface for network computers. The eSuite is designed to satisfy the enterprise users because it includes a Web browser, electronic mail, enterprise data access, and personal information management. Every task is a Java applet, and in this way, it allows users to add their own applets to meet their needs.

The eSuite is composed of the WorkPlace itself and by the Administrator application, which is in charge of customizing the environment for each user. Of course, the application for the configuration is only accessible for users with administrator access.

The WorkPlace

The WorkPlace is designed as an alternative for users who use "green screen" terminals because they are easily moved into the network computers world of the IBM Network Station.

The WorkPlace is the perfect example of an application developed for thin clients. It is written in Java (platform independent); it is task-oriented, and it is customizable.

The WorkPlace provides a set of JavaBeans-based applets including:

- eSuite calendar

- eSuite mail

- eSuite address book

- eSuite word processor

- eSuite spreadsheet

- eSuite presentation graphics

See Figure 14–9 for a view of the eSuite WorkPlace.

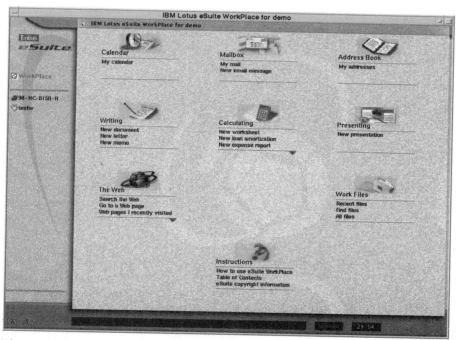

Figure 14–9 The eSuite WorkPlace

The Administrator

The Administrator is the Java applet used to configure the workplace environment of the users. Figure 14–10 on page 238 shows the Administrator Applet, which includes a tool bar with the following tabs:

- Users

- Groups

- Software

- Tasks

- Categories

Figure 14–10 The eSuite WorkPlace Administrator

Task and Categories

A task is the applet's representation in the WorkPlace. The eSuite is a customizable environment in which tasks are associated to categories. Each task is associated to a single category and is shown in that category on the eSuite WorkPlace, as shown in Figure 14–11.

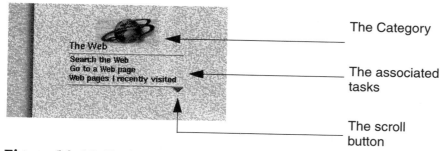

The Category

The associated
tasks

The scroll
button

Figure 14–11 Task and Categories in the eSuite

The task corresponds to activities that users perform, such as "open a presentation," "create a document" or "search the Web." The categories are used to organize the tasks. By default, every category can show three tasks on the WorkPlace at the same time. If there are more than three tasks associated to a category, a scroll button appears beside the tasks, providing access to the other tasks. If a user has no access to any task assigned to a category, the category itself is not shown on the desktop.

Software

The eSuite WorkPlace allows you to add your own Java applets and associate them to a specific task. By choosing the **Software** tab, the administrator can register an applet by specifying the applet's location, class name and purpose.

Groups and Users

The eSuite is organized so that tasks can either be assigned directly to a user or to groups of users. A user automatically gets the right to use a task if he belongs to a group to which the task is assigned. Grouping users allows much easier management.

The Users tab allows you to add or remove users, associate users with groups and if desired, assign tasks directly to a user. By default, all users belong to the *All Users* group.

Similar to the Users tab, the Group tab allows you to add or remove groups and assign tasks to the groups.

Adding a Java Applet

The following shows how to include a simple Java applet as a task to the eSuite and how to give access to this new task.

In order to perform this task, it is not necessary to understand the following Java code. It is only important that the Java class inherits from java.applet.Applet in order to be an applet. The following applet is called PerseveringScribble.java and is provided for clarification:

```java
import java.awt.*;
import java.awt.event.*;
import java.util.*;
public class PerseveringScribble extends java.applet.Applet
  {
  int last_x = 0, last_y = 0;
  Vector model = new Vector ();
  public void init ()
    {
    addMouseListener
      (
      new MouseAdapter ()
        {
        public void mousePressed (MouseEvent e)
          { last_x = e.getX (); last_y = e.getY (); }
        }
      );
    addMouseMotionListener
      (
      new MouseMotionAdapter ()
        {
        public void mouseDragged (MouseEvent e)
          {
          Graphics g = getGraphics ();
          int x = e.getX (), y = e.getY ();
          g.setColor (Color.black);
          DrawLine d = new DrawLine (last_x, last_y, x, y);
          model.addElement (d);
          d.draw (g);
          last_x = x; last_y = y;
          }
        }
      );
    }
  public void paint (Graphics g)
    {
    Enumeration e = model.elements ();
```

```
   while (e.hasMoreElements ())
     {
     ((DrawLine) e.nextElement ()).draw (g);
     }
   }
 }
class DrawLine
 {
 private int x0,
        y0,
        x1,
        y1;
 public DrawLine (int x0, int y0, int x1, int y1)
   {
   this.x0 = x0;
   this.y0 = y0;
   this.x1 = x1;
   this.y1 = y1;
   }
 public void draw (Graphics g)
   {
   g.drawLine (x0, y0, x1, y1);
   }
 }
```

The compiled class file of this sample applet should be somewhere under the eSuite directory. In this case, the code could be stored in the `applications/Perse-veringScribble` subdirectory. Note that eSuite uses `<Base.Root>/` to refer to its main directory. For the sample, the directory can be referred to as:

<Base.Root>/applications/PerseveringScribble/

The Administrator task, mentioned in "The Administrator," is now used to add the sample applet as a task to the eSuite WorkPlace.

The first thing to decide is whether the task representing the new applet is assigned to an existing category or to a new one. In case it has to be assigned to a new category called *Demo*, the steps are:

1. In the Administrator, select the *Categories* tab and click the **Add** button.

2. In the Name field, enter the name *Demo*.

3. As an option, it is possible to associate a graphic file as an icon for the category.

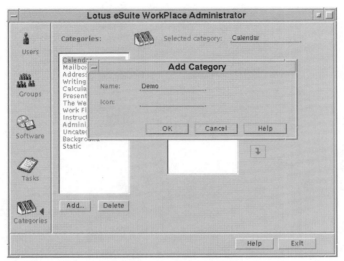

Figure 14–12 Adding a Category

To register the applet, follow these steps:

1. Select the **Software** tab, click on the **Add** button.

2. In the Codebase location, enter the path where the applet is located,
    `<Base.Root>/applications/PerseveringScribble/`.

3. Choose the **No registration file** option and add the title, `Scribble`, and the
    class name, `PerseveringScribble`. Then press **OK** to finish.

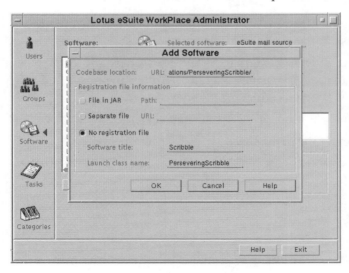

Figure 14–13 Adding a Java Applet

In order to use the applet in the WorkPlace, it must be assigned to a task. To do this:

1. Select the **Task** tab and press the **Add** button.

2. In the name field, enter a name for the task, for example Easy Scribble. This is the name of the task that appears on the WorkPlace.

3. Select the last option under the Type of task option, called **Launch an application without a document**. Then click on the **Next** button.

4. Because your applet is already registered, you can select **Persevering** from the list box and then click the **Finish** button.

5. At the right side of the window, you see a field called Category. Select the category **Demo**, added earlier.

As an option, it is possible to associate a graphic file to be the icon for the task.

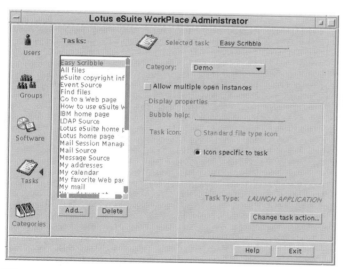

Figure 14–14 Adding a Task

Now that the applet is registered as a task and associated to a category, it can be assigned directly to a user or a group of users. In this sample case, the applet should be made available to all users and can therefore be assigned to the group *All Users*. To do this, select the **Groups** tab. Then, in the group list, select **All Users** and select the **Easy Scribble** task from the Task list. Finally, press the **Assign** button to save the changes and make them active.

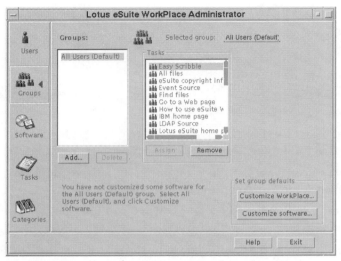

Figure 14–15 Associating a Task with a Group

Any user that logs on, from this moment on, will have access to this new task, as shown in Figure 14–16.

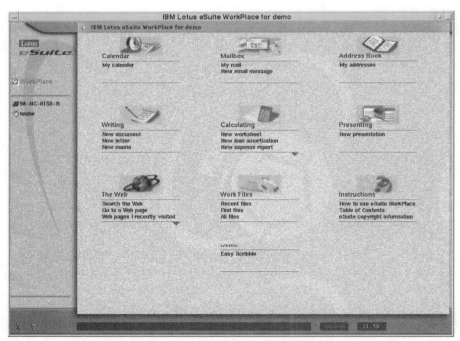

Figure 14–16 The Scribble Applet in the WorkPlace

Figure 14–17 shows the Scribble applet running on the eSuite WorkPlace. What is visible, besides our poor drawing skills, is that every applet runs embedded in, and as an unresizeable part of, the WorkPlace.

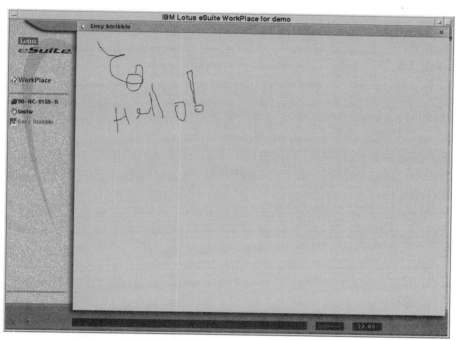

Figure 14–17 The Scribble Applet Running

Appendix A

Brief HTML Reference

This appendix provides an overview of some of the more important HTML tags used in the book. It is not the purpose of this book to detail every HTML tag. For example, minor tags and the HTML frames mechanism have been excluded. The best place to find the most current reference is on the W3C Website at:
`http://www.w3.org/MarkUp/`

Top Level Tags

These are tags that affect an entire (or large part of a) document.

`<HTML> entire-document </HTML>`

The <HTML> tag defines an HTML document. The <HTML> tag should be the first in the entire document, and the </HTML> tag should be the last.

```
<HEAD> head-section </HEAD>
```

The <HEAD> tag introduces text that describes an HTML document. Most documents have only a <TITLE> tag in the head section.

```
<TITLE> title-text </TITLE>
```

The <TITLE> tag, which is only valid in a <HEAD> section, defines the title of an HTML document. Browsers typically display document titles in their title bar and in bookmark lists.

```
<BODY attributes> document-body </BODY>
```

The <BODY> tag introduces the body of the document. It should appear after the head section and occupy the remainder of the document. Attributes are available to alter the background color of the document and the color of text, links, active links, and visited links.

Colors are specified in HTML by name (from a set of available color names) or by a six-digit hexadecimal number with the first two digits specifying the red value, the middle two the green value, and the last two the blue value.

Character Formatting Tags

These are tags that change the formatting of a set of characters and do not cause a line break.

```
<B> text </B>
```

The bold tag defines text that should be shown in boldface.

```
<I> text </I>
```

The italic tag defines text that should be shown in italics.

```
<U> text </U>
```

The underlined tag defines text that should be shown with a line underneath it.

```
<FONT attributes> text block </FONT>
```

The font tag defines that its block of text should have certain attributes, including size and color (if supported).

Block Formatting Tags

These are tags that change the formatting of a block of characters and cause a line break before and after the tag.

```
<CENTER> text</CENTER>
```

The center tag defines text that should be centered.

```
<H1 attributes> text </H1>
```

The <H1> tag defines a level 1 heading. It is typically shown in a very large bold font with several blank lines around it. It is also used by automatic indexers to describe a page. Attributes include alignment, no wrapping, and position in relation to graphics.

```
<H2 attributes> text </H2>
```

The <H2> tag defines a level 2 heading. It is typically shown in a large bold font with several blank lines around it.

Heading tags are available for six levels, with decreasing visual strength. A level 6 heading tag is typically shown in a normal font, indented, with a blank line above it.

```
<HR attributes>
```

The horizontal rule tag causes a horizontal line to be drawn across the screen. There is no </HR> tag. Attributes include horizontal width, line size, alignment, and shading characteristics.

```
<BR>
```

The line break tag breaks the current line of text. There is no </BR> tag.

```
<P attributes> text </P>
```

The paragraph tag starts a new paragraph and is equivalent to two< BR> tags. The </P> tag is optional if the tag is only to insert space between two paragraphs, but vital when attributes are applied. Attributes include text alignment and wrapping.

```
<PRE> text </PRE>
```

The preformatted text tag defines text that should be shown in a fixed-width font with the line breaks and other white space specified by the page author (all other tags ignore multiple white spaces). Within the <PRE> tag, there is no need to use <BR> tags to indicate line breaks.

```
<BLINK> block </BLINK>
```

The blink tag defines a block of content that should be shown flashing on and off.

Table Tags

These are tags used to create and lay-out tables.

```
<TABLE attributes> table-content </TABLE>
```

A table consists of an optional caption and one or more rows. Attributes include alignment, width, bordering, cell padding, and cell spacing.

```
<CAPTION attribute> text </CAPTION>
```

The caption tag defines the caption of a figure or table. It is valid only within <FIG> or <TABLE> tags. An alignment attribute is available.

```
<TR attributes> table row </TR>
```

The table row tag defines a row of cells that are defined with <TH> and <TD> tags. Attributes include alignment and background color.

```
<TH attributes> table header </TH>
```

The table header tag defines a header cell. Attributes include column and row spanning, wrapping and alignment.

```
<TD attributes> table data </TD>
```

The table data tag defines a table cell. Attributes include column and row spanning, wrapping and alignment.

List Tags

These are tags associated with lists.

```
<OL attributes> list entries </OL>
```

The ordered list tag introduces an ordered (numbered) list, which is made up of List Item <LI> tags. Attributes include compacting the list, numbering start values, type, and continuance.

```
<UL attributes> list entries </UL>
```

The unordered list tag introduces an unordered (bulleted) list, which is made up of List Item <LI> tags. Attributes include compacting the list and bullet type.

```
<MENU> list entries </MENU>
```

The menu list tag introduces a menu list, which is made up of List Item <LI> tags and does not include bullets or numbers before them.

```
<DIR attribute> list entries </DIR>
```

The directory list tag introduces a directory list, which is made up of List Item <LI> tags and does not include bullets or numbers before them. The items should be short so that they can be arranged into columns. The attribute is for compacting.

```
<LI attributes> text </LI>
```

The list item tag defines one entry in an ordered, unordered, menu, or directory list. Other tags may be embedded in a list item. Attributes include bullet style and renumbering.

Forms Tags

These are tags used to design and implement interactive forms.

`<FORM attributes> form tags </FORM>`

> The form tag introduces a form, which is made up of <INPUT> elements. Using tables and other elements, a form can take on various shapes and looks. Attributes include the action of the form and the method of submission.

`<INPUT TYPE=input-type NAME=field-name VALUE=value other-attributes>`

> Input tags are available with a number of mechanisms for the user to enter data onto an HTML form.

> Available INPUT TYPEs include:

`TYPE=CHECKBOX`

> The checkbox type input tag specifies a Boolean choice within the form that contains it. If more than one checkbox appears in the form with the same name, the user can select none, which one or several of the choices. Other attributes available include an initial selection, disabling and positioning.

`TYPE=FILE`

> The file type input tag allows the user to attach one or more files to the form for submission. Attributes include acceptable file types, disabling and positioning.

`TYPE=HIDDEN`

> The hidden type input tag specifies a hard-coded name-value pair within the form. This field is not displayed to the user.

`TYPE=IMAGE`

> The image type input tag specifies an image to be presented to the user. As soon as the user clicks on the image, the form is submitted with the selected x y coordinates of the spot on the image and the data for the other form fields. Attributes include image source and alignment.

`TYPE=PASSWORD`

> The password type input tag specifies a single-line text entry field within the form that contains it. The value entered by the user will be obscured as it is entered. Attributes include display size, maximum enterable length, disabling, and alignment.

`TYPE=RADIO`

> The radio button type input tag allows a choice among a number of options. Normally, more than one radio button will appear in the form with the same name. The user can then select only one of the choices. Attributes include initial selection, disabling and alignment.

```
TYPE=RESET
```

> The reset type input tag specifies a button. When the user clicks the button, all the fields in the form are reset to their initial values. The Value attribute defines the button's label.

```
TYPE=SUBMIT
```

> The submit type input tag specifies a button. When the user clicks the button, the form's data is submitted to the form's ACTION, using the defined METHOD, with NAME=*value* pairs. The Value attribute defines the button's label.

```
TYPE=TEXT
```

> The text type input tag specifies a single-line text-entry field within the form that contains it. Attributes include display size, maximum enterable length, disabling, and alignment.

```
<SELECT NAME=name other-attributes> option entries </SELECT>
<OPTION VALUE=value other-attributes> content
```

The select tag specifies a multiple-line selection box field within the form that contains it. The user can select one or more lines if the attribute MULTIPLE is specified. Other attributes include number of displayed selections, initial selected option, alignment and image map options (if utilized). If the VALUE attribute is not specified, the content of the option is used.

```
<TEXTAREA NAME=name other-attributes> content </TEXTAREA>
```

The text area tag specifies a multiple line text area field within the form that contains it. The NAME attribute is a required field and is used to identify the data for the field. Attributes include width and number of lines of the text area, and wrapping. The content is used as an initial value for the field. The field can be scrolled beyond the defined size to allow for larger amounts of text to be entered.

Miscellaneous Tags

These are tags that don't fit our other categories, including the important anchor tag (used for creating HyperText links) and inline image tags.

```
<A NAME=anchor> link-text </A>
<A HREF=link-address> link-text </A>
```

The anchor tag defines either an anchor in a document or in a hyperlink. The anchor tag must contain either a NAME attribute or an HREF attribute respectively, or both. An *anchor* is used to provide a point within a document that can be linked-to. A *link* defines a HyperText link, where the link-text is highlighted. If selected, the browser replaces the document in the current window with that retrieved according to the associated link address. Link addresses are commonly URIs and may include an anchor to go to a specific point within the retrieved document.

```
<!-- comment text -->
```

The comment tag is used to insert comments in your HTML code. The tag includes the actual comment text.

```
<IMG SRC=source other-attributes>
```

The inline image tag displays an image referred to by a URI. Supported image types are usually GIF and JPEG. Other attributes include alignment, bordering, height and width, alternative text to display in text-based browsers, and whether the image is an *image map*.

```
<MAP NAME=name> area tags </MAP>
```

The map tag defines a client-side image map and gives a name to a collection of AREA tags that are superimposed over an inline image to connect user clicks with links.

```
<AREA SHAPE=shape CO-ORDS=co-ords HREF=link-address>
```

The area tag defines areas that act as hotspots within an image. Typically a map will have multiple AREA tags. The SHAPE attribute can be one of RECT, CIRCLE, POLY, or DEFAULT. CO-ORDS gives the co-ordinates, in pixels, measured from the upper-left corner of the image, of the defining points for the shape. For RECT, these are left, top, right, and bottom. For CIRCLE, they are Xcentre, Ycentre and radius. For POLY, they are x1, y1, x2, y2, ... xn, yn.

```
<SCRIPT LANGUAGE=language><!-- script statements --></SCRIPT>
```

The script tag identifies script code. This can be code to be executed at this point of the document, or may contain functions for use later in the document. Netscape Navigator supports JavaScript, and Microsoft Internet Explorer 3.0 supports JScript (Microsoft JavaScript dialect) and VBScript. The statements are usually (but not required to be) enclosed in the comment tag, so that browsers that do not support scripting do not render the code as part of the page's text.

```
<APPLET attributes> applet-content </APPLET>
```

The Java applet tag instructs the browser to run a Java applet referred to by a URI. The applet-content consists of optional <PARAM> tags, ordinary text and markup to be displayed by browsers that cannot run Java applets. Attributes include code location, name, alignment, height, width, and spacing. Chapter 5 looks at Applets in more detail.

```
<SERVLET attributes> servlet-content </SERVLET>
```

The Java servlet tag instructs the connected Web server to run a Java servlet referred to by a URI. The servlet-content consists of optional <PARAM> tags, ordinary text and markup to be displayed by Web servers that cannot run Java servlets. Attributes include code location, codebase, and servlet initialization arguments. Chapter 7 looks at Applets in more detail.

Appendix **B**

Java Development: Using VisualAge for Java

This appendix introduces VisualAge for Java. It covers the following topics:

- The VisualAge family
- VisualAge Java overview
- Integrated Development Environment (IDE)
  - Java support
  - Navigating within VisualAge for Java
  - Visual Composition Editor Team development
  - Applet viewer
  - Editor/Debugger/SmartGuides
  - Proxy builder

- The Enterprise Access Builders (EAB)
  - Data Access Builder (DAX)
- System requirements
- Summary

This chapter discusses various processes and windows that you use in the development of windows and in applications using VisualAge for Java. All development for this redbook was performed using the Windows NT 4.0 version of the Enterprise Edition of VisualAge for Java. If you are using a different version or the Professional Edition, there may be some slight differences in the processes and windows discussed and shown here.

The VisualAge Family

VisualAge for Java is one of the members of the family of VisualAge products. These products cover the complete range of client/server application development topologies, clients, servers, and languages.

The VisualAge family supports the following programming environments:.

- VisualAge for Java
- VisualAge Generator (4GL)
- VisualAge for COBOL
- VisualAge for RPG
- VisualAge for C++
- . VisualAge for Smalltalk
- VisualAge for Basic
- VisualAge for e-Business
- VisualAge for PacBase
- VisualAge Financial Foundation
- VisualAge 2000
- VisualAge WebRunner

In addition, the VisualAge product set supports application development across the following client and server platforms.

Note: Not all VisualAge products support all the client and servers listed here.

- OS/2

- Windows 3.1 and 3.11

- Windows NT

- Windows 95

- AIX

- OS/390

- OS/400

VisualAge uses a construction-from-parts paradigm, which eases the migration to client/server, object-oriented, and Web-based technologies. With the Visual Composition Editor, which is available with VisualAge for Java, you can develop programs by visually arranging and connecting prefabricated parts. You can also create your own reusable parts. For a complete description of each of the VisualAge family members and supported environments, visit the VisualAge Family Web page at:

http://www.software.ibm.com/ad/.

VisualAge for Java Overview

IBM VisualAge for Java is one of the first enterprise-wide, team enabled, incremental application development environments for Java in the industry. It is designed to connect Java clients to existing server data, transactions, and applications. This enables developers to extend server-based applications to communicate with Java clients on the Internet or intranet, rather than rewrite the application from scratch. VisualAge for Java creates 100 percent pure Java-compatible applications, applets, and JavaBeans.

VisualAge for Java is available in three versions:

- **Entry**: Free, with a five hundred class limit. This version is available on the enclosed CD-ROM.

- **Professional Edition**: Includes the Integrated Development Environment (IDE)

- **Enterprise Edition**:
  - Includes all Professional Edition support
  - Includes the Enterprise Access Builders
  - Supports the AS/400 Toolbox for Java (will be included in the Enterprise Access Builder in the future)
  - Team support will be included in the future.

Beyond the current batch-based Java tools available today, VisualAge for Java provides:

- Superior enterprise connectivity
- Project-based team development
- A true incremental *rapid application development* environment for Java.

VisualAge for Java is part of the VisualAge family of products and shares some of the components from the other VisualAge products. For example, VisualAge for Java shares the team environment repository and image concepts (and implementation) with the VisualAge for Smalltalk product. It also shares the Visual Composition Editor component, which is common across all the development environments.

With VisualAge for Java, the developer can develop 100 percent Java-compliant JDK 1.1 applications and applets all from the same development environment. This enables customers and Business Partners to migrate to Java-based Web applets at their own pace along an incremental path, including:

- Implementing Java extensions to their applications
- Developing whole Java applications
- Moving to client/server Java applications
- Developing Web-based Java applets

The Integrated Development Environment incorporated within the product enables the developer to code/compile/test/debug single lines of code as well as full-scale applications, enabling the application to scale with the business requirement. The IDE is built around the industry leading ENVY/Developer team development environment from OTI (an IBM subsidiary company), which is well recognized within the object technology marketplace for its ability to provide management facilities for small- and large-scale application development projects. The IDE enables a developer to build and run applications, applets, and code snippets interactively without the need to run the compile statement (JavaC) from the command line. All applications can be run from within the IDE without the need to export the Java source or class files. This is achieved through the provision of a JDK 1.1-compliant Virtual Machine (VM) within the IDE. Because you can interactively modify code and run it without compilation, developers are able to debug code on the fly, spotting errors in their code with the debugger, changing it, and continuing without bringing the running application down. . .all within the VisualAge for Java IDE.

VisualAge for Java is an open IDE, and developers can easily import and export Java source and class files as well as JavaBeans that may have been purchased by the company or made available on the WWW. The JavaBeans support in VisualAge for Java also enables a developer to take an existing JavaBean (for example, from the WWW), import it into VisualAge for Java, modify the bean, and export it again for use within another JDK 1.1-compliant development environment (for example, Symantec Cafe and Borlands JBuilder).

Version 1 of VisualAge for Java supports JDK 1.1 (the most recent version at the time of publication). Along with the current JDK support, VisualAge for Java also supports all the most current standards for Java development (for example, Java Database Connectivity (JDBC) and so forth), which is discussed later. Because of the portability of JDK 1.1-compliant Java code, code that is developed using VisualAge for Java should be able to run on any Java Virtual Machine.

The initial release of the product runs on OS/2 Warp Version 4.0, Windows NT 4.0 or Windows 95.

VisualAge for Java comes with the following core components:
- Integrated Development Environment:
  - Hierarchy browser
    - Projects Packages
    - Classes Methods
  - Editor Debugger
  - Applet viewer
  - Team support (Enterprise edition)
  - Java class libraries
  - Visual Composition editor
- Enterprise Access Builders (EAB)
  - Data Access Builder
  - CICS Access Builder
  - RMI builder
  - C++ builder

All of the preceding components utilize the JDK 1.1 and Java Virtual Machine support of VisualAge for Java.

Integrated Development Environment (IDE)

This section of the appendix covers the Integrated Development Environment (IDE) component of VisualAge for Java.

Java Support

Java is a collection of classes built from the ground up, following object-oriented (OO) principles. In Java, everything is an object except for the standard data types inherited at the top of the hierarchy from the root class, object.

Java classes are contained in packages. The concept of a package in Java is a useful way of grouping classes that are related.

JDBC is the Java standard to manipulate enterprise data stored in relational databases. It is the Java equivalent to ODBC, a widely accepted standard developed by Microsoft. JDBC provides a standard SQL database access interface. Constructs such as database connections, SQL statements, result sets, and database metadata are included. With JDBC, it is possible to develop Java applications independently of the target relational database management system (RDBMS). Many vendors already provide (or will provide in the near future) JDBC drivers targeted at accessing dozens of database management systems.

In conjunction with JDBC, JavaSoft is releasing a JDBC-to-ODBC bridge. Such a bridge provides a way for Java applications developed to the JDBC standard to gain access to any database using the existing ODBC drivers.

Remote Method Invocation (RMI) lets programmers create Java objects whose methods can be invoked from another Java Virtual Machine. RMI is equivalent to a Remote Procedure Call in the nonobject world.

The JavaBeans API defines a portable, platform-neutral set of APIs for software components. JavaBeans components can plug into existing component architectures such as IBM's OpenDoc, Microsoft's OLE/COM/Active-X architecture, or Netscape's LiveConnect.

Java Native Interface (known previously as the native method interface in JDK 1.0) provides the capability for a Java object to call a native platform function typically written in C, C++, or any other language.

The internationalization support allows the development of localized applets and applications. The global Internet demands global software; that is, software that can be developed independently of the countries or languages of its users, and then localized for multiple countries or regions. JDK 1.1 provides a rich set of

Internationalization APIs for developing global applications. These APIs are based on Unicode 2.0 character encoding and include the ability to adapt text, numbers, dates, currency, and user-defined objects to any country's conventions.

Java Archive (JAR) is a platform-independent file format that aggregates many files into one, similar in concept to a ZIP file. Multiple Java applets and their requisite components (class files, images, and sounds) can be bundled in a JAR file and subsequently downloaded to a browser in a single HTTP transaction, greatly improving the download speed. The JAR format also supports compression, which reduces the file size and further improves the download time. In addition, the Applet author can digitally sign individual entries in a JAR file to authenticate their origin. It is fully backward-compatible with existing applet code and is fully extendible, being written in Java.

The Core Java JDK 1.1 API includes the following packages:

- Java.lang:

  This package contains all the classes and interfaces of the base Java language. It also includes the subpackage:

  - Java.lang.reflect:

    This package enables the Java program to examine the structure of Java classes and to reflect upon its own structure.

- Java.util:

  This is the utility package containing various utility classes and interfaces, including random numbers, system properties, and other useful classes. This package includes the subpackage:

  - Java.util.zip:

    This package provides classes for data-string checksum and compression and archive of data streams.

- Java.io:

  This package provides the input/output classes and the interfaces for files and streams. It includes also support for object serialization.

- Java.net:

  This package is composed of classes and interfaces for handling network operations such as TCP/IP, sockets and URLs.

- Java.awt:

  This is the abstract windowing package that allows for definition of GUI constructs that are portable to multiple windowing systems. It also provides printing support. The following subpackages are part of the Java.awt package:

  - Java.awt.image:

    Provides the classes necessary to handle images in various formats, such as GIF and JPEG.

  - Java.awt.peer:

    Provides hidden classes that map their Java.awt equivalents and are designed to implement the GUI constructs on specific platforms, such as Apple's Macintosh, Microsoft's Windows 95 or UNIX's Motif.

  - Java.awt.datatransfer:

    Defines a generic framework for interapplication data transfer including clipboard and cut-and-paste. Most classes rely on the object serialization API from the Java.io package.

  - Java.awt.event:

    This packages defines three categories of classes and interfaces:

    - Event classes that represent events
    - Event listeners, interfaces that define necessary methods for an object to be modified by occurrence of a particular event
    - Event adaptors, no-op event listener interfaces, needed for subclassing

- Java.applet:

  This package is designed to provide the behavior specifically for applets.

- Java.text:

  This package provides classes and interfaces for internationalization purposes.

- Java.sql:

  This package provides the JDBC APIs. It allows programs to send SQL queries to databases and retrieve results.

- Java.beans:

  This package constitutes the JavaBeans APIs for creating and using embeddable and reusable software components.

- Java.math:

  This package provides two classes used in cryptographic support.

- Java.security:

  This package provides classes and interfaces that represent abstractions of cryptographic security (private and public keys, certificates, digital signature). Two subpackages are available:

  - Java.security.acl: for manipulating access control lists

  - Java.security.interfaces: for independent implementation design

- Java.rmi:

  This package defines fundamental classes and interfaces used for Remote Method Invocation. Three subpackages provide additional functionalities:

  - Java.rmi.dgc: classes and interfaces needed for distributed garbage collection

  - Java.rmi.registry: classes and interfaces required for a Java client to look up for services and for a Java server to advertise the services it provides

  - Java.rmi.server: classes and interfaces that allow a Java program to create an object that can be used remotely by other Java programs.

For a full description of the Java class library and core API, visit the JavaSoft JDK 1.1 (currently 1.1.5 in April 1998) Web page at:
`http://java.sun.com/products/jdk/1.1/docs/index.html`.

Navigating within VisualAge for Java

This section of the appendix introduces the fundamental elements of the VisualAge for Java IDE that are accessed from the Workbench window in the IDE. It covers:

- Starting VisualAge for Java

- The Workbench and its hierarchy:

  - Projects

  - Packages

  - Classes

  - Interfaces

  - Unresolved problems

- Browsers:

  - Project

  - Package

  - Class

Starting VisualAge for Java

During the installation of VisualAge for Java, an item is added to the Windows NT 4.0 Taskbar, **IBM VisualAge for Java for Windows**. This item has a number of subitems, and selecting IBM VisualAge for Java starts VisualAge for Java. Follow a similar process if you are using OS/2 or Windows 95.

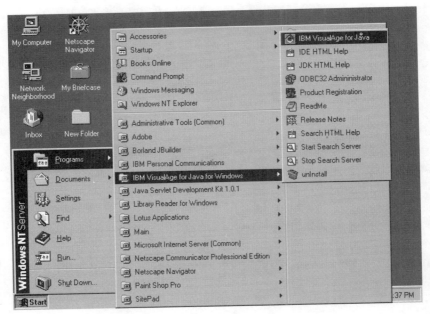

Figure B–1 Starting IBM VisualAge for Java—Windows NT 4.0 Taskbar

During the startup process, VisualAge for Java loads the development image. Because this image can be 8 MB or larger (typically in the 15 MB-25 MB range), the startup process can take one to two minutes because the entire image must be loaded into memory. The development image is also known as the workspace, and these two terms are used interchangeably in this appendix.

If this is the first time VisualAge for Java has been started, the first window displayed is the Quick Start window.

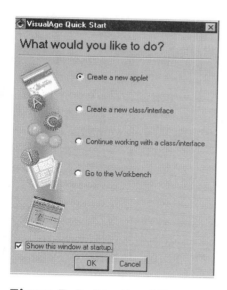

Figure B–2 Starting IBM VisualAge for Java—Quick Start

The Quick Start window provides a single point to perform most of the simple tasks. However, as you become more experienced using VisualAge for Java, you may decide to stop this window from appearing at startup.

Select **Go to the Workbench** and press **OK** to go to the Workbench window.

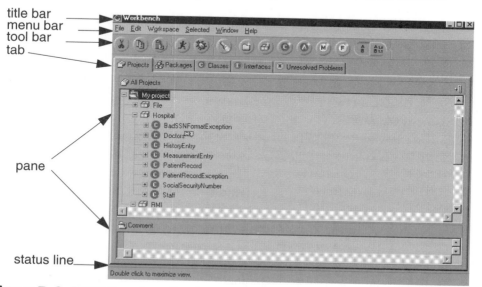

Figure B–3 IBM Visualage for Java—Workbench

The Workbench is the main window into the workspace. You organize your work from the Workbench. From here, you can open several other windows to help with your tasks. As you open windows, navigate in them, create source code, and perform other tasks, the workspace is modified. From the Workbench, you can open specialized windows (called browsers) on individual program elements in the workspace.

The Workbench window is split into a number of areas that are common across most of the VisualAge for Java windows:

- Title bar
- Menu bar
- Tool bar: Provides fast access to menu items
- Notebook tabs: Provides views of the four fundamental components of VisualAge for Java (projects, packages, classes, and interfaces) as well as a tab for displaying any unresolved problems.
- Panes:
  - Hierarchy pane: Typically, displays the component being browsed in context with its containing components. For example, a project browser shows all of its packages, and each package is expandable to show all of the classes/interfaces it contains, and so forth.
  - Source pane: If a method is highlighted in the hierarchy pane, the method source code is displayed in the source pane. Similarly, if a class/interface is highlighted in the hierarchy pane, the class/interface definition is displayed in the source pane.
- Status line: Provides feedback to the user on the current action/mouse position/selection, and so forth.

Component Hierarchy

Source code is stored as structured objects in the following hierarchy of VisualAge program elements:

```
Projects
    Packages
        Classes or Interfaces
            Methods or constructors
```

You are probably already aware of the package, class or interface, and method or constructor components that are part of the standard Java language. In addition, VisualAge for Java includes a higher grouping level called projects, which enables the grouping together of various packages.

Each higher-level component can have multiple lower-level components. For example, a project can contain one or more packages.

Various icons are used in each of the browsers to depict each component. Examples of the icons used are:

Figure B–4 Project, Package, Class, Method, and Run Icons

Workbench Window

In the following Workbench window (Projects tab), the project has been expanded to show its packages. One of these packages, the File Package, has been expanded to show its classes and interfaces (classes only in this case). One of these classes, the GenPR Class, has been expanded to show its method(s). The main (java.lang.String[ ]) method has been selected, and its source is shown in the source pane.

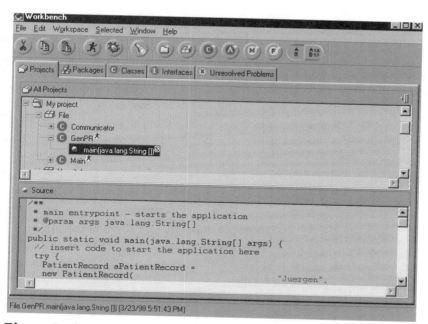

Figure B–5 IBM VisualAge for Java—Workbench Window

There is also a graphical view of the classes contained in this package, but a high-resolution screen is required to gain maximum benefit from this particular view.

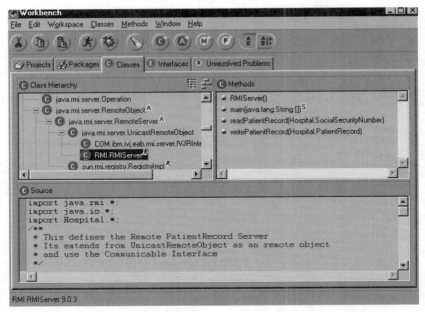

Figure B–6 IBM VisualAge for Java—Class Hierarchy

Component Browsers

The next section discusses the four component browsers used extensively within VisualAge for Java (project, package, class, and interface). Each of the browsers is displayed from the Workbench window by selecting a component in the **Hierarchy Browser Pane** of the Workbench (for example, a package) and then selecting **Open** from its pop-up menu.

Project Browser

The project browser displays details on all the components within the project, including the packages, classes, interfaces, methods, and method source across the first three different views (tabs). The final tab on all the browsers is an Editions tab, which displays the version/edition information about this component, enabling the developer (even in the Professional Edition of VisualAge for Java) to manage multiple versions/editions of packages/classes/interfaces/methods.

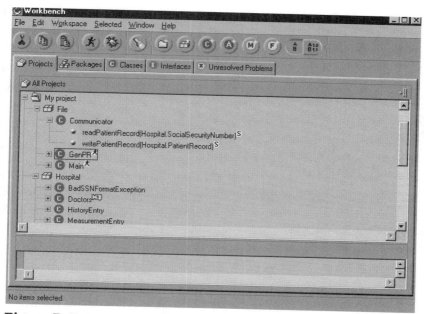

Figure B–7 IBM VisualAge for Java—Project Browser

Package Browser

The package browser displays details on all the components within the package, including the classes, interfaces, methods, and method source across the first two different views (tabs). As with the project browser, the package browser has the editions tab to help manage multiple editions of the package.

The most-used view shows the contained classes in the hierarchy in tree format.

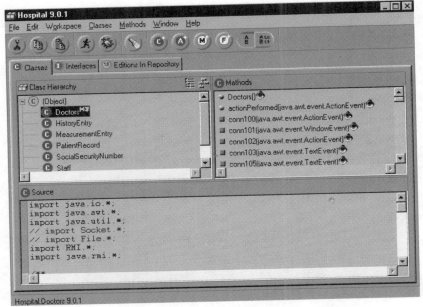

Figure B–8 IBM VisualAge for Java—Package Browser

Class Browser

The class browser is a little different in its implementation when compared with the project and package browsers. The class browser still displays all the subcomponents (methods) it contains: the method source in the lower pane, and an editions tab for managing multiple editions of the components. But in addition, there are four extra tabs:

- The Hierarchy tab displays the position of the class in the hierarchy showing all the superclasses, both in tree and graphical format.

- The Editions in Repository tab shows the editions available for the class in the repository.

- The Visual Composition tab is used primarily for the design of visual classes.

- The Bean Info tab displays information about the features that have been defined for the class (if any) and allows the Bean Info to be modified.

A lot of work is performed using the Visual Composition builder and this is discussed in the next sections. To open this browser, you select a class, click the right mouse, and select Open.

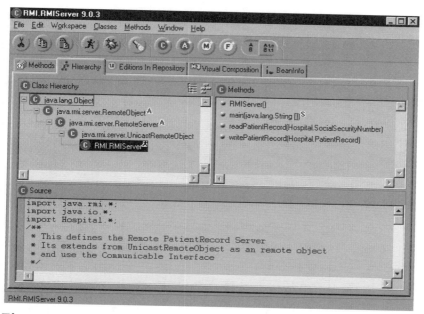

Figure B–9 IBM VisualAge for Java—Class Browser

How It Fits Together

VisualAge for Java uses three basic components to build reusable JavaBeans and to use JavaBeans that may have been built by other tool vendors. These three components are the Visual Composition editor, the Features editor, and the Script editor.

VisualAge for Java comes with a large number of reusable beans or parts that are stored either in the VisualAge image/workspace or that can be brought into the image/workspace from the repository (sometimes called the Parts/Beans Warehouse). Once a class or bean is in the image, a developer can use the Visual Composition editor to connect multiple beans together to perform the required function.

The product can also be used to develop reusable beans or to modify existing beans. This is achieved by using a combination of the Feature editors for properties, methods, and events, and the Script editor for actually writing the Java code that is invoked by the various features.

JavaBeans and Classes

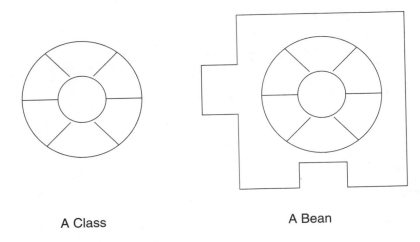

A Class   A Bean

Figure B–10 Class and Bean

A class is a template for objects that have similar behavior (methods) and data elements (variables, properties). To use classes in visual builders (for example, VisualAge for Java, Symantic Cafe), the class needs to have features defined for it that allow it to be connected to other beans within a visual development environment.

JavaBeans add standardized features and object introspection mechanisms to classes, allowing builder tools to query components (classes or groups of classes) about their properties, behavior, and events, thus allowing visual builders to connect beans together that are implemented to the same JavaBeans standard.

Individual JavaBeans vary in functionality, but most share certain common defining features:

- Introspection—allowing a builder tool to analyze how a bean works
- Events—allowing beans to fire events, and informing builder tools about both the events they can fire and the events they can handle
- Properties—allowing beans to be manipulated programatically
- Methods—allowing beans to perform functions implemented by the underlying class methods
- Customization—allowing a user to alter the appearance and behavior of a bean
- Persistence—allowing beans that have been customized in an application builder to have their state saved and restored.

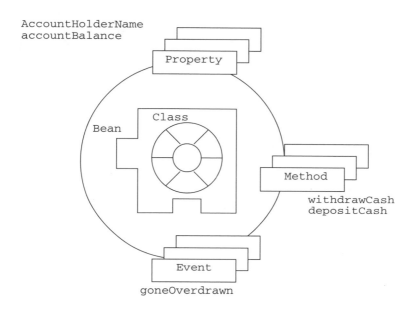

Figure B–11 JavaBeans—Classes, Properties, Methods and Events

In the preceding diagram, an account class has been defined with functions/methods and variables. In addition to the account class definition, bean features have been defined for the following definitions:

- Variable/Property

  AccountHolderName
  AccountBalance

- Method

  WithdrawCash
  DepositCash

- Event

  GoneOverdrawn

In this example, there is probably a one-to-one relationship between the accountHolderName and accountBalance bean properties with instance variables of the same name (defined in the class). There are also the withdrawCash and deposit-Cash methods with bean method features of the same name. However, in addition to these four features, the bean has an event, goneOverdrawn, which is fired from within the `withdrawCash` method. Other JavaBeans can listen for this event before taking action. For example, an `OverDrawnAccounts` object may listen for account objects to fire this event. When the account object fires the `goneOverdrawn` event, the `OverDrawnAccounts` object senses this automatically (because it is listening) and takes its appropriate action (sends a letter informing the account holder of the account status and of the charges that have been applied).

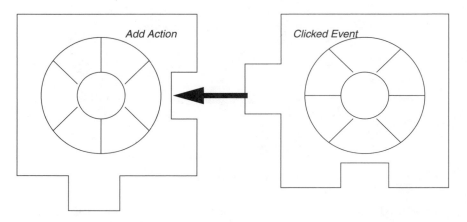

Figure B–12   Events and Actions between JavaBeans

In the preceding figure, there are two classes packaged as beans. The right-most bean (for example, a push button) has a connection to the left-most bean (for example, a listbox) and when the clicked event occurs, the listbox performs the add function. In VisualAge for Java, this connection is made through a series of simple steps that do actually connect the two beans together.

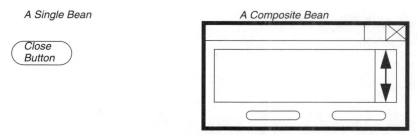

Figure B–13   Single Bean Versus Composite Bean

Beans can either be single beans made up of individual beans/classes, or they can be composite beans made up of two or more classes/beans. In the preceding figure, the pushbutton is a single bean; whereas the window is a composite bean made up of a pushbutton and a list.

The preceding figure represents single and composite beans that are visual. Similar concepts apply to nonvisual classes/beans. For example, an array contains a number of strings.

The previous discussion introduced the concepts (albeit, in overview) of visual builders and of JavaBeans. In VisualAge for Java, you visually construct many modules of your application by connecting various JavaBeans using the Visual Composition editor (VisualAge's visual builder).

The following list summarizes the types of connections that the Composition editor provides. The return value is supplied by the connection's `normalResult` property. If you want to:

- Cause one data value to change another
  - Use the connection type **Property-to-property**
  - The color is dark blue
  - No return Value
- Call a behavior whenever an event occurs
  - Use the connection type **Event-to-method**
  - The color is dark green
  - Return Value
- If you want to supply an input argument
  - Use the connection type **Parameter**
  - The color is violet
  - No return Value

A property-to-property connection links two property values together. This causes the value of one property to change when the value of the other changes. A connection of this type appears as a bidirectional dark blue line with dots at either end. The solid dot indicates the target, and the hollow dot indicates the source. When your part is constructed in the running application, the target property is set to the value of the source property. These connections never take parameters.

An event-to-method connection calls the target method whenever the source event occurs. An event-to-method connection appears as a unidirectional dark green arrow with the arrowhead pointing to the target.

A parameter connection supplies a parameter value to a method by passing either a property's value or the return value from another method. This connection appears as a bidirectional violet line with dots at either end. The solid dot indicates the target, and the hollow dot indicates the source. In addition, the parameter names are included in the connection's pop-up menu. The parameter is always the source of the connection because the parameter cannot store any values. If you connect the parameter as the target, VisualAge reverses the direction of the connection to make the parameter the source.

The Composition editor uses a dashed line to give you a visual clue so that you know when a parameter connection is needed. For example, if you connect an event to a method that requires parameter values, the connection line between the event and the method is dashed.

In the preceding discussion, the source and target points of a connection were introduced.

A connection is directional; it has a source and a target. The direction in which you draw the connection determines the source and target. The part on which the connection begins is the source, and the part on which it ends is the target. When you make an event connection, the Composition editor draws an arrow on the connection line between the two parts. The arrow points from the source to the target. If information can pass through the connection in both directions (as it can in property-to-property connections), a hollow circle indicates the source, and a solid circle indicates the target.

Often, it does not matter which part you choose as the source or target, but there are connections where direction is important. For example, in an event connection, the event is always the source. If you try to make an event the target, VisualAge automatically reverses it for you.

If the target of the connection takes input parameters, the connection line initially appears dashed to show that it is incomplete. Many events pass data through the connection to the target; so the connection line might appear solid even if the target takes one input parameter and you have not otherwise provided one.

The target of a connection can have a return value. If it does, you can treat the return value as a no-set property of the connection and use it as the source of another connection. This return value appears in the connection menu for the connection as normalResult.

Building a Sample Application Window

The objective of this section of the appendix is to build a simple application using VisualAge for Java. The sample application enables an end-user to add parts to a list as if the user were ordering them in a parts ordering application.

Earlier in this appendix, VisualAge for Java was started, and you navigated past the Quick Start window to the Workbench window.

From the **Workbench** window, select the **Selected** menu item; then select the **Add Project**... submenu item

> *Note*
>
> In all future scripts, selected submenu items are formatted the same as this:
> **Selected --> Add Project...**.

The SmartGuide—Add Project window is shown: Type in the name of your Project, Team01Project, and click **Finish**.

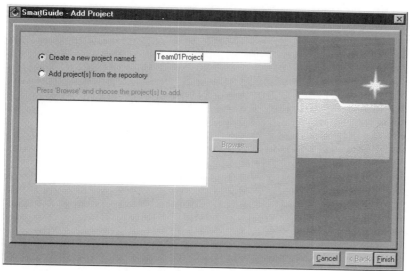

Figure B–14 Add Project SmartGuide

A project named Team01Project is created; you are returned to the Projects tab of the Workbench window, and the Team01Project is highlighted.

Open the Team01Project

Bring up the Team01Project's pop-up menu and select **Open**:

The Team01Project window opens. The title of this window is Team01Project(dd/mm/yy hh:mm:ss am). The time stamp element of the window title is an indication of the date/time when this edition of the project was created. If the Team01Project window does not open up maximized, then maximize it.

Add a New Package (Team01Lab1) to the Team01Project Project

To add a new package, click the right mouse button in the **Packages** pane and select **Add Package** from the pop-up menu.

Select the **Packages --> Add Package...** menu item from the Team01Project window.

Enter Team01Project as the name of the project to which this class is added (this is the default). Enter **Team01Lab1** as the package name and click **Finish** to create it.

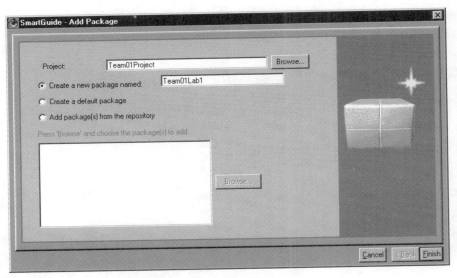

Figure B–15 Add Package SmartGuide

A new package, Team01Lab1, is created in the Team01Project. The new package is shown highlighted in the Packages pane of the Team01Project window.

Add a New Class (Team01OrderEntry) to the Team01Lab1 Package

Select the **Classes/Interfaces --> New Class/Interface...** menu item. Enter **Team01OrderEntry** as the class name. Enter **java.awt.Frame** as the superclass name.

Notice that class names are case sensitive. You are creating a visual class, and most visual classes have java.awt.Frame as their superclass.

Select the **Design the class visually** radio button. Click **Finish** to create the class.

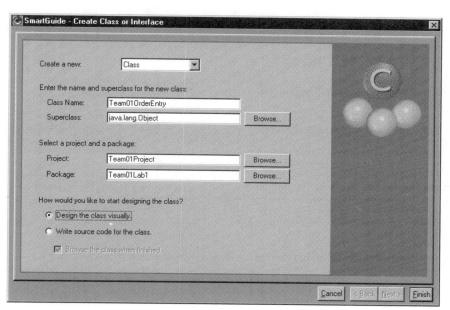

Figure B–16 Add Class SmartGuide

A new class, Team01OrderEntry, is created in the Team01Lab1 package in the Team01Project project. The new class is shown in the classes and interfaces pane of the Team01Project window, and the Visual Composition editor for the Team01OrderEntry class is opened and in focus.

Maximize the Team01Lab1.Team01OrderEntry(dd/mm/yy hh:mm:ss am) window.

The title of the window is Team01Lab1. Team01OrderEntry(dd/mm/yy hh:mm:ss am). The suffix time-stamp element of the window title is an indication of the date/time when this edition of the class was created, and the prefix shows you which package.class you are working on.

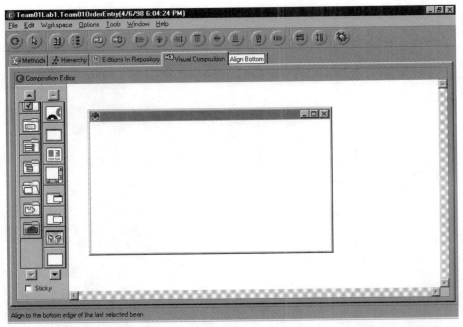

Figure B–17 IBM VisualAge for Java—Visual Composition Editor

Take a moment to review the preceding window to see the various components on the Visual Composition editor.

Window: The window being built, usually in the top-left corner of the free-form surface.

Free-form surface: The white space surrounding the window being built. The free-form surface is usually used to drop nonvisual parts (for example, a timer) that you want to utilize in your class but that you do not want to show to the end user at run time.

Parts palette: The area on the left of the Visual Composition editor window that contains.

> Parts categories (the left-most column/scrollbar) - a container for parts.
>
> Parts (the right-most column/scrollbar) - the parts
>
> > **Sticky**: The checkbox at the bottom of the parts palette. The sticky check-box enables you to load the cursor with a part and to perform multiple drops of that part onto the free-form surface or window.

Add the Visual Components to the Window

The completed window at run time for this section looks similar to this:

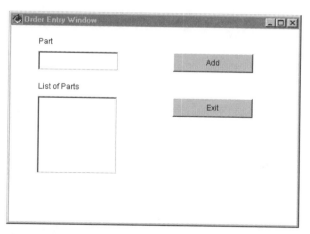

Figure B–18 Order Entry Window Example

Note

Do not be too concerned with the placement and alignment of parts as you are building the window. Later, we will make it look good.

Also increase the size of the window at this point. This makes it easier to add parts. To size a part, click on it to select it. There is a block in each corner that indicates that it is selected. These are called resize handles. Move the mouse pointer over one of these resize handles and press and hold the left mouse button to drag the part to its desired size.

Now we build the Graphical User Interface by selecting parts from the parts palette and placing them on the window. Use the completed window shown previously as a guide. Add:

- One TextField
- Two buttons
- One list
- Two labels

> **Note**
>
> Use the hover help to recognize the parts in the parts palette. Move the mouse pointer over the top of the part and view the online help.

Move the cursor over the parts palette and left-click on the data entry category. Left-click on the **TextField** part. This loads the cursor with the TextField. Move the cursor over the window, near to the left edge (about 10 percent in) and 20 percent down. Left-click to drop the TextField into position. Now left-click on the **Buttons** category. Left-click on the **Button** part. Move the cursor to the right side of the window, about 25 percent in from the right edge and 20 percent down, and drop a button with a left-click; and then drop another button just below the first one. Left-click on the lists category and then on the list part.

Figure B–19 Parts—List

Move the cursor to the left side of the window about 10 percent in and 50 percent up. Left-click to drop the List. Left-click on the **Data Entry** category, and left-click on:

Figure B–20 Labels

Move the cursor to just above the TextField that you dropped earlier and left-click to drop it. Add another TextField just above the list that you dropped earlier.

Make the Window Look Good

Move the cursor over the label just above the TextField. Hold the **Alt** key and left-click (Alt-left). You can now type in the text that is shown on the label. Type the word Part: and then left-click on the free-form surface to stop editing the label text. Move the cursor over the other label and Alt-left. Type List of Parts. Move the cursor over the top button and Alt-left. Type Add. Move the cursor over the bottom button and Alt-left. Type Exit. Move the cursor to the free-form surface and left-click to stop editing. Move the cursor over the Window title bar and double-click to open the Properties Dialog for the window. Left-click in the value column of the title row and type in **Order Entry Window** for the title of the window. Close this window by click on the x in the upper right corner.

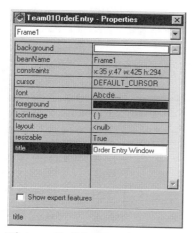

Figure B–21 Window Properties

Move the cursor over the TextField and left-click. Move the cursor over the list and then left-click while holding down the Ctrl key (Ctrl-left). Both parts are now selected. You can tell a part is selected by the re-size handles. When you have two or more parts selected, the alignment smarticons are enabled.

Figure B–22 Align Buttons

This allows you to align left, center, right, top, middle, bottom, space horizontally, vertically, same width, and height.

> *Note*
>
> To learn the function of a smarticon, move the mouse over it and view the help text.

Move the cursor to the bottom right re-size handle of the list. Click and hold the left mouse button, and drag the re-size handle to make the list wider. Release the button when you are happy with the width of the list. Notice that the TextField stretches as well. Now select the Match Width smarticon. This makes the Text-Field the same width as the list. The list is the part of reference because it has the darker re-size handles. Still with the list and Textfield selected, click on the Align-Left smarticon to align their left sides. Move the cursor to the free-form surface and left-click to deselect the part. You now know how to align and size parts. Using your own style and GUI building skills, align the various parts to make the window look cool! Test the application. It does not have any function, but you can see how it looks. Save the Order Entry Window and click on the **Test** smarticon; then click on run on the **Command Line Argument** window to test the application.

Figure B-23 Test Button

You receive a message saying "Generating run-time code". This is the Visual Composition editor saving the layout information into Java code. The developed window is shown. Review it and close the window. You return to the VisualAge Visual Composition window.

Before testing, make sure you have a main method similar to:

```
/**
 * main entrypoint - starts the part when it is run as an application
 * @param args java.lang.String[]
 */
public static void main(java.lang.String[] args) {
    try {
        Team01Lab1.Team01OrderEntry aTeam01OrderEntry = new
            Team01Lab1.Team01OrderEntry();
        aTeam01OrderEntry.getFrame1().setVisible(true);
    } catch (Throwable exception) {
        System.err.println("Exception occurred in main() of"
            +java.lang.Object");
    }
}
```

Add the Function

Move the cursor over the Exit button and left-click to select it. With the cursor still over the Exit button, right-click to bring up the Buttons pop-up menu. Select **Connect** and **action.actionPerformed(java.awt.event.ActionEvent)**.

Figure B–24 Connection

Selecting Connect brings up the features available to you as defined on the button JavaBean. The action.actionPerfomed feature listens or watches for the default action being performed for the part. For a button, the default action is the button being pressed or clicked.

The spider is shown. The spider allows you to connect parts (beans) together. Move the spider to the window title bar and left-click. The connection target pop-up window is displayed.

What happens when the Exit button is pressed? You want the window to be closed/disposed.

Select **dispose()** from the pop-up window. A green connection is displayed between the Exit button and the window.

You are now ready to visually perform the function to add text entries from the TextField to the list. Move the cursor over the Add button and left-click to select it. With the cursor still over the Add button, right-click to bring up the Buttons pop-up menu. Select **Connect**, and **action.actionPerformed**. Move the spider to the list and left-click. The connection target pop-up window is displayed.

What happens when the Add button is pressed? You want the text/string entered in the TextField to be added to the list. Select **add** (java.lang.String) from the pop-up window.

A dashed green connection is displayed between the Add button and the list. You have now completed half of this connection. You have told VisualAge that when the Add button is pressed, something is added to the list, but you have not specified what is added. You can do this now.

Move the cursor over the dashed green connection from the Add button to the list. Left-click over the connection. Selection handles are shown along the connection to show that it has been selected. With the cursor still over the connection (but not on a selection handle), right-click to bring up the Connections pop-up menu and select **Connect --> Item**.

Figure B–25 Connection

Move the resulting spider over the TextField. Left-click and select **Text**. A purple arrow joins the TextField to the green connection. Do not forget that VisualAge colors each connection depending on its type. You have now completed the window for this section.

Test it out by selecting the **Test** smarticon. Enter some values in the TextField and check if the Add button adds them to the list. Test the Exit button.

This is how our completed VisualAge window looks; your window may look similar.

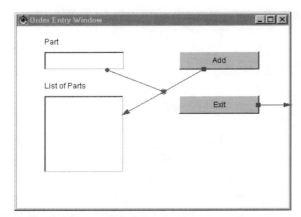

Figure B–26 Designing Connections

Version Your Application

Left-click on the **Hierarchy** tab. The class hierarchy is displayed showing the Team01OrderEntry class and its superclasses. Left-click on **Team01Lab1.Team01OrderEntry** to select it. Select the **Classes-->Version...** menu item. Make sure the **Automatic** radio button is selected and click on the **Finish** button.

Your class is now versioned. You can change the class at any time but you can also go back to this version of the Team01OrderEntry class whenever you need to.

Extending the Application

The application is now extended, and the following actions are performed:

- Add a quantity field.

- Modify the behavior so that the Add pushbutton invokes a script to concatenate the part and quantity details and then displays them in the list.

- Add a Delete button to delete existing entries in the list.

- Enable/disable the Delete button when an item is selected/deselected in the list.

- Add a Java script breakpoint and modify code when the breakpoint is invoked.

At the end of this section of the appendix, the completed development window should look similar to this:

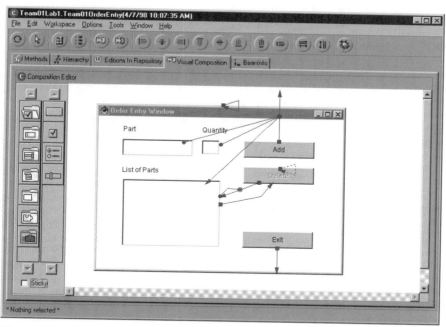

Figure B–27 New Application Connections

Add Standard GUI Parts

Click on the Visual Composition tab to get back to the Visual Composition editor.

- Add a Delete button to the window.

  Disable the Delete button. To modify a component's properties, double left-click on the component to bring up its Properties window. Check on expert features, then single left-click inside the value column for the property name you want to modify (to bring focus to the value) and change the value as appropriate. Change the enabled property to false and the label to Delete.

- Add a TextField that allows the quantity of parts to be input (called the Quantity TextField later).

  Place it level with and a little to the right of the part TextField. You may need to move some components around, and you may even have to make the window a little larger. To resize any component, single left-click and hold down over a resize handle and drag the mouse to the required size. Release the mouse button to end resizing.

- Add a label part and change its text property to Quantity.

Delete Connections

You can add items from the TextFields to the list using a script in this section. Therefore, the current connection from the Add button (action.actionPerformed) to the list (add(java.lang.String)), taking the Text property from the TextField, is removed. Move the cursor to the green connection from the Add button to the list (the one just described). Single left-click over the connection and resize handles should appear on it. If they do not appear, you are not exactly over the connection; move the cursor and try again if this is the case. Press the **Delete** key and select **OK** when prompted by the confirmation message. The connection and any connections it was supporting are deleted.

Write a New Java Method to Add Part/Quantity Text to the List

To add both the part and quantity text to the list, write a script to concatenate the two TextFields together. Single left-click on the **Methods** tab and select the **Methods --> New Method...** menu item. In the Method Name entry field of the Method Properties Window, enter String formatLine (String part, String qty) and select the **Finish** button.

Figure B–28 Add Method SmartGuide

A new method called `formatLine` is created that takes two String variables (part and quantity) and returns a string (the concatenated string).

```
/** * This method was created by a SmartGuide.
* @return java.lang.String
* @param part java.lang.String
* @param qty java.lang.String
*/
public String formatLine(String part, String qty) {
return;
}
```

Modify the `formatLine` method source as shown in the following example and use **Ctrl-S** to save the modified method.

```
return part + " " + qty;
```

Single left-click on the **Visual Composition** tab to return to editing the window.

Make the Connections to Add the Part/Quantity to the List

Start the connection from the action.actionPerformed event of the Add button and drop the spider over the free-form surface. The free-form surface is outside the window that you are building. The connection target pop-up menu appears. Select the **Event to Script...** menu item. The following window is shown that lists all of the scripts you can connect to for the class being developed.

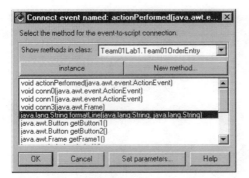

Figure B–29 Connections to Add Part/Quantity to List

Select the **java.lang.String formatLine(java.lang.String, java.lang.String)**
script and select **OK**.

A light green dashed connection is shown from the Add button to the free-form
surface. A dashed connection means that the connection requires parameters that
have not yet been supplied. Connect the part parameter for the preceding light
green dashed connection to the text property of the part TextField.

- Connect the quantity parameter for the preceding light green dashed connection to the text property of the quantity TextField.

- Connect the `normalResult` parameter for the preceding light green dashed
  connection to the `addItem(java.lang.String)` method of the list.

- Try testing the application to see if you can add parts to the list using the
  script that you just created.

- Return back to the Visual Composition editor.

Make the Connections for the Delete Button

Connect the `action.actionPerformed` event of the Delete button to the
`remove(java.lang.String)` action of the list. There is a dashed green line connection from the Delete button to the list.

- Click on the list to select it.

- Connect the `selectedItem` property of the list to the item parameter of the connection between the Delete button and the list. The green connection now
  should become a solid green line.

- Connect the `itemStateChanged` event (that is, an event is fired when the
  selected item changes) of the list to the enabled() action of the Delete button.
  There is a dashed green connection between the list and the delete button.

- Double-click on the dashed green connection to open it. Click on **Expert features** and then use the **Set parameters** button to set the value to **True**. This enables the button when an item is selected in the list.

- Connect the `action.actionPerformed` event of the Delete button to the `enabled()` action of the Delete button. You can leave the parameter default as false; this disables the button.

Test the part and add some part/quantity items to the list. Try to select some items from the list to see if you can delete them. The Delete button should only be enabled when an item is selected in the list. Keep the test window running and continue with the next section.

Debugging Code, Setting Breakpoints, and Changing Code

With the Test window still running, return to the class browser/editor Methods tab page. Modify the code of the `formatLine` method so that the line return part + " " + qty; now reads return part + " : " + qty. Save the part with **Ctrl-S**. Add another part/quantity item and see that the code you changed was used to add this new part. Your test window should look similar to this:

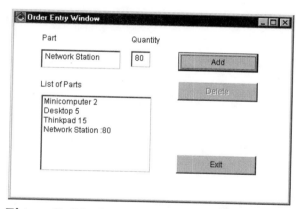

Figure B–30 Running the Application

With the Test window still running, return to the Class browser/editor Methods tab page. Move the cursor to the method source pane on the
```
return part + " : " + qty;
```
line. Right-click the mouse and select **Insert/Remove Breakpoint**. A blue breakpoint marker is shown. This is the point where the code stops prior to executing it and opens up a debugger window. If the blue breakpoint marker does not appear, you probably were not in the first column, or you were on an incorrect line.

```
Source
/**
 * This method was created by a SmartGuide.
 * @return java.lang.String
 * @param part java.lang.String
 * @param qty java.lang.String
 */
public String formatLine (String part, String qty) {
    return part + "." + qty;
}
```

Figure B–31 The IBM VisualAge for Java Debugger - Source Window

Add another part/quantity item to the running test window. The debugger window is shown.

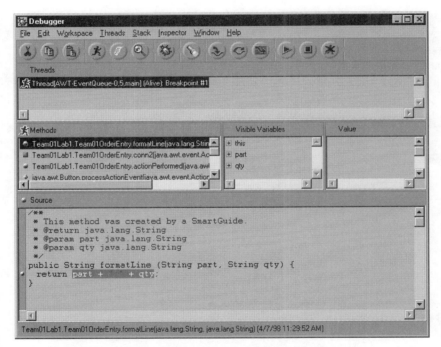

Figure B–32 IBM VisualAge for Java—The Debugger

The code has stopped prior to executing the statement. The uppermost pane shows the current thread when the debugger was invoked. In the three middle panes, the left-hand pane shows the call stack with the most recent method at the top (call stack pane), the center pane shows the variables that are accessible (variables pane), and the right pane shows the value of the currently selected variable (variable value pane). The bottom pane shows the current line in the current method (method source pane). Single left-click on the part variable in the variables pane. The variable value pane is updated and displays the string value of whatever you typed into your part TextField. As you are aware, a string is an array of characters. Expand the part variable you have selected with a single left-click on the plus (+). Then expand the resulting char [ ] value entry. Select entry **0**, then **1** (this assumes you typed in a part with two or more characters). The variable value pane shows you the values of the first two characters you typed into your part TextField.

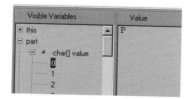

Figure B–33 The IBM VisualAge for Java Debugger—Variables

Now single left-click on the Team01Lab1.Team01OrderEntry.connx(java.awt.event.ActionEvent) entry in the call stack pane (notice your entry is similar to conn1). You see that the variables pane, variable value pane, and method source pane are all updated. In the method source pane, the actual code that called the current method is highlighted (this.formatLine(getTextField12().getText(), getTextField11().getText());). Navigate to the Methods pane of the Team01OrderEntry Class editor/browser, traverse the list of methods, and select the **connx** (for example, conn1) method. This is the method that you are currently looking at in the debugger. Return to the debugger window. Select the top entry in the call stack pane, **Team01Lab1.Team01OrderEntry.formatLine(java.lang.String)**. Now modify the code so that the string " : " now reads " :- ". **Ctrl-S** to save the method. Select the **Resume** button. The debugger window blanks out as that thread has now run to completion. Close the debugger window and navigate back to the running test window. Your part/quantity entry has been added and with the " :- " separator between the part and quantity.

Anywhere you have a method source window, you can modify the method, save it, and it runs immediately with the updated code. Now select an entry in the list of the running test window. The Delete button is now enabled. Test it out by deleting the entry. The entry is deleted, and the Delete button is disabled (until you select another entry in the list).

Close It Down and Version

Close the Team01Lab1.Team01OrderEntry Class editor/browser. Version the class by either accepting the default version name or by entering your own. Save the workspace.

Team Development

Team development will be enabled in VisualAge for Java with the incorporation of the ENVY/Developer from OTI, an IBM Subsidiary company. Team development will be available as part of VisualAge for Java Enterprise.

> **Important Information**
>
> Team support is not available in the currently released product, but is planned in a later release.

For an individual, this allows a developer the freedom to develop code independently from the rest of the development team, yet still within the scope of the overall project. A developer can recall at any time a history of individual changes made to any component made within the developer's image/workspace and retrieve prior versions of a component should this be appropriate. This total flexibility in development allows a developer to try things out in the knowledge that, at any time, a prior frozen version of a component can be recalled. The component to be recalled can be an individual method, an entire class/interface, a package, or a complete project.

Version control within the team development provides facilities to freeze the development of a component (class, package, or project) so that no changes can be made to that component. This is extremely useful when checkpointing components within a development cycle.

With the Enterprise Edition, multiple developers can, if appropriate, work on any component (project, package, class, or method) concurrently. In a normal check-in, check-out philosophy, this is impossible, but within the VisualAge for Java Enterprise Edition, this can be achieved. Despite this flexibility, component integrity is never compromised. For further information, see the VisualAge for Java documentation.

In the Professional Edition, each developer has a unique repository that stores every component available, although the developer may only have a subset of components in the image. However, in the Enterprise Edition, every developer shares a common repository, allowing all the work to be shared and accessed concurrently, online and in real time.

Just as in the Professional Edition, the Enterprise Edition records all changes made to any component and who made that change. In the Enterprise Edition, there are facilities to enable the access control rights for individual developers to every component within the repository.

Therefore, because of the ease of development with fallback facilities, the development in a RAD type environment is positively encouraged by the tool but with all the management controls should they be necessary.

The configuration of VisualAge for Java places a development image/workspace on the client and a repository on the client/file server in the Professional Edition. In the Enterprise Edition, the repository has to be placed on a shared file server. The repository holds a copy of every version of every component for the development team, whereas the image/workspace contains only the requested version of a subset of components. As an example, Developer1 may be working on GUI projects, packages, and classes, and Developer2 may be working on Data access packages, packages, and classes. The shared repository (the Enterprise Edition) holds every edition/version of all these components, but, for example, the Developer2 image/workspace holds only the Data access components and not the GUI components.

In a team development environment using a file server for the repository code, changes made by a developer to any component get written back immediately to the repository. Therefore, the component change is immediately made available to all other developers who may be using the component. On a nightly basis (as part of the regular systems management procedures), the repository should be backed up to external media.

When a developer starts VisualAge for Java, the image/workspace gets copied from disk into memory, and it is this copy of the image that the developer works with when adding/deleting/changing components. It is vital that the developer saves this "in-memory" image to disk on a regular basis (for example, once per hour). It is not catastrophic if the developer receives a GPF after an entire series of changes since every component is still available in the repository. However, rebuilding the image from scratch may take an hour or two.

In addition, at regular intervals (for example, at lunch time and at end-of-day), each individual developer should copy their working image/workspace to the file server, and these again should be backed up on a nightly basis.

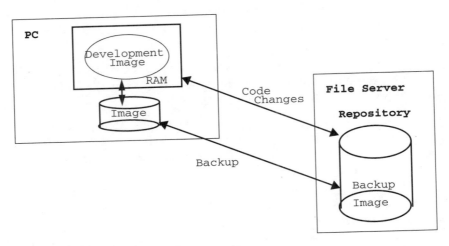

Figure B–34 Change Management

The team development facilities enable the versioning and editing of components. This is a simple process where the developer can create a version of a component at any time where a version is a frozen component that cannot be changed. Therefore, in the following diagram, there are three separate versions of the component. The developer can assign each version a unique name, and in the example, the versions are 1.0, 1.1, and 2.0. As with most things in VisualAge for Java, a component can be any class/interface, package, or project, and the developer explicitly versions these components. Methods are the exception, and these get versioned automatically every time a change is made to them.

Figure B–35 Versioning

The big question is..."If a component is a version and a version is just another name for a frozen component that cannot be changed, then how do I change a versioned component?" The answer to this is to create an edition of the component. An edition of a component is editable, but the original version of the component remains in the repository should the developer need to go back to it at any time. Therefore, the process for creating, freezing, and changing a component (let's say Class A) is as follows:

- Create Class A (it gets created as an edition):

  Write methods

  Define variables

- Version Class A as Class A 1.0:

  Class A is frozen and cannot be changed.

- Edition Class A:

  Class A can now be edited again, but version 1.0 is still available and it needs to be restored.

- Version Class A as Class A 2.0

Change Management

VERSION: A totally frozen entity, class, project (V 1.1)

VERSIONING: Making a frozen entity from an edition

EDITION: An editable entity, class, application (time stamping)

EDITIONING: Making editable an entity from a version

Applet Viewer

The VisualAge for Java Applet Viewer is incorporated into the IDE. This enables a developer to develop Java applets and to test them without having to boot up a separate Web browser (for example, Netscape). The applet viewer is a primitive viewer and should only be used for debugging purposes, with the final testing being performed in a real-life Web browser. However, because the applet viewer comes with VisualAge for Java, it supports the level of the JDK supported by the IDE (currently JDK 1.1), whereas you may not be certain of this level of support in some Web browsers. For example, the current level of Netscape supports most but not all JDK 1.1 APIs.

VisualAge for Java has an applet creation SmartGuide that is accessed through its smarticon on the toolbar.

The applet creation SmartGuide walks the developer through the process of creating an applet and completing the tasks that usually are hand-coded into the applet. One of the windows that is displayed as part of the SmartGuide is included here as an example of the type of information the applet creation Smart-Guide can process. The SmartGuide - Applet Properties window allows the setting of applet/application and thread details. Many applets can be run as stand-alone applets and stand-alone applications. In the latter case, a `main()` method needs to be created. In addition, should the applet perform a long-running task or repeatable task (such as repeating animation), it is advisable to write this as a separate thread. Again, the SmartGuide provides the option of creating the applet to use its own thread.

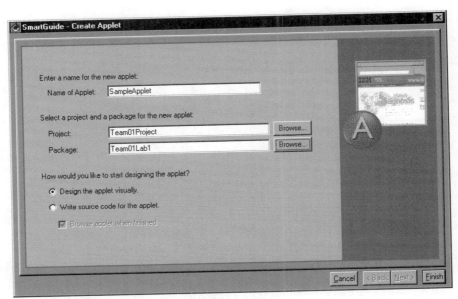

Figure B–36 Create Applet SmartGuide

After the applet has been created from the SmartGuide, use the class browser to view it and to see its place in the class hierarchy. As you expect, the applet inherits from java.applet.Applet, and its required methods are generated also (`init()`, `start()`, `stop()`, `destroy()`, `paint()`).

From the applets pop-up menu, select the **run --> In Applet Viewer** menu item to run the applet in the applet viewer. Outside of the IDE, an HTML file is required to wrapper the applet so it can run in a Web browser. The HTML file specifies the width, height, parameters, and so on of the applet. Within the VisualAge for Java IDE, this HTML file is not required. As part of the applet viewer, the Settings window is displayed that asks the developer to input these HTML settings prior to the applet running.

Settings for Team01Lab1.SampleApplet

Enter the applet's attributes and parameters:

Attributes

WIDTH: 200

HEIGHT: 200

NAME:

Parameters

\<param name=... value=...\>
Example: \<param name=timesToRun value=5\>

Classpath

..\project_resources\Team01Project;

Codebase

SampleApplet will run with CODEBASE = file:///C:/IBMVJava/ide/project_resources/Team01Project

Run   Cancel   Save   Reset

Figure B-37 Run Applet

Editor/Debugger/SmartGuides

In an object-oriented application development environment, developers need to perform many similar tasks as procedural developers, but in addition, they perform a number of different tasks as part of a RAD development process. Specific to Java, these tasks include: add a project, package, or class interactively.

A new project, package, or class can be added interactively (for example, a new class can be created from many different places in the IDE including the Workbench, Project Browser, Package Browser, and so on).

- Add or change a method:

    Adding or changing a method is probably the most important task of an application developer because this is the code that is actually executed in the running application. VisualAge for Java provides the capability to change a method at virtually any point. All browsers allow method source editing, and the debugger also allows methods to be added and edited.

- Evaluate an expression:

    Wherever a method can be entered or edited, an expression can be evaluated. For example, a developer may write a complex, concatenated line of Java code that needs to be tested. Instead of running the complete application, in many cases, VisualAge for Java allows the code snippet to be highlighted and run as is (provided it is a stand-alone piece of code).

For example, in any Method Source pane, the following code can be entered, selected, and run:

```
System.out.println("Hello World!")
```

Hello World is displayed on the console window (the standard output device of the IDE).

- Invoke methods:

  As previously discussed, most code can be evaluated "on the spot" without running an application; it follows from this that most methods can also be evaluated/invoked "on the spot."

- Test, debug, set breakpoints:

  The debugger within the IDE is a powerful aid to the developer. It enables breakpoints to be set, to hop over methods, to hop into methods, to run methods to completion, to interactively patch code, and to add new method classes while the running thread is held.

- Patch code:

  As previously stated, code can be patched at any time within the development cycle without losing the original code. This includes patching running code that may have caused the debugger to be invoked.

- Compile class/method incrementally:

  Outside of the IDE, a developer must modify the class as a complete unit. Therefore, if only one line of a method needs modifying, then the entire .JAVA file needs to be edited and compiled. Within the VisualAge for Java IDE, individual methods can be edited and saved incrementally without the need to recompile the entire class that contains the method being changed.

- Maintain project database:

  The team development environment has already been introduced in this chapter, and it is this team development environment that provides a complete project database for the development team.

- Syntax check code:

  VisualAge for Java detects syntax errors that occur when code violates Java syntax rules. If, for example, you misspell a keyword or forget a semicolon, a message dialog box informs you of the type of syntax error when you try to save the code. In addition, the input cursor in the Source pane automatically selects the piece of code that caused the problem.

The Editor Pane

The editing pane (elsewhere called the Method Source pane) allows the developer to:

- Perform editing operations

- Undo/Redo:

  This option is accessed from the Edit--Revert menu item.

- Search in the workspace (image) for highlighted text:

  A developer can highlight some text and then select **Search** from the pop-up menu to search the workspace for references to or declarations of the highlighted text.

- Insert and remove breakpoints for debugging:

  A breakpoint is inserted/removed by moving the cursor to the left margin of the line requiring a breakpoint and double-clicking. In the IDE, this forces the debugger window to appear just before execution of this line.

- Save your changes:

  When changes are saved for a method, the entire method is syntax-checked before it is saved. At any time, the previous version can be restored.

- Cancel your changes:

  If changes have been made to a method and the developer selects another method to change without saving the pending changes, a warning dialog is displayed asking whether the pending changes should be saved or not.

- Editor setup:

  The editor has some default settings and these can be modified. The default settings are as follows:

  - Browser Font—Serif 10

  - Comment—Red

  - Default Text—Courier 10

  - Error—Red

  - Keyword—Blue

  - Literal String—Green

The Debugger

As you work in the integrated development environment, you need not launch a special debugger virtual machine or start the virtual machine in debug mode. The debugger opens automatically when you need it. It opens when:

- Execution hits a breakpoint that you inserted

- An uncaught exception occurs

- You select the debug button on any menu bar

You can use the debugger to step through code and inspect and change variables. You can also fix a bug by modifying the source from within the debugger.

VisualAge activates the debugger when one of a program's threads encounters a breakpoint. The top pane (the threads pane) displays the current thread that was created when you started the applet/application and the debugger invoked for whatever reason. In VisualAge, you create a thread (or multiple threads) whenever you run a program or evaluate code in the Scrapbook. When the debugger opens on a breakpoint, the threads pane displays the thread that caused the debugger to open. The entry consists of an internal identifier for the thread and an indication of what caused the debugger to open.

The middle part is divided into three panes that give more details of the current state of processing the code. From left to right, they are:

- Stackframes pane
- Variables pane: A text pane that displays the current value of a selected variable in the variables pane
- Source pane

The stackframes pane (or thread stack pane) displays a stack trace as a list of stackframes. Each stackframe corresponds to a method that was called. Stackframes are in reverse chronological order (the most recent stackframe is the top item). The debugger lets you manipulate thread execution by dropping to a particular stackframe in the stackframes pane. This is particularly useful if the debugger opens on an uncaught exception, since it lets you back up and repeat the steps that caused the exception to be thrown.

The Source pane displays the source of the selected method.

The Variables pane displays a list of all the locally visible variables for the current stackframe. If you select a variable, its current value is displayed in the text/variable pane.

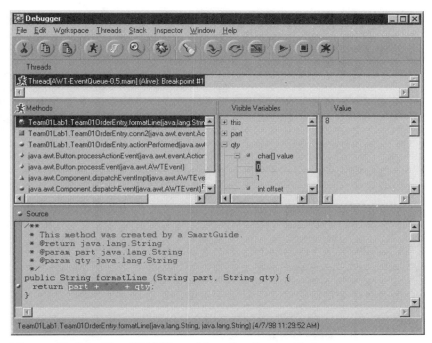

Figure B–38 The IBM VisualAge for Java—Debugger

Stepping through Methods

With the debugger's navigation buttons, you can step through the current method. You can use the buttons to process the current statement (which is the one that is automatically selected), step into it, execute until the method returns, or resume processing the thread. When the debugger opens on a breakpoint, all the navigation buttons are enabled. By contrast, if the debugger opens because of an uncaught exception, the navigation buttons are disabled because the current process has hit a dead end. In this case, you must first drop the stackframe that throws the exception to reset the current status of processing.

- Into:

  Steps into the current statement and invokes the method (if any). A new stackframe is added to the list, and the Source pane displays the source of the method that you stepped into. Use this button to follow a method and determine what it does.

- Over:

  Executes the statement that is currently selected in the Source pane. The values of local variables are updated.

- Return:

  Executes all statements in the method that is currently selected in the stack-frame's pane until the method is about to return and then stops. All local variables are updated.

- Resume:

  Continues processing. Select this button to continue running the program. If the program is resumed successfully, its thread is removed from the debugger.

Inspectors

You can use an inspector to view the state of objects or variables that hold objects. With the inspector, you can:

- Inspect the result of evaluating a code fragment in the Scrapbook or in the Variables pane of the debugger

- Open a browser on the declarations of an object's class

- Evaluate code fragments in the context of an object

- Change the value of an object

Using the Inspector: As an example, open an inspector on a string array object by copying the following code to a page in the scrapbook.

```
String[ ] [ ] info = {
{ "Red", "Number", "R of RGB" },
{ "Green", "Number", "G of RGB" },
{ "Blue", "Number", "B of RGB" }};
return info;
```

Select the code and select **Inspect** from the pop-up menu. The inspector appears and shows the array object stored in the info variable. The title bar displays the identifier for the class of the inspected object (a two-dimensional string array). The title bar also shows the context from which you opened the inspector (from Page 1).

The Fields pane shows the elements of the array. The Value pane shows the value of a selected field.

The info array maps to a table with three rows and three columns (indexed 0 through 2). The top-level items in the Fields pane map to the three rows. By expanding items 0 through 2, you see that each row consists of three columns.

Select the second row in the first column (**info[1][.0]**). It holds the parameter name Green. Internally, the string Green is represented as an array of characters that you can view in more detail by expanding the tree in the Fields pane. The icon () to the left of the character array indicates that the internal representation is private.

Changing the Value of an Object

You can change the value of fields while you are inspecting an object. Follow these steps.

1. In the Fields pane, select the field that you want to modify.

2. In the Value pane, replace the text with the value you want in the field.

3. Select **Save** from the pop-up menu.

The expression in the Value pane is evaluated, and if the result can be assigned to the object, it is. When the code resumes, it uses the value. If the result cannot be assigned, the inspector displays an error message.

Other VisualAge for Java Windows

The following section describes other VisualAge for Java windows.

The Scrapbook

The Scrapbook helps you organize code fragments and notes. You can run any Java statement or expression from the scrapbook and control the context in which it is compiled.

To open the scrapbook, select **Scrapbook** from any window pull-down menu. The scrapbook appears with an empty page. From the scrapbook, you can run the code fragment or open an inspector on the object that is returned as the result of running the code. To open an inspector, select **Inspect** from the pop-up menu of the selected code fragment.

For example, most programming languages and environments take developers through the "Hello World" application as the first exercise in learning a new language/environment. With VisualAge for Java, this can be achieved in under a minute.

Hello World in Under a Minute:

1. Select **Scrapbook** from the Window pull-down menu.

2. Type: `System.out.println("Hello World!");`

3. Select the line of code that you typed in Step 2.

4. Select **Run** from the pop-up menu.

The console (the standard output device) appears and displays the string Hello World!. The example works. The code was automatically compiled by the built-in Java compiler and then run by the built-in Java Virtual Machine.

The Console

The console is the standard output device (System.out) for Java programs that you run in VisualAge.

The Repository Explorer

With the Repository Explorer, you can explore the repository to view program components that are not present in the workspace/image.

The Log

The log displays messages and warnings from VisualAge

SmartGuides/Wizards

The VisualAge for Java IDE comes with various SmartGuides (also known as Wizards in other IDEs) that guide the developer through the repeatable process of creating a component.

For example, the Class Creation SmartGuide takes the developer through the standard process of creating a class including the following setup parameters:

- Is this a class or an interface?
- Which project is the class defined in?
- Which package is the class defined in?
- What is the class name?
- Which class is the superclass?
- What happens when the SmartGuide completes?
  - Open a Visual Composition editor (for example, if the class inherits from java.awt.Frame).
  - Open a class browser.
  - Do not open a browser.
- Which interfaces (if any) does the class implement?
- Which modifiers should be implemented?
  - Public
  - Abstract
  - Final
  - Should stub methods be generated?

There are a number of SmartGuides, including class creation, interface creation, method creation, and applet creation.

Proxy Builder

The VisualAge for Java development environment includes a Java proxy builder that allows the development of JavaBeans to enable a local JavaBean to access another JavaBean located in another Java Virtual Machine (local or remote) by using a Java proxy object.

In VisualAge for Java, the RMI access builder can generate proxy code for a Java-Bean in such a way that this JavaBean can be made accessible remotely through the builder-generated proxy code. A client-side server proxy, server-side server proxy, and supporting interface code are generated for each user JavaBean. A distributed client/server application can easily be created using these proxies. A client application can use the generated client-side server proxy as if it were a local object even though service requests to the client-side server proxy are actually sent over to the user JavaBean through RMI.

> *Note*
>
> In this release, you can only create servers out of JavaBeans that are generated by the C++ access builder. The tool to create distributed access for user-written JavaBeans is not yet available.

To enable a Java application to access a Java server over RMI:

1. Create or modify the packages.
2. Create the JavaBeans.
3. Import the JavaBeans into the Enterprise Access Builders.
4. Generate the distribution proxies as JavaBeans.
5. Export the generated JavaBeans.
6. Import the generated JavaBeans into the IDE.
7. Write the business logic.
8. Assemble the client.
9. Assemble the server.
10. Build the application.
11. Deploy the application.
12. Run the application.
    Regenerate code.

Enterprise Access Builders (EAB)

The Enterprise Access Builders provides a graphical method to organize, create, and package parts generated by the following subcomponents:

- Enterprise Access Builder for data (Data Access Builder)
- Enterprise Access Builder for CICS (CICS Access Builder)

These subcomponents produce JavaBeans for access to transactions and databases.

The following operations are available from the Enterprise Access Builders:

- Create a package to organize parts into Java packages.
- Create data access parts to provide access to the Data Access Builder.
- Create CICS parts to access CICS transactions using CICS ECI.
- Create Jar file to package multiple parts into a JAR file.

In this appendix, we focus only on the Data Access Builder.

Data Access Builder (DAX)

VisualAge for Java—Enterprise Access Builder for Data (referred to as Data Access Builder or DAX) is an application development tool that you can use to create data access classes customized for your existing relational database tables. It allows you to create object-oriented applications quickly and reliably by generating the source code for you. These data access classes (which are JavaBeans) can be used directly in your Java programs and by the VisualAge for Java IDE.

Some of the key features of the Data Access Builder are:

- JDBC to access your database:

  Data Access Builder generates code that uses JDBC to access your database. You can use the JDBC driver in IBM DB/2, JDBC-ODBC bridge in JDK Version 1.1 or other JDBC drivers with the generated code.

- Flexibility in specifying source:

  Data Access Builder generates code from database tables, from database views, or from SQL statements that you type in.

- Quick and simple to use:

  You can simply specify a database table name and Data Access Builder can access the table information and generate Java source code that allows you to add, update, delete, or retrieve the data in that table.

- Data manipulation operations:

  Generated classes customized to your data help you perform common database tasks such as adding, retrieving, updating, and deleting data. Classes are also generated to allow you to use a cursor to fetch rows from database queries that return result sets.

- Add your own methods:

  You can add your own methods by typing in SQL statements; Data Access Builder generates the Java source code for you.

- Stored procedure support:

  You can use Data Access Builder to generate code that calls stored procedures.

- Generate code for table joins:

  You can specify table joins using SQL statements, and Data Access Builder can generate Java classes for them.

- Connection and transaction services:

  Separate services are provided for connection and disconnection from your databases. In addition, commit and rollback methods are generated to handle transaction services.

System Requirements

The current release of VisualAge for Java has the following system requirements:

- Processor: 32-bit processor (Pentium or higher, or compatible processor)

- Display: SVGA 800 x 600 minimum (1024 x 768 recommended)

- Operating system: Windows NT 4.0, Windows 95, or OS/2 Warp 4.0

- Other software: TCP/IP, DAX with DB2 at the appropriate level on the server side. Support for other databases through ODBC is also available. An ODBC driver is required and is not shipped with VisualAge for Java.

- Memory: 32 MB minimum (64 MB or more recommended)

- Disk space:

  EAB = 55 MB
  EAB + IDE = 90 MB
  Swap space = 30 MB

Summary

In summary, VisualAge for Java is a full member of the VisualAge family. It allows application developers to develop applications and Web-based applets using the Java language.

VisualAge for Java includes a powerful and full-function integrated development environment. The IDE is JDK 1.1 compliant, allowing the edit/compile/test of Java applications within the IDE prior to exporting the code for running in other JDK 1.1-compliant virtual machines and Web browsers. Because of its compliance with the JDK 1.1 API, the VisualAge for Java environment supports Java APIs for accessing remote components through the RMI and JDBC APIs.

Because of the portability of JDK 1.1-compliant Java code, code that is developed using VisualAge for Java should be able to run anywhere without change.

The IDE enables a developer to build and run applications, applets, and code snippets interactively without the need to run the compile statement (JavaC) from the command line. All applications can be run from within the IDE without the need to export the Java source or class files. This is achieved through the provision of a JDK 1.1-compliant Virtual Machine (VM) within the IDE and an applet viewer. Because you can interactively modify code and run it without compilation, developers are able to debug code on the fly, spot errors in their code with the debugger, change it, and then continue without bringing the running application down—all within the VisualAge for Java IDE.

VisualAge for Java is an open IDE, and developers can easily import and export Java source and class files as well as JavaBeans, which may have been purchased by the company or made available on the WWW. The JavaBeans support in VisualAge for Java also enables a developer to take an existing JavaBean (for example, from the WWW), import it into VisualAge for Java, modify the bean, and then export it again for use within another JDK 1.1-compliant development environment (for example, Symantec Cafe and Borlands JBuilder).

The Enterprise Access Builder (EAB) provides components to aid connection to DB2-compliant data sources, CICS transactions, and other programs. It extends the VisualAge for Java capabilities to make client/server programming easier.

Appendix C

Special Notices

This publication is intended to help program designers to develop applications for thin Java clients such as the IBM Network Station 1000. The information in this publication is not intended as the specification of any programming interfaces that are provided by Javasoft. See the PUBLICATIONS section of the IBM Programming Announcement for the IBM Network Station and Sun's Java for more information about what publications are considered to be product documentation.

References in this publication to IBM products, programs or services do not imply that IBM intends to make these available in all countries in which IBM operates. Any reference to an IBM product, program, or service is not intended to state or imply that only IBM's product, program, or service may be used. Any functionally equivalent program that does not infringe any of IBM's intellectual property rights may be used instead of the IBM product, program or service.

This document has not been subjected to any formal review and has not been checked for technical accuracy. Results may be individually evaluated for applicability to a particular installation. You may discuss pertinent information from this document with a customer, and you may abstract pertinent information for presentation to your customers. However, any code included is for internal information purposes only and may not be given to customers. If included code is identified as incidental programming, its use must conform to the guidelines in the relevant section of the sales manual.

Information in this book was developed in conjunction with use of the equipment specified, and is limited in application to those specific hardware and software products and levels.

IBM may have patents or pending patent applications covering subject matter in this document. The furnishing of this document does not give you any license to these patents. You can send license inquiries, in writing, to the IBM Director of Licensing, IBM Corporation, 500 Columbus Avenue, Thornwood, NY 10594 USA.

Licensees of this program who wish to have information about it for the purpose of enabling: (i) the exchange of information between independently created programs and other programs (including this one) and (ii) the mutual use of the information which has been exchanged, should contact IBM Corporation, Dept. 600A, Mail Drop 1329, Somers, NY 10589 USA.

Such information may be available, subject to appropriate terms and conditions, including in some cases, payment of a fee.

The information contained in this document has not been submitted to any formal IBM test and is distributed AS IS. The information about non-IBM ("vendor") products in this manual has been supplied by the vendor and IBM assumes no responsibility for its accuracy or completeness. The use of this information or the implementation of any of these techniques is a customer responsibility and depends on the customer's ability to evaluate and integrate them into the customer's operational environment. While each item may have been reviewed by IBM for accuracy in a specific situation, there is no guarantee that the same or similar results will be obtained elsewhere. Customers attempting to adapt these techniques to their own environments do so at their own risk.

Any performance data contained in this document was obtained in a controlled environment based on the use of specific data and is presented only to illustrate techniques and procedures to assist IBM personnel to better understand IBM products. The results that may be obtained in other operating environments may vary significantly. Users of this document should verify the applicable data in their specific environment. No performance data may be abstracted or reproduced and given to non-IBM personnel without prior written approval by Business Practices.

The following document contains examples of data and reports used in daily business operations. To illustrate them as completely as possible, the examples contain the names of individuals, companies, brands, and products. All of these names are fictitious and any similarity to the names and addresses used by an actual business enterprise is entirely coincidental.

Reference to PTF numbers that have not been released through the normal distribution process does not imply general availability. The purpose of including these reference numbers is to alert IBM customers to specific information relative to the implementation of the PTF when it becomes available to each customer according to the normal IBM PTF distribution process.

You can reproduce a page in this document as a transparency, if that page has the copyright notice on it. The copyright notice must appear on each page being reproduced.

The following terms are trademarks of the International Business Machines Corporation in the United States and/or other countries:

400	AIX
AS/400	BookManager
CICS	DB2
IBM®	OS/2
OS/390	OS/400
PROFS	RS/6000
S/390	San Francisco
VisualAge	

The following terms are trademarks of other companies:

C-bus is a trademark of Corollary, Inc.

Java and HotJava are trademarks of Sun Microsystems, Incorporated.

Microsoft, Windows, Windows NT, and the Windows 95 logo are trademarks or registered trademarks of Microsoft Corporation.

OLE, COM, Active-X are trademarks or registered trademarks of Microsoft Corporation.

PC Direct is a trademark of Ziff Communications Company and is used by IBM Corporation under license.

Pentium, MMX, ProShare, LANDesk, and ActionMedia are trademarks or registered trademarks of Intel Corporation in the U.S. and other countries.

UNIX is a registered trademark in the United States and other countries licensed exclusively through X/Open Company Limited.

OS/2, OS/390 and OS/400 are trademarks of International Business Machine Corporation.

Other company, product, and service names may be trademarks or service marks of others.

Appendix **D**

Related Publications

The publications listed in this section are considered particularly suitable for a more detailed discussion of the topics covered in this redbook.

International Technical Support Organization Publications

For information on ordering these ITSO publications see "How To Get ITSO Redbooks" on page 317.

* *RS/6000 - IBM Network Station Companion Guide,* SG24-2016

Redbooks on CD-ROMs

Redbooks are also available on CD-ROMs. **Order a subscription** and receive updates 2-4 times a year at significant savings.

CD-ROM Title	Subscription Number	Collection Kit Number
System/390 Redbooks Collection	SBOF-7201	SK2T-2177
Networking and Systems Management Redbooks Collection	SBOF-7370	SK2T-6022
Transaction Processing and Data Management Redbook	SBOF-7240	SK2T-8038
Lotus Redbooks Collection	SBOF-6899	SK2T-8038
Tivoli Redbooks Collection	SBOF-6898	SK2T-8039
AS/400 Redbooks Collection	SBOF-7270	SK2T-2849
RS/6000 Redbooks Collection (HTML, BkMgr)	SBOF-7230	SK2T-8040
RS/6000 Redbooks Collection (PostScript)	SBOF-7205	SK2T-8041
RS/6000 Redbooks Collection (PDF)	SBOF-8700	SK2T-8043
Application Development Redbooks Collection	SBOF-7290	SK2T-8037
Personal Systems Redbooks Collection	SBOF-7250	SK2T-8042

Other Publications

These publications are also relevant as further information sources:

- *Java in a Nutshell*, O' Reilly, ISBN 1-56592-262-X

- *Java Examples*, O' Reilly, ISBN 1-56592-371-5

- *Webmaster in a Nutshell*, O'Reilly, ISBN 1-56592-229-8

How To Get ITSO Redbooks

This section explains how both customers and IBM employees can find out about ITSO redbooks, CD-ROMs, workshops, and residencies. A form for ordering books and CD-ROMs is also provided.

This information was current at the time of publication, but is continually subject to change. The latest information may be found at http://www.redbooks.ibm.com.

How IBM Employees Can Get ITSO Redbooks

Employees may request ITSO deliverables (redbooks, BookManager BOOKs, and CD-ROMs) and information about redbooks, workshops, and residencies in the following ways:

- **PUBORDER** – to order hardcopies in United States
- **GOPHER link to the Internet** – type GOPHER WTSCPOK.ITSO.IBM.COM

- **Tools disks**

  To get LIST3820s of redbooks, type one of the following commands:
  ```
  TOOLS SENDTO EHONE4 TOOLS2 REDPRINT GET SG24xxxx PACKAGE
  TOOLS SENDTO CANVM2 TOOLS REDPRINT GET SG24xxxx
    PACKAGE (Canadian users only)
  ```

  To get lists of redbooks:
  ```
  TOOLS SENDTO USDIST MKTTOOLS MKTTOOLS GET ITSOCAT TXT
  ```

  To register for information on workshops, residencies, and redbooks:
  ```
  TOOLS SENDTO WTSCPOK TOOLS ZDISK GET ITSOREGI 1996
  ```

  For a list of product area specialists in the ITSO:
  ```
  TOOLS SENDTO WTSCPOK TOOLS ZDISK GET ORGCARD PACKAGE
  ```

- **Redbooks Web Site on the World Wide Web**

  ```
  http://w3.itso.ibm.com/redbooks
  ```

- **IBM Direct Publications Catalog on the World Wide Web**

  ```
  http://www.elink.ibmlink.ibm.com/pbl/pbl
  ```
  IBM employees may obtain LIST3820s of redbooks from this page.

- **REDBOOKS category on INEWS**

- **Online** – send orders to: USIB6FPL at IBMMAIL or DKIBMBSH at IBM-MAIL

- **Internet Listserver**

  With an Internet E-mail address, anyone can subscribe to an IBM Announcement Listserver. To initiate the service, send an E-mail note to announce@webster.ibmlink.ibm.com with the keyword subscribe in the body of the note (leave the subject line blank). A category form and detailed instructions will be sent to you.

How Customers Can Get ITSO Redbooks

Customers may request ITSO deliverables (redbooks, BookManager BOOKs, and CD-ROMs) and information about redbooks, workshops, and residencies in the following ways:

- **Online Orders** (Do not send credit card information over the Internet) – send orders to:

	IBMMAIL	Internet
In United States	usib6fpl at ibmmail	usib6fpl@ibmmail.com
In Canada	caibmbkz at ibmmail	lmannix@vnet.ibm.com
Outside North America	dkibmbsh at ibmmail	bookshop@dk.ibm.com

- **Telephone orders**

United States (toll free)	1-800-879-2755
Canada (toll free)	1-800-IBM-4YOU

Outside North America	(long distance charges apply)
(+45) 4810-1320 - Danish	(+45) 4810-1020 - German
(+45) 4810-1420 - Dutch	(+45) 4810-1620 - Italian
(+45) 4810-1540 - English	(+45) 4810-1270 - Norwegian
(+45) 4810-1670 - Finnish	(+45) 4810-1120 - Spanish
(+45) 4810-1220 - French	(+45) 4810-1170 - Swedish

- **Mail Orders** – send orders to:

IBM Publications	IBM Publications	IBM Direct Services
Publications Customer Support	144-4th Avenue, S.W.	Sortemosevej 21
P.O. Box 29570	Calgary, Alberta T2P 3N5	DK-3450 Allerød
Raleigh, NC 27626-0570	Canada	Denmark
USA		

- **Fax** – send orders to:

United States (toll free)	1-800-445-9269	
Canada	1-800-267-4455	
Outside North America	(+45) 48 14 2207	(long distance charge)

- **1-800-IBM-4FAX (United States) or (+1) 408 256 5422 (Outside USA)** – ask for:

  Index # 4421 Abstracts of new redbooks
  Index # 4422 IBM redbooks
  Index # 4420 Redbooks for last six months

- **Direct Services** – send note to softwareshop@vnet.ibm.com

On the World Wide Web

Redbooks Web Site	http://www.redbooks.ibm.com
IBM Direct Publications Catalog	http://www.elink.ibmlink.ibm.com/pbl/pbl

- **Internet Listserver**

  With an Internet E-mail address, anyone can subscribe to an IBM Announcement Listserver. To initiate the service, send an E-mail note to announce@webster.ibmlink.ibm.com with the keyword subscribe in the body of the note (leave the subject line blank).

IBM Redbook Order Form

Please send me the following:

Title	Order Number	Quantity

First name   Last name

Company

Address

City   Postal code   Country

Telephone number   Telefax number   VAT number

☐ Invoice to customer number   _____

☐ Credit card number   _____

Credit card expiration date   Card issued to   Signature

We accept American Express, Diners, Eurocard, Master Card, and Visa. Payment by credit card not available in all countries. Signature mandatory for credit card payment.

List of Abbreviations

AFC	Advanced Function Classes	*CGI*	Common Gateway Interface
APA	All Points Addressable	*CLI*	Call Level Interface
APDU	Application Protocol Data Unit	*CORBA*	Common Object Request Broker Architecture
API	Application Program Interface	*COS*	Card Operating System
ATM	Asynchronous Transfer Mode	*DAX*	Data Access builder, part of EAB
ATR	Answer-To-Reset	*DCE*	Distributed Computing Environment
BPE	Business Process Engineering	*DF*	Dedicated File
		DNS	Domain Name Service
CAE	Client Application Enabler	*DTD*	Document Type Definition

EAB	Enterprise Access Builder, part of IBM VisualAge for Java	JAR	Java Archive
		JDBC	Java data base connectivity
EEPROM	Electrically Erasable Programmable Read Only Memory	JDK	Java Development Kit
		JIT	Just-In-Time compiler
		JPEG	Joint Photographic Expert Group
EF	Elementary File	JVM	Java Virtual Machine
FTP	File Transfer Protocol	LMC	Lunar Medical Center
GIF	Graphic Information Format	MF	Master File
GIS	Geospatial Information Systems	MFC	Multi Function Card
HTML	HyperText Markup Language	MIME	Multipurpose Internet Mail Extension
HTTP	HyperText Transfer Protocol	NC	Network Computer
HTTPS	Secure HTTP	NCOS	Network Computer Operating System
IAD	Internet Access Device	NFS	Network File System
IBM	International Business Machines Corporation	NSM	Network Station Manager
ICMP	Internet Control Message Protocol	NVRAM	Non-Volatile Random Access Memory
IDE	Integrated Development Environment, graphic development component of IBM VisualAge for Java	ODBC	Open Data Base Connectivity
		OMG	Object Management Group
		OO	Object Oriented
IETF	Internet Engineering Task Force	OSF	Open Software Foundation
		PDA	Personal Digital Assistant
IFC	Internet Foundation Classes	POST	Power-On Self-Test
IIOP	Internet InterOperability Protocol	PROFS	Professional Office System
IP	Internet Protocol	RAM	Random Access Memory
ISO	International Standards Organization	RDBMS	Relational Database Management System
ITSO	International Technical Support Organization	RM-ODP	Reference Model for Open Distributed Processing
		RMI	Remote Method Invocation
JAF	JavaBeans Activation Framework	ROM	Read Only Memory

RPC	Remote Procedure Call
SDK	Servlet Development Kit
SGML	Standard Generalized Markup Language
SMTP	Simple Mail Transfer Protocol
SQL	Structured Query Language
SSI	Server-Side Includes
SSL	Secure Sockets Layer
STB	Set-Top Boxes
TCP	Transmission Control Protocol
TFTP	Trivial File Transfer Protocol
UDP/IP	User Datagram Protocol/ Internet Protocol
URI	Universal Resource Identifier
URL	Universal Resource Locator
VM	Virtual Machine
WBT	Windows-Based Terminal
W3C	World Wide Web Consortium
WWW	World Wide Web

Index

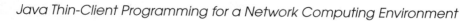

LICENSE AGREEMENT AND LIMITED WARRANTY

READ THE FOLLOWING TERMS AND CONDITIONS CAREFULLY BEFORE OPENING THIS SOFTWARE PACKAGE. THIS LEGAL DOCUMENT IS AN AGREEMENT BETWEEN YOU AND PRENTICE-HALL, INC. (THE "COMPANY"). BY OPENING THIS SEALED SOFTWARE PACKAGE, YOU ARE AGREEING TO BE BOUND BY THESE TERMS AND CONDITIONS. IF YOU DO NOT AGREE WITH THESE TERMS AND CONDITIONS, DO NOT OPEN THE SOFTWARE PACKAGE. PROMPTLY RETURN THE UNOPENED SOFTWARE PACKAGE AND ALL ACCOMPANYING ITEMS TO THE PLACE YOU OBTAINED THEM FOR A FULL REFUND OF ANY SUMS YOU HAVE PAID.

1. **GRANT OF LICENSE:** In consideration of your payment of the license fee, which is part of the price you paid for this product, and your agreement to abide by the terms and conditions of this Agreement, the Company grants to you a nonexclusive right to use and display the copy of the enclosed software program (hereinafter the "SOFTWARE") on a single computer (i.e., with a single CPU) at a single location so long as you comply with the terms of this Agreement. The Company reserves all rights not expressly granted to you under this Agreement.

2. **OWNERSHIP OF SOFTWARE:** You own only the magnetic or physical media (the enclosed disks) on which the SOFTWARE is recorded or fixed, but the Company retains all the rights, title, and ownership to the SOFTWARE recorded on the original disk copy(ies) and all subsequent copies of the SOFTWARE, regardless of the form or media on which the original or other copies may exist. This license is not a sale of the original SOFTWARE or any copy to you.

3. **COPY RESTRICTIONS:** This SOFTWARE and the accompanying printed materials and user manual (the "Documentation") are the subject of copyright. You may not copy the Documentation or the SOFTWARE, except that you may make a single copy of the SOFTWARE for backup or archival purposes only. You may be held legally responsible for any copying or copyright infringement which is caused or encouraged by your failure to abide by the terms of this restriction.

4. **USE RESTRICTIONS:** You may not network the SOFTWARE or otherwise use it on more than one computer or computer terminal at the same time. You may physically transfer the SOFTWARE from one computer to another provided that the SOFTWARE is used on only one computer at a time. You may not distribute copies of the SOFTWARE or Documentation to others. You may not reverse engineer, disassemble, decompile, modify, adapt, translate, or create derivative works based on the SOFTWARE or the Documentation without the prior written consent of the Company.

5. **TRANSFER RESTRICTIONS:** The enclosed SOFTWARE is licensed only to you and may not be transferred to any one else without the prior written consent of the Company. Any unauthorized transfer of the SOFTWARE shall result in the immediate termination of this Agreement.

6. **TERMINATION:** This license is effective until terminated. This license will terminate automatically without notice from the Company and become null and void if you fail to comply with any provisions or limitations of this license. Upon termination, you shall destroy the Documentation and all copies of the SOFTWARE. All provisions of this Agreement as to warranties, limitation of liability, remedies or damages, and our ownership rights shall survive termination.

7. **MISCELLANEOUS:** This Agreement shall be construed in accordance with the laws of the United States of America and the State of New York and shall benefit the Company, its affiliates, and assignees.

8. **LIMITED WARRANTY AND DISCLAIMER OF WARRANTY:** The Company warrants that the SOFTWARE, when properly used in accordance with the Documentation, will operate in substantial conformity with the description of the SOFTWARE set forth in the Documentation. The Company does not warrant that the SOFTWARE will meet your requirements or that the operation of the SOFTWARE will be uninterrupted or error-free. The Company warrants that the media on which the SOFTWARE is delivered shall be free from defects in materials and workmanship under normal use for a period of thirty (30) days from the date of your purchase. Your only remedy and the Company's only obligation under these limited warranties is, at the Company's option, return of the warranted item for a refund of any amounts paid by you or replacement of the item. Any replacement of SOFTWARE or media under the warranties shall not extend the original warranty period. The limited warranty set forth above shall not apply to any SOFTWARE which the Company determines in good faith has been subject to misuse, neglect, improper installation, repair, alteration, or damage by you. EXCEPT FOR THE EXPRESSED WARRANTIES SET FORTH ABOVE, THE COMPANY DISCLAIMS ALL WARRANTIES, EXPRESS OR IMPLIED, INCLUDING WITHOUT LIMITATION, THE IMPLIED WARRANTIES OF MERCHANTABILITY AND FITNESS FOR A PARTICULAR PURPOSE. EXCEPT FOR THE EXPRESS WARRANTY SET FORTH ABOVE, THE COMPANY DOES NOT WARRANT, GUARANTEE, OR MAKE ANY REPRESENTATION REGARDING THE USE OR THE RESULTS OF THE USE OF THE SOFTWARE IN TERMS OF ITS CORRECTNESS, ACCURACY, RELIABILITY, CURRENTNESS, OR OTHERWISE.

IN NO EVENT, SHALL THE COMPANY OR ITS EMPLOYEES, AGENTS, SUPPLIERS, OR CONTRACTORS BE LIABLE FOR ANY INCIDENTAL, INDIRECT, SPECIAL, OR CONSEQUENTIAL DAMAGES ARISING OUT OF OR IN CONNECTION WITH THE LICENSE GRANTED UNDER THIS AGREEMENT, OR FOR LOSS OF USE, LOSS OF DATA, LOSS OF INCOME OR PROFIT, OR OTHER LOSSES, SUSTAINED AS A RESULT OF INJURY TO ANY PERSON, OR LOSS OF OR DAMAGE TO PROPERTY, OR CLAIMS OF THIRD PARTIES, EVEN IF THE COMPANY OR AN AUTHORIZED REPRESENTATIVE OF THE COMPANY HAS BEEN ADVISED OF THE POSSIBILITY OF SUCH DAMAGES. IN NO EVENT SHALL LIABILITY OF THE COMPANY FOR DAMAGES WITH RESPECT TO THE SOFTWARE EXCEED THE AMOUNTS ACTUALLY PAID BY YOU, IF ANY, FOR THE SOFTWARE.

SOME JURISDICTIONS DO NOT ALLOW THE LIMITATION OF IMPLIED WARRANTIES OR LIABILITY FOR INCIDENTAL, INDIRECT, SPECIAL, OR CONSEQUENTIAL DAMAGES, SO THE ABOVE LIMITATIONS MAY NOT ALWAYS APPLY. THE WARRANTIES IN THIS AGREEMENT GIVE YOU SPECIFIC LEGAL RIGHTS AND YOU MAY ALSO HAVE OTHER RIGHTS WHICH VARY IN ACCORDANCE WITH LOCAL LAW.

ACKNOWLEDGMENT

YOU ACKNOWLEDGE THAT YOU HAVE READ THIS AGREEMENT, UNDERSTAND IT, AND AGREE TO BE BOUND BY ITS TERMS AND CONDITIONS. YOU ALSO AGREE THAT THIS AGREEMENT IS THE COMPLETE AND EXCLUSIVE STATEMENT OF THE AGREEMENT BETWEEN YOU AND THE COMPANY AND SUPERSEDES ALL PROPOSALS OR PRIOR AGREEMENTS, ORAL, OR WRITTEN, AND ANY OTHER COMMUNICATIONS BETWEEN YOU AND THE COMPANY OR ANY REPRESENTATIVE OF THE COMPANY RELATING TO THE SUBJECT MATTER OF THIS AGREEMENT.

Should you have any questions concerning this Agreement or if you wish to contact the Company for any reason, please contact in writing at the address below.

Robin Short
Prentice Hall PTR
One Lake Street
Upper Saddle River, New Jersey 07458

Java™ Development Kit, Version 1.1.x, Binary Code License

This binary code license ("License") contains rights and restrictions associated with use of the accompanying software and documentation ("Software"). Read the License carefully before installing the Software. By installing the Software you agree to the terms and conditions of this License.

1. Limited License Grant. Sun grants to you ("Licensee") a non-exclusive, non-transferable limited license to use the Software without fee for evaluation of the Software and for development of Java™ compatible applets and applications. Licensee may make one archival copy of the Software. Licensee may not re-distribute the Software in whole or in part, either separately or included with a product. Refer to the Java Runtime Environment Version 1.1 binary code license (http://www.javasoft.com/products/JDK/1.1/index.html) for the availability of runtime code which may be distributed with Java compatible applets and applications.

2. Java Platform Interface. Licensee may not modify the Java Platform Interface ("JPI", identified as classes contained within the "java" package or any subpackages of the "java" package), by creating additional classes within the JPI or otherwise causing the addition to or modification of the classes in the JPI. In the event that Licensee creates any Java-related API and distributes such API to others for applet or application development, Licensee must promptly publish an accurate specification for such API for free use by all developers of Java-based software.

3. Restrictions. Software is confidential copyrighted information of Sun and title to all copies is retained by Sun and/or its licensors. Licensee shall not modify, decompile, disassemble, decrypt, extract, or otherwise reverse engineer Software. Software may not be leased, assigned, or sublicensed, in whole or in part. Software is not designed or intended for use in on-line control of aircraft, air traffic, aircraft navigation or aircraft communications; or in the design, construction, operation or maintenance of any nuclear facility. Licensee warrants that it will not use or redistribute the Software for such purposes.

4. Trademarks and Logos. This License does not authorize Licensee to use any Sun name, trademark or logo. Licensee acknowledges that Sun owns the Java trademark and all Java-related trademarks, logos and icons including the Coffee Cup and Duke ("Java Marks") and agrees to: (i) to comply with the Java Trademark Guidelines at http://java.com/trademarks.html; (ii) not do anything harmful to or inconsistent with Sun's rights in the Java Marks; and (iii) assist Sun in protecting those rights, including assigning to Sun any rights acquired by Licensee in any Java Mark.

5. Disclaimer of Warranty. Software is provided "AS IS," without a warranty of any kind. ALL EXPRESS OR IMPLIED REPRESENTATIONS AND WARRANTIES, INCLUDING ANY IMPLIED WARRANTY OF MERCHANTABILITY, FITNESS FOR A PARTICULAR PURPOSE OR NON-INFRINGEMENT, ARE HEREBY EXCLUDED.

6. Limitation of Liability. SUN AND ITS LICENSORS SHALL NOT BE LIABLE FOR ANY DAMAGES SUFFERED BY LICENSEE OR ANY THIRD PARTY AS A RESULT OF USING OR DISTRIBUTING SOFTWARE. IN NO EVENT WILL SUN OR ITS LICENSORS BE LIABLE FOR ANY LOST REVENUE, PROFIT OR DATA, OR FOR DIRECT, INDIRECT, SPECIAL, CONSEQUENTIAL, INCIDENTAL OR PUNITIVE DAMAGES, HOWEVER CAUSED AND REGARDLESS OF THE THEORY OF LIABILITY, ARISING OUT OF THE USE OF OR INABILITY TO USE SOFTWARE, EVEN IF SUN HAS BEEN ADVISED OF THE POSSIBILITY OF SUCH DAMAGES.

7. Termination. Licensee may terminate this License at any time by destroying all copies of Software. This License will terminate immediately without notice from Sun if Licensee fails to comply with any provision of this License. Upon such termination, Licensee must destroy all copies of Software.

8. Export Regulations. Software, including technical data, is subject to U.S. export control laws, including the U.S. Export Administration Act and its associated regulations, and may be subject to export or import regulations in other countries. Licensee agrees to comply strictly with all such regulations and acknowledges that it has the responsibility to obtain licenses to export, re-export, or import Software. Software may not be downloaded, or otherwise exported or re-exported (i) into, or to a national or resident of, Cuba, Iraq, Iran, North Korea, Libya, Sudan, Syria or any country to which the U.S. has embargoed goods; or (ii) to anyone on the U.S. Treasury Department's list of Specially Designated Nations or the U.S. Commerce Department's Table of Denial Orders.

9. Restricted Rights. Use, duplication or disclosure by the United States government is subject to the restrictions as set forth in the Rights in Technical Data and Computer Software Clauses in DFARS 252.227-7013(c) (1) (ii) and FAR 52.227-19(c) (2) as applicable.

10. Governing Law. Any action related to this License will be governed by California law and controlling U.S. federal law. No choice of law rules of any jurisdiction will apply.

11. Severability. If any of the above provisions are held to be in violation of applicable law, void, or unenforceable in any jurisdiction, then such provisions are herewith waived to the extent necessary for the License to be otherwise enforceable in such jurisdiction. However, if in Sun's opinion deletion of any provisions of the License by operation of this paragraph unreasonably compromises the rights or increase the liabilities of Sun or its licensors, Sun reserves the right to terminate the License and refund the fee paid by Licensee, if any, as Licensee's sole and exclusive remedy.

ABOUT THE CD

CONTENTS

The CD included with this book includes trial versions of DB2 and Lotus Domino Go, the shareware SitePad Pro and full versions of the MindQ VisualAge for Java tutorial and the VisualAge for Java Entry version. Possible limitations are stated in the license agreement of each product. The CD is intended to complement the book by offering tools and products to reconstruct the samples created in the book. The CD also includes the HTML and Java source code created in the book as well as a javadoc created documentation for most of the code. Please also see Trademarks section below.

SYSTEM REQUIREMENTS

This CD-ROM has been created for the Windows 95 or Windows NT 4.0 operating system. It uses the Joliet file system and makes use of long file names. Other operating systems might be able to browse the documents, but not to install the products coming with this CD-ROM.
The CD-ROM is HTML guided, therefore you need a Web browser such as Microsoft Internet Explorer or Netscape Navigator. The HTML documents have been tested with Netscape Navigator 4.x and Internet Explorer 2.0 and 4.0. Best results can be expected with Internet Explorer 4.0, because of its integration in the operating system.
DB2 is coming with several documents available as postscript files. You may either need a PostScript printer to print these files or a PostScript viewer such as GhostView.

The CD is organized into the following directories:

\DB2UDB	DB2 Universal Database V5 Trial
\GoWebserver	Lotus Domino Go Webserver for Windows 95 and Windows NT
\JDK	Java Development Kit 1.1.6
\MINDQ	MindQ tutorial "Java Programming Using VisualAge for Java"
\ModelWorks	SitePad Pro Java IDE
\PTR	Java and HTML source code created in the book
\PTRgraphics	Graphics used for HTML navigation on this CD-ROM
\VAJava	VisualAge for Java - Entry Version

In order to use the HTML navigation on the CD-ROM, load the \indext.html file into your browser.

TRADEMARKS

The following terms are trademarks of the IBM Corporation in the United States or other countries or both: IBM, DB2, VisualAge. Microsoft, Windows, Windows NT, and the Windows 95 logo are trademarks or registered trademarks of Microsoft Corporation. Java, JavaBeans, VisualAge, and JDK are trademarks or registered trademarks of Sun Microsystems, Inc. MindQ is a registered trademark of MindQ Publishing, Inc. SitePad Pro is a trademark of Model Works Software. Lotus Domino Go Webserver is a registered trademark of the Lotus Development Corp.

TECHNICAL SUPPORT

Technical support for this CD is not provided by Prentice Hall nor by the authors. However, if you feel that your CD is damaged, please contact Prentice Hall for a replacement:
disc_exchange@prenhall.com.